Seductive Forms

Seductive Forms

Women's Amatory Fiction
from 1684 to 1740

ROS BALLASTER

CLARENDON PRESS · OXFORD

1992

Oxford University Press, Walton Street, Oxford OX2 6DP
Oxford New York Toronto
Delhi Bombay Calcutta Madras Karachi
Petaling Jaya Singapore Hong Kong Tokyo
Nairobi Dar es Salaam Cape Town
Melbourne Auckland
and associated companies in
Berlin Ibadan

Oxford is a trade mark of Oxford University Press

Published in the United States
by Oxford University Press, New York

British Library Cataloguing in Publication Data
Data available

Library of Congress Cataloging in Publication Data
Ballaster, Ros.
Seductive forms: women's amatory fiction from 1684–1740: with
particular reference to Aphra Behn, Delarivier Manley, and
Eliza Haywood/Ros Ballaster.
Includes bibliographical references and index.
1. English fiction—Women authors—History and criticism.
2. Behn, Aphra, 1640–1689—Criticism and interpretation.
3. Manley, Mrs. (Mary de la Rivière), 1663–1724—Criticism and interpretation.
4. Haywood, Eliza Fowler, 1693?–1756—Criticism and interpretation.
5. Women and literature—Great Britain—History—18th century.
6. Women and literature—Great Britain—History—17th century.
7. Erotic stories, English—History and criticism.
8. Fiction—Authorship—Sex differences. 9. Seduction in literature.
10. Literary form. I. Title.
PR858.W6B34 1992   823'.085099287'09032—dc20   91–43583
ISBN 0–19–811244–0

Typeset by Cotswold Typesetting Ltd, Cheltenham
Printed and bound in
Great Britain by Biddles Ltd,
Guildford and King's Lynn

Acknowledgements

My thanks to Janet Todd for patient and diligent supervision and Marilyn Butler for early direction and counsel. Members of the Oxford Feminist Theory Group from 1984 to 1988 provided invaluable intellectual support and inspiration—in particular, Dianne Chisholm, Kate Lilley, Clair Wills, Stephanie Flood, Karen Van Dyck, Hero Chalmers, Clare Brant, and Diane Purkiss. My students and colleagues at Oxford University, Oxford Polytechnic, and the University of East Anglia challenged and refined my ideas. Discussions with and advice from Toril Moi, Roger Lonsdale, Isobel Grundy, Linda Hardy, Lee Wallace, Su Wiseman, and Lorna Hutson have all been formative in the development of this book. Financial aid and the opportunity for uninterrupted work were provided by the British and American Federations of University Women and the Fulbright Association. The Bodleian, Houghton and Widener libraries were endlessly patient with enquiries and requests. Phil Harriss's editing skills and comments were invaluable. Thanks also to Andrew Lockett and Kim Scott Walwyn at Oxford University Press for making the production and editing of this book so pleasant an experience.

Those who have borne with my continuing obsession with the seduction narrative in all its forms are too numerous to mention by name. Special thanks go to my mother for constantly, if irritatingly, asking me when I would be finished and to all my family for love and support. Above all, to Jeri Johnson whose contribution to both thesis and book is incalculable—friend, counsellor, editor, and always my best critic.

Contents

Introduction

In 1684 Aphra Behn published the first volume of her epistolary fiction, *Love-Letters between a Nobleman and his Sister*.[1] The *Love-Letters* were a new phenomenon in both the history of British prose fiction and that of women's writing. Sexually explicit and outspokenly partisan in their politics, they were authored by a woman whose only source of income was her pen and who was associated with the most notorious political and literary figures of the day. In 1740, by contrast, Samuel Richardson published the first two volumes of his epistolary fiction, *Pamela; or, Virtue Rewarded*.[2] Written by a man, whose main source of income was his own publishing house, these letters were explicitly moral, and lacking in overt political statement.

Like Behn's heroine, Sylvia, Pamela is the victim of a seduction plot on the part of a young male libertine. Yet, significantly, Pamela resists where Sylvia succumbs and is rewarded with the comforts of bourgeois marriage. Whereas Behn's aristocratic Tory heiress adopts the life of a classless adventuress as a result of her passion for an illicit sexual object, Richardson's working-class Whiggish heroine is elevated to the life of a benevolent country gentlewoman by virtue of her resistance to an illicit sexual proposition.

The distance between Behn's *Love-Letters* and Richardson's *Pamela* is, as this book hopes to demonstrate, both less and more wide than it at first appears. Both, Sylvia and Pamela are 'rewarded' with their respective fates by virtue of their power as writers. Both, in their different ways, come to control the scene of representation of their own amatory histories. It is, after all, Pamela's papers, her secretly scribbled accounts of her trials at the hands of her tormentors, that finally win her the respect of her lover. It is Sylvia's education in the duplicities of the letter and her consequent ability to manipulate epistolary representation that enable her to engineer her way out of the position of a discarded victim of seduction into that of female libertine. However, whereas Pamela triumphs (ostensibly at least) because of her innocence, her lack of self-consciousness, and

---

[1] Aphra Behn, *Love Letters between a Nobleman and his Sister* (London, 1684).
[2] Samuel Richardson, *Pamela, or, Virtue Rewarded* (London, 1740).

integrity of mind, Sylvia triumphs because of her manipulative arrogance.

The contrasting destinies of these two early heroines of the letter indicate the gulf between late seventeenth- and mid- to late eighteenth-century conceptions of both the literary practice of the woman writer, and her relation to amatory and political discouse. Perceptions of the 'proper' form of the woman writer changed during this period from the narcissistic, practised artifice of Sylvia to the spontaneous and innocent literary effusions of Pamela. How, then, are we to account for this shift? This book attempts to give an account of the conditions that enabled some women writers in the late seventeenth and early eighteenth century to 'profit', both materially and ideologically, from the narcissistic strategies that Behn's heroine learns through the course of her novel.

A study of women's novelistic writing in England prior to the rise of sentimental myth inaugurated by Richardson's *Pamela* considerably enriches our understanding of the importance of ideologies of gender in the construction of genre. The first section of this book examines twentieth-century theories of the early modern novel and late seventeenth-century traditions in feminocentric prose fiction, in order to situate the work of Behn, Manley, and Haywood more precisely in relation to their predecessors and successors in love fiction. Chapter 1 provides a survey and evaluation of twentieth-century accounts of the late seventeenth- and eighteenth-century novel, arguing for a more sophisticated analysis of the role of sexual fantasy and party-political metaphor in the literature of seduction. The predominance of realist teleologies in historical studies of the rise of the novel has obscured the continuing appeal of fantasy and non-realist forms (traditionally associated with the romance and feminine literary consumption) for writers of early prose fiction.

Chapter 2 takes issue with the 'myth' of the female reader in the eighteenth century, which, it argues, has tended to represent women's amatory fiction as a sub-cultural form servicing degraded popular taste and bearing little or no relation to the political and ideological mainstream. The depiction of the woman reader in contemporary periodical and prose fiction was, it is suggested, not a realistic representation, but a formal device that served to introduce new concepts concerning the male political subject and his relation to the state. Chapter 2 goes on to outline the prevailing conventions in amatory fiction in the last decades of the seventeenth century in

Britain, developed from French models; it explores the specific formal and ideological properties of the French romance, the *nouvelle*, the scandal chronicle and epistolary fiction.

The second section of the book looks in more detail at the fiction of Behn, Manley, and Haywood and their transformations of these feminocentric French forms in the context of late seventeenth- and early eighteenth-century party politics and gender ideologies. Behn and Manley seek to privilege the female writer as a political agent, precisely by virtue of her position at the margins of the political order. They indulge in a complex form of (auto)biographizing that constructs the woman writer as an erotic enigma for her male and female readers. Eliza Haywood's romances of the 1720s and 1730s, by contrast, refuse such autobiographical impulses and bring us closer to the conventions of domestic fiction. The woman writer is here identified with her suffering, silenced heroines, rather than privileged because of her distance from them. However, Haywood's deployment of the trope of the masquerade reveals a continued interest in the heroinizing of artifice and fictional duplicity.

Finally, the conclusion offers a brief account of the critical fate of the prose fiction of Behn, Manley, and Haywood in the mid- to late eighteenth century. These early amatory fictions were persistently 'written out' of the novel tradition in this period in the attempt to make it respectable. The novel, identified at every stage as a 'female form', was, in this period, refined by purging it of its disreputable associations with female sexuality and the subversive power of female 'wit', or artifice. Women writers could now only gain status in the newly respectable form of the novel by denying any association with the infamous Behn, Manley, and Haywood.

I

Gender and Genre

1

The Rise of the Novel: Gender and Genre in Theories of Prose Fiction

The question of the literary genre is not a formal one: it covers the motif of the law in general, of generation in the natural and symbolic senses, of birth in the natural and symbolic senses, of the generation difference, sexual difference between the feminine and masculine genre/gender, of the hymen between the two, of an identity and difference between the masculine and feminine.[1]

The attempt to give an account of the birth of a genre, the novel, has occupied literary theorists and critics from the late eighteenth century to the present day. The novel proves itself an errant child in this genealogical project, subjecting the literary critic to a seemingly unresolvable romance quest for definitive origin. The novel is read and reread for the marks of its ancestry, variously located in the epic, the fable, the romance, the ballad, the discourse of journalism, the rise of the middle class, the decline of the aristocracy, the emergence of a female reading public, and the development of a commercial book trade. The inability to resolve the question of the novel's origin lies, it appears, not in a paucity of evidence but rather a super-abundance of it. Not surprisingly, the ascription of gender identity to this most ambiguous of genres has come to play an increasingly important part in the quest. This chapter explores and analyses twentieth-century theories of the rise of the novel and the place or displacement of the role of gender difference in their making; it serves as a critical starting point for my own consideration of the discursive power of sexuality in prose fiction by women of the late seventeenth and early eighteenth century.

Historicism versus Formalism

Broadly speaking, most theories of the novel fall into one of two schools, here denoted by the terms historicism and formalism. For the

---

[1] Jacques Derrida, 'The Law of Genre', *Critical Inquiry*, 7 (1980), 74.

former (drawing in the main upon the insights of New Criticism, structuralism, and Russian formalism), the hybrid form of the novel has one of two origins. It is born either of a synthesis of a number of formal properties displayed by different genres and sub-genres prior to its emergence, or in reaction to previous genres in the conventional move of 'defamiliarization' or 'making strange' that Russian formalists have isolated as the generating principle of literary history.[2] In this history of the novel's development, then, the 'novel-effect' is the product of purely formal causes. Literary history bears little or no relation to social, economic, or political history. It renews and transforms itself only when literary and rhetorical strategies have become conventional and 'worn out'.

Historicist critics, in contrast, ascribe generic development to apparently 'non-textual' causes, that is, to changes in social, economic, or political conditions. As in formalist analyses, however, the novel is figured as an essentially 'problem-solving', or syncretic, genre, but in this critical context it resolves class or gender (rather than generic) conflict on the level of ideology. Within this perspective, which most commonly find its origins in Marxist theory, changes in the mode of production, in social organization and philosophical notions of the human subject are registered and responded to in the novel form. Inevitably historicist criticism's major failing has been its inability to explain satisfactorily why the novel form should be pre-eminent as a cultural response to changes in class structure. In other words, while historicist criticism may provide us with an account of the rise of the bourgeois hero or heroine in narrative fiction of the early modern period, it does not ultimately explain the specific links between bourgeois political hegemony and the cultural hegemony of the novel form.

The central problem, then, in both formalist and historicist analyses of the 'rise of the novel' has been one of causality, compounded by the heterogeneity of the novel form itself. Whether the heroic protagonist of this narrative of narrative is a specific author or body of authors (Defoe, Richardson, and Fielding simultaneously humanize aristocratic romance and purge a debased popular culture to dominate the field of narrative fiction) or form

[2] For Russian formalist theories of 'defamiliarization', see Viktor Shklovsky, 'Art as Technique' (1917), and 'Sterne's *Tristram Shandy*: Stylistic Commentary', (1921) in *Russian Formalist Criticism: Four Essays*, trans. and ed. Lee T. Lemon and Marion J. Reis (Lincoln, Nebr., 1965), 3–57.

itself (the plain style, narrative subjectivism, and 'realism' defeat
both the idealist objectivism of epic and romance and the prurient
voyeurism of ballad, chapbook, and 'history'), narrative theory
appears to be caught in a teleological trap.

Within this narrative of narrative theory, Ian Watt and Northrop
Frye become the central antagonists, taking up arms for the formalist and historicist perspective respectively in the 1950s and
replaying the critical dichotomies for which Richardson and Fielding
were so famed in the 1750s.[3] Ironic reflexivity and self-conscious
literariness confronts plain-speaking representationalism, or, in a
well-worn critical opposition of the eighteenth century itself, fiction
confronts fact. Frye's *Anatomy of Criticism* (1957) provided a much
needed corrective to the reduction of all prose fiction to the novel, in
particular reinstating the importance of the romance as a distinct
rule-governed form in narrative history rather than an abortive early
attempt at novelistic 'realism'. Frye insisted on the possibility of clas-
sifying forms of narrative without expanding the generic category of
the novel into a meaningless panacea, nor producing infinite taxono-
mies of modes and sub-modes of fiction.

Frye's archetypalist criticism has, of course, long been under
attack for its essentially ahistorical reductionism. Indeed, the
Anatomy of Criticism ultimately provided little more than a linear history of formal transformations in narrative, making no attempt to
account for the causes behind them. In contrast, Ian Watt's *The Rise
of the Novel* (1957) sought to explain formal change as a register of
social change in the early to mid-eighteenth century under the sway
of two new or 'novel' social forces, those of Puritanism and capi-
talism. Watt's thesis provides an alternative to the archetypal
descriptivism of Frye's 'anatomy' in its emphasis on historical specificity and its willingness to position the discourse of fiction in relation
to other discourses of power—sexual, economic, and religious.

However, Watt's compulsive valorization of 'realism' in opposition
to 'romance' and the radical selectivity of his study (the 'rise' of the
novel is represented in the work of three novelists, only one of
whom, Richardson, fully embodies the characteristics of the 'formal

[3] In fact, Watt and Frye published their two major critical works in the same year.
See Ian Watt, *The Rise of the Novel: Studies in Defoe, Richardson and Fielding* (London,
1957) and Northrop Frye, *Anatomy of Criticism* (Princeton, NJ, 1957). For an outline of
the more direct and personal rivalry between Richardson and Fielding, see Alan D.
McKillop, 'The Personal Relations between Richardson and Fielding', *Modern
Philology*, 28 (1931), 423–5.

realism' Watt outlines) has been challenged by his successors in historicist criticism. At this stage it is enough to note that Watt's thesis
too readily assumes that the primary aim of prose fiction in the
early eighteenth century was to provide, through a number of innovative formal strategies (contiguous narrative, the use of proper
names, almanacs, histories, chronicles, plots drawn from life rather
than art, etc.), a convincing representation of middle-class experience and ideology. In doing so, he underplays the continuing potency
of the language and plots of romance for, and the diversity of narrative forms available to, the eighteenth-century writer and reader.

If Frye takes an Augustan perspective on the origins of the novel,
struggling to produce a reformulated classical taxonomy in order to
lift the genre from its shameful roots in popular culture, Watt might
be characterized as the equivalent of the eighteenth-century
'modern', appropriating feminine sensibility as the model for a new
relation between the masculine subject and social order while
refusing women any active shaping role in culture beyond their role
as literary objects and consumers. Within this model, women are no
more than the embodiment of sensibility, and thus its victims,
lacking the necessary distance from it to be capable of shaping it
into a properly literary form without the example of masculine
founding fathers before them:

The majority of eighteenth-century novels were actually written by women,
but this had long remained a purely quantitative assertion of dominance; it
was Jane Austen who completed the work that Fanny Burney had begun,
and challenged masculine prerogative in a much more important matter. Her
example suggests that the feminine sensibility was in some ways better
equipped to reveal the intricacies of personal relationships and was therefore
at a real advantage in the realm of the novel. (339)

Watt's realist teleology and valorization of Richardsonian domestic or sentimental fiction cannot accommodate, except as an
unfortunate aberration, the explicitly amorous, politically engaged,
and fantasy-oriented fiction by women which took up so large a
share of the prose-fiction market in the late seventeenth and early
eighteenth century. As Nancy Armstrong's illuminating study of
domestic fiction from Richardson's *Pamela* to Virginia Woolf's
Orlando shows, the development of the figure of the domestic
woman in fiction and its attendant ideal of feminine sensibility is
indeed instrumental in the production of bourgeois hegemony. Armstrong asserts that this 'redefinition of desire' in terms of domes-

ticity is 'a decisive step in producing the densely interwoven fabric of common sense and sentimentality that even today ensures the ubiquity of middle-class power'.[4] The continuing dominance of this bourgeois paradigm of femininity as domesticity should not blind us to the recognition that it is a culturally produced and historically specific ideology, the genesis of which can be traced to the mid- and late eighteenth century and, in particular, to the novel of that period.

Our readings of prose fiction before the 1740s, then, must be open to different interpretations of the ideological significance of gender conflict. Indeed for much of this book I will refer less to amatory fiction's role in a generalized conflict between bourgeois and aristocratic ideologies which seems to me more relevant to a later period, than to its role in the specific party political distinctions of Whig and Tory that dominate the ideological scene from Charles II's restoration in 1660 to at least a decade after the death of Queen Anne in 1714. The period from 1684 to 1740, I will argue, provided significant and distinctive conditions of access for the woman writer into explicitly political discourse, before the full development of the 'naturalizing' mechanisms of bourgeois ideology for which the figure of the 'hystericized' domestic woman proved so central.[5] This is not to say that before the 1740s in Britain there were no class or gender ideologies at work, but rather that these were more frequently articulated through a discourse of party politics than they were in a later period.

Inevitably no feminist account of the rise of the novel can be purely formalist in its approach, since its primary interest lies in elaborating both the means by which gender identity is discursively produced as a form of social control in a given culture and the ways in which women as historical subjects and agents have negotiated their relation to that discourse. This book, then, confronts epistemological and formal questions of genre and its formation, related to the 'pre-novelistic' period of fiction from 1684 to 1740, with sociopolitical and ideological questions of gender associated with new

---

[4] Nancy Armstrong, *Desire and Domestic Fiction: A Political History of the Novel* (Oxford, 1985), 5.

[5] See Roland Barthes's essay 'Myth Today', in his *Mythologies* (1957), trans. Annette Lavers (London and New York, 1973). Barthes comments that 'bourgeois norms are experienced as the evident laws of a natural order—the further the bourgeois class propagates its representations, the more naturalized they become' (140). On the 'hystericization' of women, see Michel Foucault, *The History of Sexuality, i: An Introduction* (1976), trans. Robert Hurley (Harmondsworth, 1981), 122–7.

models and representations of sexual and class differences in the
same period through the consideration of one particular mode of
fiction, the amatory or seduction narrative. In so doing, it neither
seeks to read women's writing as simple evidence of women's
experience, nor to represent the 'feminization' of culture in this
period as solely a formal, or literary historical, concern.

The Novel as Discourse

Watt's and Frye's successors in the theory of the novel have increasingly turned to the study of these prose fictional forms before the
watershed of 1740, and have also attempted to combine formal and
historical analysis in a more dialectical fashion than either achieved.
Two of the most significant works, Lennard Davis's *Factual Fictions*
(1983) and Michael McKeon's *The Origins of the English Novel* (1987),
look to other theoretical sources—the work of Michel Foucault and
Mikhail Bakhtin respectively—in order to invigorate and problem-
atize their critical understanding of literary history.[6] For both Davis
and McKeon the novel is not a stable category but rather a discursive field that is constituted through a complex interchange of socio-
historical and formal factors.

Davis argues that until the early eighteenth century popular prose
constituted an undifferentiated 'news/novel matrix' in the shape of
ballads and journalistic prose. A close analysis of new initiatives in
press censorship and libel laws in the early eighteenth century
combined with interpretation of early theoretical statements on the
nature of prose fiction in the same period, leads Davis to conclude
that the novel is formed out of the division of this matrix. The
distinctive characteristics of the novel from this rupture onwards are
its exploitation of an epistemological confusion between fact and
fiction and an increasing 'eroticization' of the reading process
through 'a decreasing of the perceptual distance between reader and
text' (67).

Davis finds the 'origins' of the English novel, then, in the non-
literary sources of contemporary politics and popular forms, and so
firmly rejects any linear relation between the novel and its supposed
literary antecedent, the romance. This rejection is in keeping with

---

[6] Lennard J. Davis, *Factual Fictions: The Origins of the English Novel* (New York,
1983) and Michael McKeon, *The Origins of the English Novel 1600–1740* (Baltimore and
London, 1987).

Davis's own commitment, in line with Foucault, to a 'disjunctive history' (9), but it poses serious problems for the twentieth-century critic of women's fiction in this period. Davis pays Delarivier Manley considerable attention in his analysis of early theories of fiction, largely by virtue of her preface to a scandal chronicle entitled *Queen Zarah* (1705), which repudiates the 'romance' as a model for the new prose 'history'.[7] Yet he dismisses the prose fiction of Eliza Haywood and Mary Davys from the realm of his discussion of the novel with the comment that they 'seem to lack ambivalence and a special attitude toward fact and fiction' (121–2). Thus, Haywood and Manley, the two major scandal fiction writers of the early eighteenth century are firmly divided by Davis's criteria for determining advances in the novel. Davis's schema does not accommodate the importance of gender ideology in the construction of a novelistic discourse in this period. The popular association of the late seventeenth-century (French) romance with a female readership and female literary production established a continuity between the female-authored 'novel' in England and the earlier romance despite their significant differences, which even Manley's preface could not dispel.[8] Davis's blindness to the proximity of genre and gender differentiation in the discourse of the early modern novel means that he is forced to explain away Haywood's and Davys's fictions as '[unable], in formal terms . . . to create or belong to a genre' (122). Davis's reading ultimately produces little more than a new version of an old history of the novel whereby the 'masculine' tradition of news reporting, journalism, and ballads displaces the 'feminine' one of the romance to provide a more respectable, if populist rather than 'literary', backdrop to the emergence of the novel proper. It comes as no surprise when Davis concludes his book with three chapters on Defoe, Richardson, and Fielding in deference to his own precursor, Ian Watt.

Michael McKeon also does little to displace the hegemony of this triumvirate in the history of the rise of the English novel, although

[7] Delarivier Manley, the 'Preface' to *The Secret History of Queen Zarah and the Zarazians* (1705), repr. in Ioaon Williams (ed.), *Novel and Romance: A Documentary Record* (London, 1970), 33–9.

[8] See Dieter Schulz, ' "Novel", "Romance", and Popular Fiction in the First Half of the Eighteenth Century', *Studies in Philology*, 70 (1973), 77–91. Schulz argues that Defoe's, Richardson's, and Fielding's attacks on 'romance' are a reaction to the 'sensationalism and erotic sensualism' of Behn's, Manley's and Haywood's fiction, rather than the idealism of the seventeenth-century French romance (90).

he adds Bunyan, Cervantes, and Swift to his list. Like Watt, both McKeon and Davis are unwilling to consider the female writer's relation to the formal conflicts at work in the novel as a distinct and separate object of enquiry. Clearly women's fiction in this period is not an entirely autonomous genre free of the determinations that go into the making of the novel. Rather the perception of women's different, and frequently disruptive use of fictional forms is precisely *instrumental* in the novel's formation.

McKeon's innovative book insists on the dialectical structures at work in the process of 'novelization'. His consideration of classical and medieval constructions of the realm of fiction aligns his work with that of Frye, while his attention to historical particularity and his conviction that literary change can only be understood in relation to social forces links him with the critical heritage of Ian Watt. McKeon's object is to produce a new methodology of genre which will allow the development of the novel to be better understood. Thus, he asserts that 'what is required is a theory not just of the rise of the novel but how categories, whether 'literary' or 'social' exist in history: how they first coalesce by being understood in terms of—as transformations of—other forms that have thus far been taken to define the field of possibility' (4). McKeon, like others before him, views the novel as essentially a problem-solving genre, but one which operates on two inter-related levels, the literary and the social. The novel achieves its status as a 'simple abstraction' in the mid-eighteenth century by virtue of its ability to negotiate 'problems of categorial instability' (20). Problems of generic categorization, or what McKeon labels 'questions of truth' (how to 'tell the truth' in narrative) and problems of social categorization, or 'questions of virtue' (how to determine the relation of the social order to its members) are articulated in tandem.

For McKeon, novelistic narrative deals primarily with problems of signification, exploring the means by which narrative signifies 'truth' (moral or empirical) and by which the individual signifies his or her 'virtue' (inherited or inherent). A dialectical movement through the alternatives offered as resolutions of this double epistemological and ethical crisis brings about generic and social change. On the formal level with regard to questions of truth, sixteenth-century 'romance idealism' is negated by seventeenth-century naive 'empiricism' which is in turn negated by early eighteenth-century 'extreme skepticism'. The double negation of the latter entails a partial resubmission to 'romance idealism'. On the social level, a parallel movement is in train with regard to questions of virtue through a number of ideological positions that correlate to these formal categories. Sixteenth-century 'aristocratic ideology' is negated by seventeenth-century 'progressive ideology', which is in turn negated by a 'conservative ideology' which resubmits to 'aristocratic ideology', despite its attempts to complete a double negation. Thus, ideological positions relate to particular literary forms.

McKeon's schema enables a sophisticated reading of individual texts and ideological conflict in the early modern period, since it refuses any simple cause-and-effect model of the relations between literature and history. Like Davis, McKeon sees the novel as developing through a process of parody, internalization, and negation of a variety of forms, rejecting the kind of linear or sequential model that almost inevitably results in the advocacy of the 'triumph of realism'. Further, he insists on the specificities of class differentials in this period, challenging Watt's double thesis of the rise of the middle class and the decline of the romance on the grounds that status and formal distinctions in the early modern period are far less unified and coherent than Watt would have them be.

This new schematization can, like Frye's 'modes', appear merely taxonomical and rigidly deterministic. However, its central premise that prose fiction narrative in this period negotiates problems of the relation of epistemological to ethical authority, is, for the purpose of this book at least, a valuable one. In similar vein to McKeon, Nancy Armstrong has argued that 'the internal composition of a given text is nothing more or less than the history of its struggle with contrary forms of representation for the struggle to control semiosis' (23). McKeon is rightly suspicious of those readings of the eighteenth-century novel that would ignore the political and ideological centrality of a discourse of female 'chastity' to the formation of new social hierarchies in the mid-eighteenth century, preferring to see the privileging of chastity as a simple exercise of patriarchal power and control over women:

In associating female virtue with chastity, the eighteenth century is commonly thought to mark a low point of careless patriarchal cynicism. But it may be more accurate to see that association in the context of patrilineal honor, a critique in which women, besieged by discredited aristocratic honor, come to embody the locus and refuge of honorous virtue. (158)

An idealized notion of a female 'virtue' as a form of resistance to aristocratic despotism, which reaches its nadir with Richardson's *Pamela* in 1740, is, then, part of the 'progressive' language of emergent social classes. The insight that a discourse on 'woman' or valorization of the 'feminine' in a particular culture may not signify either feminist protest or a retrenchment of patriarchal power, is an important one for feminist criticism, if it is to avoid the equation of (masculine) class interest with feminist sentiment.

However, *The Origins of the English Novel* does not consider the position of women writers as in any way distinct from that of their male contemporaries in terms of the representation of gender conflict. Aphra Behn, Delarivier Manley, and Eliza Haywood all, for the first time in histories of the rise of the novel, receive serious attention and critical reading in McKeon's book, but precisely not as *women* novelists. In his section entitled 'The Gendering of Ideology',
→ McKeon notes that love or amatory narrative is deployed in the service of both progressive (Behn and Davys) and conservative (Manley and Haywood) positions (255–65). The progressive narrative reveals aristocratic honour to be mere avarice and appetite acted out against the industrious virtue of the merchant and/or woman, while the conservative narrative identifies this same avarice and appetite as the motivation behind the supposed 'virtue' of the progressive male or female protagonist. Thus the amatory plot is revealed to be itself a mere disguise for another interest, the elaboration of a particular political ideology.

McKeon does not employ his usual dialectical method with regard to these women writers for whom sexual and party politics are plotted in a constant dynamic. Women's amatory plots in this period are, of course, on one level, political allegories, but, I will argue, they refuse to be read solely as such. They attempt to articulate sexual and party political interest simultaneously, with reference both to the struggle for a specifically female authority in sexual and party political representation and to the more general struggle to resolve ethical and epistemological crises in the social order through narrative form.

Myth, Seduction, and the Novel

In contrast, J. J. Richetti's earlier book, *Popular Fiction before Richardson* (1969) does consider early women novelists as playing a

distinctive and separate role in the making of early modern prose
fiction. Richetti's exploration of the workings of 'popular' fiction
and its affective goals with stress on the 'seductive' capacity of
narrative, have all provided rich sources of investigation for this
book. Richetti dismisses Watt's equation of the rise of the middle
class with realist technique in fiction on grounds of anachronism:
'What is involved is nothing less than a gratuitous imposition of the
social and philosophical norms (summed up in such terms as
bourgeois democracy and pragmatism) and the narrative effects
(summed up in the term realism) we value most upon a body of
writing which was at least partly unaware of, if not hostile to,
them.'[9]

Richetti turns his critical attention to the 'sub-genres' of the novel
before the advent of domestic fiction, considering rogue and whore
biographies, travel and pirate narratives, scandal chronicles, the
amatory novella, and the pious polemic as ideological apparatuses
for articulating a central conflict between secular and religious belief
in the first decades of the eighteenth century. In doing so, he shifts
our attention from the moment of production in prose narrative to
that of consumption, arguing that narratives only 'become "fictions"
during the process of consumption' (7). Popular forms of fiction are
described as 'fantasy-machines' (9), satisfying readers' voyeuristic
erotic desires and their moral expectations simultaneously.

In other words, for Richetti popular fiction works as ideology
'command[ing] immediate, emotional and inarticulate assent' on the
part of its reader (11). Richetti attributes Manley and Haywood's
popular success to their ability to exploit latent sexual and social
antagonism in the same narrative form of the 'scandal chronicle'
(124). Their use of a 'myth of persecuted innocence' to drive
narrative structure is interpreted as a sign of 'an eighteenth-century
feminism, not yet a political movement, of course, but a set of
apparently stirring moral and emotional affirmations' (181), a
nascent feminism which the pious polemic of Penelope Aubin and
Jane Barker in the 1720s succeeded in repressing in favour of an
essentially conservative sentimental moralism.

However, Richetti's argument raises as many problems as it
answers. He points out that theories of literary history establish
themselves on the basis of a 'rigorous selection of texts ... that have

[9] J. J. Richetti, *Popular Fiction before Richardson: Narrative Patterns 1700–39* (Oxford,
1969), 4.

slithered through the fine nets of posterity' (4) and rightly insists that we cannot understand the development of prose fiction in the eighteenth century without recognizing its status 'as a significant step in the emergence of a "mass art"' (5). Yet he all too willingly concedes that early prose fiction is in the main 'morally indefensible' and 'bad art' (5), leaving his reader with the impression that any study of it is merely a tedious duty undertaken for the sake of historical accuracy alone. Moreover, Richetti retreats into Watt's historical methodology of employing literary texts as sociological data. In the light of the lack of historical evidence with regard to readers, he tells us, 'it seems . . . perfectly valid to generalize about this audience by treating their texts as evidence, by analysing them, and deducing their audience's features from them' (9). Since he else-where asserts that we must recognize that art 'provides fantasies which allow pleasurable identification and projection' (5), rather than simply historical reflection, this method of procedure must come under scrutiny. In particular, Richetti leaves unquestioned the assumption that the readership of amatory fiction was female. Yet if we can 'deduce', as Richetti does, that Manley and Haywood were presenting erotic fantasy under the guise of moral exempla—in other words that neither writer tells the truth about her text, how can we be sure that their claims to present a female audience with stories of tragic love did not conceal an address to male and female readers alike in terms of party politics?

Further, Richetti consistently interprets the ideological strategies of 'popular' texts as simple. Fantasy-machines, he informs us, need only straightforward literacy skills on the part of their reader, rather than sophisticated reading techniques (9). Ideology, then, is nothing more or less than what Marxists would term 'false consciousness'. Terry Eagleton has noted the shortcomings of this conception of ideology as 'a screen interposed between men and their history', in that 'it fails to grasp ideology as an inherently complex formation which, by inserting individuals into history in a variety of ways, allows of multiple kinds and degrees of access to that history'.[10]

Richetti sees the popular fictions of the early eighteenth century as succeeding in the presentation of historically specific gender and class conflict in terms of absolute mythic opposition. While this may be broadly true of its fictional strategy, it seems mistaken to assume

[10] Terry Eagleton, *Criticism and Ideology: A Study in Marxist Literary Theory* (London, 1976), 69.

that the supposedly limited capacities of popular imagination *dictate* such a movement, or that readers with only adequate literacy skills are inevitably incapable of grasping ideological complexity. We might contrast Richetti's vision of an eminently simple world of mythic opposition offered to the eighteenth century reader with Lennard Davis's argument that epistemological ambiguity in these same texts served to construct a 'paranoid' reader:

What writers seem to have been faced with was a threat to the mechanism of signification caused by a reading which demanded that the reader look beyond and discard the literal text. Reading of this type can be seen as becoming something of a paranoid venture in which seemingly insignificant details would yield the true, but concealed, meaning of a written work, and endless levels of meaning could be plumbed without certainty as to which was the 'real' text.[11]

Richetti's tendency to interpret popular fiction as mere 'allegory' conceals the complexity of the reading act initiated in this pre-novelistic period. The readers of women's amatory fiction are required to read by a process of constant movement between sexual and party political meaning, rather than strip off the cloak of party political satire to reveal the 'true' narrative of sexual opposition, as Richetti suggests, or lift the veil of the love plot to reveal the party political one, as McKeon implies.

Women's Traditions and the Novel

Feminist critics, of course, cannot be accused of failing to take note that women writers in this period were differently situated in relation to epistemological and ethical questions by virtue of their sex. Indeed, here the consideration of women as *writers* has tended to be neglected. Women's contribution to the formal development of the novel has been subordinated to the project of exploring their literature for sociological evidence of the position of women in general. In fact, with the exception of Bridget MacCarthy's 1944 book, *Women Writers: Their Contribution to the English Novel*, feminist critics have only recently turned their attention to the large number of women writers in the eighteenth century.[12] The major works of

---

[11] Lennard Davis, *Factual Fictions*, 150.
[12] Bridget MacCarthy, *Women Writers: Their Contribution to the English Novel 1621–1744* (Cork, 1944). MacCarthy, however, took a highly censorious view of the salacious and erotic content of Behn's, Manley's, and Haywood's writing.

feminist literary history in the 1970s were inclined to see women's fiction in the eighteenth century as at best consisting of a few tentative attempts to depict female experience faithfully, a process which the nineteenth century brought to fruition. Thus Elaine Showalter in her otherwise ground-breaking *A Literature of their Own* (1976) dismisses eighteenth-century women writers with the comment that 'they refused to deal with a professional role, or had a negative orientation toward it . . . they did not see their writing as an aspect of female experience, or as an expression of it'.[13]

This kind of feminist criticism proves itself to be as trapped in realist teleologies as its masculinist counterpart. The image of the modest and amateur eighteenth-century woman of letters owes its genesis to the literary personae of Fanny Burney and Jane Austen and is born out of a reaction to the high level of professionalism and blatant eroticism practised by women writers earlier in the century. Like Showalter, Sandra Gilbert and Susan Gubar in their *Madwoman in the Attic* (1979) produce a determinedly linear account of female literary history viewed as a series of increasingly sophisticated aesthetic responses to the restrictions imposed by a 'patriarchal poetics':

Detached from herself, silenced, subdued, this woman artist tried in the beginning . . . to write like an angel in the house of fiction: with Jane Austen and Maria Edgworth, she concealed her own truth behind a decorous and ladylike facade, scattering her own wishes to the winds or translating them into incomprehensible hieroglyphics. But as the time passed and her cave-prison became more constricted, claustrophobic, she 'fell' into the gothic/Satanic mode, and with the Brontes and Mary Shelley, she planned mad or monstrous escapes, then dizzily withdrew—with George Eliot and Emily Dickinson—from those open spaces where the scorching presence of the patriarchal sun . . . emphasized her vulnerability. (101–2)

Formal change in women's narrative fiction, in this account, is caused by the inability of previous forms to maintain an effective resistance to, or protection from, the energies of patriarchal power. Gilbert and Gubar do succeed in abandoning a strictly 'representationalist' view to women's narrative fiction, reading it for its covert messages and formal strategies, rather than as a straightforward

---

[13] Elaine Showalter, *A Literature of Their Own: British Women Novelists from Bronte to Lessing*, rev. edn. (London, 1982), 18–19. For other major feminist histories of the woman's novel, see Sandra Gilbert and Susan Gubar, *The Madwoman in the Attic: The Woman Writer and the Nineteenth Century Literary Imagination* (London and New Haven, Conn., 1979) and Ellen Moers, *Literary Women: The Great Writers* (London, 1977).

reflection of female experience on the level of content. However, the message they find behind women's narrative manipulations is always the same. Rage at patriarchal oppression is the 'truth' behind every woman's fiction and the feminist critic's job is to discover and uncover its strategies of concealment.

In the 1980s feminist critics have given new attention to women novelists in the early eighteenth century. The work to date has, however, largely consisted of bibliographical and biographical research.[14] While this kind of 'rediscovery' provides a vital source for critical analysis, it is the contention of this book that, in relation to this period of intense generic confusion and disturbance, women's writing must be analysed within a history of genre if it is to find a satisfactory place in accounts of the 'rise' of the novel. Feminist criticism, as the example of Gilbert and Gubar suggests, has been inclined to interpret women's choices to write within a particular genre or form as motivated solely by the attempt to escape patriarchal oppression as though the history of women's writing was somehow exempt from the pressures of generic convention within which male writers operate.

Notable exceptions to this rule are two recent studies of early modern women's writing from Jane Spencer and Janet Todd, which endeavour to provide a more specific account of the woman writer's changing status in the realm of fiction and of the figure of the woman in the discourse of fiction in the eighteenth century.[15] Spencer's *The Rise of the Woman Novelist* offers a meticulous history of women's relationship to literary 'authority' from the mid-seventeenth to the late eighteenth century. Thematic responses to the 'woman question' in a variety of prose fictions by women are sought out and identified under the headings of protest, conformity, and escape. Spencer does not seek to produce a linear history of a single female tradition in the novel. She neither views women's writing as entirely self-determining in isolation from male-authored texts, nor subsumes the category 'woman writer' into a general study of the novel. In her introduction she asserts that 'the rise of the novel

---

[14] See, in particular, Janet Todd (ed.), *A Dictionary of British and American Women Writers 1600–1800* (London, 1984) and Dale Spender, *Mothers of the Novel: One Hundred Good Women Writers before Jane Austen* (London, 1986).

[15] Jane Spencer, *The Rise of the Woman Novelist: From Aphra Behn to Jane Austen* (Oxford, 1986); Janet Todd, *The Sign of Angellica: Women, Writing and Fiction 1660–1800* (London, 1989).

cannot be understood fully without considering how its conventions were shaped by the contributions of a large number of women, their writing deeply marked by the 'femininity' insistently demanded of them by the culture to which they belonged' (p. vii).

Spencer is rightly suspicious of the assumption that women's writing must inevitably occupy an oppositional position in relation to patriarchal society, and that the rise of the professional woman writer necessarily indicates a more general rise in the social status of women. Indeed, she argues, it might imply that women were suffering an increasing alienation from direct political and economic agency: 'at the same time as encouraging women to write, this feminization of literature defined literature as a special category supposedly outside the political arena, with an influence on the world as indirect as women's was supposed to be' (p. xi).

The Rise of the Woman Novelist provides a thematic or content-oriented analysis which pays little attention to formal distinctions within the category of the novel. Thus, epistolary fictions, scandal narratives, romances, histories are aligned according to the different responses their plots manifest to contemporary ideologies of proper femininity. Women's prose fiction in this period is accorded three trajectories or traditions which 'overlap and influence one another, but are nonetheless sufficiently distinct to be discussed under three headings' (108). While this method of consideration enables Spencer to cover an extensive and diverse body of texts, it sacrifices the question of formal specificity to one of thematic unity. In this respect, Spencer's three traditions are highly reminiscent of Elaine Showalter's three 'stages' in the history of women's writing outlined in her *A Literature of their Own*.[16] Both Showalter and Spencer represent their different 'traditions' as marked by a particular attitude on the part of the female author to an abstracted and culturally sanctioned definition of the 'feminine'. Women's writing is thus seen as an ongoing response to masculine cultural authority, its primary concern the construction of alternative models and means of winning female power. Yet generic conventions are at least as important as ideological concepts in the making of women's fiction

---

[16] In her first chapter, Showalter identifies three stages in the history of women's writing: the feminine (1840–1880), dominated by the imitation of male models and subservience to the presentation of the 'feminine' woman: the feminist (1880–1920), representing women's protest and marked by the dramatization of wronged woman-hood and/or female utopia: the female (1920 onwards), a stage in which women writers attempt self-definition and insist on artistic autonomy (3–36).

and the shaping of representations of femininity in this transitional period. They can neither be reduced to nor substituted for contemporary gender ideologies. A categorization of fiction by and for women simply on the basis of content and theme ignores the dialectical relations *between* content and form that go to make up novelistic discourse.

If Spencer rejects a strictly linear history of women's novelistic fiction that ignores its relation to the writing of men and to other literary forms, she continues to subscribe to the commonplace of eighteenth-century literary studies that there was a rise of the novel in this period. By contrast, Todd's *The Sign of Angellica* opens with the bold claim that 'literature is not progressive; there is not really a *rise* of the male or the female novel' (2). She supports her argument by pointing to the 'sophisticated insights and techniques' employed by Behn and Manley in comparison with the unswerving position of 'moralist's authority' adopted by women novelists of the mid- to late eighteenth century such as Sarah Fielding and Ann Radcliffe. The rise in prestige of the novel form through the century does not necessarily betoken increasing sophistication in narrative technique, nor should we allow our analysis of eighteenth-century fiction to be overly determined by the realist aesthetics that came to dominate in the century that followed. Todd's book offers accounts and interpretations of individual texts by women from 1660 to 1800 alongside analysis of prevailing political, social, and cultural conditions in the three periods she identifies as producing significantly different variations in fictional prose by women (the Restoration and early eighteenth century, the mid-eighteenth century and the late eighteenth century). As a result, she provides only a cursory study of the novels of Behn and Manley, while Haywood receives consideration solely as the author of moralistic courtship fiction in the 1750s.

Seductive Forms both expands on the serious attention *The Sign of Angellica* accords to the narrative ambiguity and explicit eroticism of the female-authored novel of the Restoration and early eighteenth century and takes issue with some of Todd's assertions about the application of critical theory to feminist literary history. Todd argues that, since 'psychoanalytical or deconstructionist criticism ... sees feminine writing less as writing by women than as a modality open to either sex' (7), it ignores the importance of female *signature*, privileging the writing of the figure 'woman' over the question of women's writing. While I concur with this judgement, I would suggest that we cannot dispense with the insights of psychoanalysis and deconstruction in feminist criticism *in so far* as they point to the complexity and ambiguity of meaning in language and particularly the discourse of sexual desire. They ask us, then, to question those assumptions that I have already highlighted as limiting our understanding of the eighteenth-century woman writer's intervention in party and sexual politics—the stability of generic distinction, the primacy of romance and the 'woman question' as concerns in texts by women, the superiority of realist technique in narrative fiction. Above all, it seems to me that psychoanalytic criticism offers one, if not the only, route toward an understanding of the importance of the role of fantasy in the production of textual meaning.

Fantasy, Narrative, and Seduction

This book considers one 'thematic' concern of early prose fiction consistently identified with female authorship, the representation of 'amatory' intrigue, in the light of the epistemological and ethical questions that distinctive narrative forms raise in the period 1684 to 1740. One of its central premises remains that 'formal' questions are by no means abstract or apolitical, but rather profoundly ideological. In this respect, I would concur with Michael McKeon's assertion that 'the distinctive feature of novelistic narrative is its internalization or thematization of formal problems on the level of content'.[17] Seduction narratives provide a peculiarly complex instance of this process in that their content and their form appear to mirror each other. The telling of a story of seduction is also a mode of seduction. The struggle for control over the identification and interpretation of amatory signs between male and female protagonists which is enacted on the level of content can be taken as a metaphorical substitution for the struggle for epistemological authority between male and female readers and writers on the level of form.

In a different context Ross Chambers has noted the connection between the development of a metaphor of seduction to describe the power of narrative and a certain alienation of the 'literary' from the social. At the point where writing becomes a form of labour and the literary work a commodity, a crisis of authority is instigated in the realm of textual production:

when narrative ceases to be (perceived as) a mode of direct communication

[17] McKeon, *Origins of the English Novel*, 266.

of some pre-existing knowledge and comes instead to figure as an oblique way of raising awkward, not to say unanswerable questions, it becomes necessary for it to trade in the manipulation of desire (that is, the desire to narrate must seek to arouse some corresponding desire for narration) to the precise extent that it can no longer depend, in its hearers or readers, on some 'natural' thirst for information.[18]

In other words, the alienation of the producer from his product results in reification. Other critics have noted that the increasing substitution of patronage with commercial publication as the major mode of material production in literature and a concomitant increase in the legitimating power of print (itself part of a larger transformation in the mode of production in the late seventeenth century from feudal to early capitalist relations) produces just such an 'alienation' for the writer from his or her work.[19]

While this change in the mode of literary production liberated the aspiring woman writer in that she could now earn a living by her pen and compete in a more 'open' market, these gains did not exempt her from experiencing the same problems of 'authorization' as her male counterpart. Narratorial power was now accorded by a reading market, rather than the political and economic influence of a patron. Literary texts became increasingly specialized in this new market, since publishers, in order to make profits, had to target particular large sections of their potential audience. In this sense, then, what Ross Chambers describes as the 'transactional status' of the narrative text, shifts 'from a sense of (seductive) *authority* exerted by the text to a sense of the (still seductive) *dependency* of the text on the act of reading that [was] to realize it, in its complexity and plurality, as writing' (14). Seduction narratives, as this book demonstrates, precisely dramatize such an uneasy relationship toward their readership within the tale of love. Interpretation of the 'signs' of love and their truthfulness or duplicity becomes a field of conflict in these female-authored texts, a conflict that is

[18] Ross Chambers, *Story and Situation: Narrative Seduction and the Power of Fiction* (Manchester University Press Theory and History of Literature Ser., 12; Manchester, 1984), 13.
[19] See Lennard Davis, *Factual Fictions*, 144–6, and Raymond Williams, *Marxism and Literature* (Oxford, 1977), 154–64. See also Leo Lowenthal and Margaret Fiske, 'The Debate over Art and Popular Culture: English Eighteenth Century as a Case Study', in Leo Lowenthal (ed.), *Literature, Popular Culture and Society* (Englewood Cliffs, NJ, 1961), 52–108.

recognized throughout as deeply implicated in the struggle for political and literary authority between the two genders.

Recent developments in psychoanalytic criticism have drawn our attention to the parallelism between the metonymic drive of narrative and the metonymic structure of desire, drawing on Roman Jakobson's identification of the two poles of language, metaphor and metonym, with the 'poetic' and 'narratological' aspects of literary production, as well as Freud's conception of desire as an ongoing pursuit of an imaginary 'lost' wholeness with the mother on the part of the child.[20] Here too, then, narrative is associated with 'alienation', considered on the psychic plane of separation from the mother's body and entrance into language as a symbolic substitution for that loss (in other words, the shift from demand to desire), as opposed to the social alienation Marxists and social historians have recognized as the characteristic quality of capitalist modes of production (the shift from use to exchange and, hence, surplus value).

The discourses of psychoanalysis and semiotics provide a more sophisticated model of the workings of desire in language and, specifically, the role of fantasy in popular narrative, than the central texts of eighteenth-century novel criticism have hitherto offered. Although the application of a late nineteenth-century clinical methodology to the reading of early eighteenth-century texts may appear anachronistic, psychoanalysis's understanding of the processes of 'reading' and the duplicities of narrative acts, evolved through the experience of the analytic exchange, has a peculiar appropriateness to a period in which the problem of differentiating 'fact' from 'fiction' dominated the field of narrative. Sigmund Freud is himself one of the best known readers of the seduction narrative and the texts which are the focus of this book can be usefully interpreted in the light of his changing perceptions of the importance of the tale of seduction to the formation of the (female) subject.

---

[20] See Roman Jakobson and Morris Halle, *Fundamentals of Language* (The Hague, 1956), 76–82; Jacques Lacan, 'The Agency of the Letter in the Unconscious', *Écrits: A Selection*, trans. Alan Sheridan (London and New York, 1977), 146–78; Robert Con Davis (ed.), *Lacan and Narration: The Psychoanalytic Difference in Narrative Theory* (Baltimore and London, 1983). For a useful account of structural psychoanalysis's understanding of the Freudian child's entry into language, see Elizabeth Wright, *Psychoanalytic Criticism: Theory in Practice* (London, 1984), 107–22.

Freud's renunciation of his seduction theory in the late 1890s was to be formative in the evolution of a theory of fantasy. His own narration in an essay entitled 'On the History of the Psychoanalytic Movement' (1914) of the epistemological crisis engendered by his unwillingness to believe that so many of his 'hysterical' female patients could have experienced sexual abuse, or what he terms 'seduction' at the hands of their fathers at an early age, is a telling one:

One was readily inclined to accept as etiologically significant the statements made by patients in which they ascribed their symptoms to passive sexual experiences in the first years of childhood—to put it bluntly, to seduction. When this etiology broke down under the weight of its own improbability and contradiction in definitely ascertainable circumstances, the result at first was helpless bewilderment. Analysis had led back to these infantile sexual traumas by the right path, and yet they were not true. The firm ground of reality was gone. . . . At last came the reflection that, after all, one had no right to despair because one has been deceived in one's expectations. If hysterical subjects trace their symptoms to traumas that are fictitious, then the new fact which emerges is precisely that they create such scenes in fantasy, and this psychical reality requires to be taken into account alongside practical reality. This reflection was soon followed by the discovery that these fantasies were intended to cover up the autoerotic activity of the first years of childhood, to embellish it and raise it to a higher plane.[21]

It is beyond the scope of this book to provide a history of the negative effects of Freud's scepticism in the clinical world of psycho-analysis, but his exploration here of the confusions of fact and fiction in the seduction narrative can be usefully employed with respect to the work of art.

Freud asks us to read narrative on two levels, that of mimetic representation and that of desiring projection. Thus, the compuls-ively repetitive structure of seduction and betrayal in women's amatory fiction may express, on the mimetic level, women's sense of oppression at the hands of patriarchy, and, on the level of fantasy, their active desire for control over amatory representation. According to Freud, the narrating female subject converts her own

---

[21] Sigmund Freud, 'On the History of the Psychoanalytic Movement', *The Standard Edition of the Complete Psychological Works of Sigmund Freud*, trans. and ed. James Strachey *et al.* (London, 1953–74), xiv. 17 (cited as *SE* with vol. number). For a critique of Freud's renunciation of the seduction theory, see J. M. Masson, *Freud: The Assault on Truth* (London, 1984).

tale of passivity in the face of seduction into an act of seduction in itself, in that she tells the tale in order to seduce her auditor or reader.

Psychoanalytic concepts of 'transference' remind us that the analysand seeks to 'affect' the analyst.[22] As Meredith Anne Skura, in her own consideration of the uses of psychoanalysis in literary analysis, points out, fantasy narration is inherently transactional and its main object, far from 'telling the truth', may be to seduce its consumer.[23] Psychoanalytic theory makes us aware that fantasy in narrative is far more complex than Richetti's 'false consciousness' model suggests. As Skura goes on to argue, fantasy cannot be understood merely as wish-fulfillment, or, with respect to the literary text, catharsis. It takes the form of a dispersed 'set of ingredients or a structure of conflict' which resonates throughout the text (59).

This conceptualization of the nature of fantasy also undermines the critical belief in a straightforward process of 'identification' or projection in both the consumption and production of the literary text. Critics of twentieth-century popular romantic fiction for women are inclined to assume that women readers identify solely with the dominant female subject position represented in the text, that is, that of the embattled heroine.[24] Fantasy can entail the pleasure of undermining a fixed subject position for the reader or consumer through the experience of textual pleasure, as well as identification with available subject positions in the text.[25] A reading of textual fantasy requires that the critic recognize that imaginary pleasures are invested across an entire spectrum of literary techniques and phenomena, whereby desires are constantly displaced

[22] On 'transference', see J. Laplanche and J.-B. Pontalis, 'Transference', in *The Language of Psycho-Analysis*, trans. Donald Nicholson-Smith (The International Psycho-Analytical Library, 94; London, 1983), 455–62.

[23] Meredith Anne Skura, *The Literary Use of the Psychoanalytic Process* (London and New Haven, Conn., 1981), 10.

[24] See Tania Modleski's otherwise illuminating readings of romantic fiction, the Gothic, and soap opera in her *Loving with a Vengeance: Mass-Produced Fantasies for Women* (London and New York, 1984); Carol Thurston, *The Romance Revolution: Erotic Novels for Women and the Quest for a New Sexual Identity* (Urbana and Chicago, 1987) and Ann Barr Snitow, 'Mass Market Romance: Pornography for Women Is Different', in Ann Barr Snitow, Christine Stansell, and Sharon Thompson (eds.), *Desire: The Politics of Sexuality* (London, 1984), 258–75.

[25] See Cora Kaplan, 'The Thorn Birds: Fiction, Fantasy, Femininity', in *Sea Changes. Culture and Feminism* (London, 1986), 131; Laplanche and Pontalis on 'Phantasy (or Fantasy)', 314–19; and Rosemary Jackson, *Fantasy. The Literature of Subversion* (London, 1981), 61–82.

and transformed, rather than simply acted out through a single literary character.

The parallels between twentieth-century romantic fiction for women and amatory fiction by women in the early eighteenth century are by no means absolute. We can have no access to the reading responses of the majority of women readers in this period, although diaries and letters of individual women such as Dorothy Osborne and Mary Montagu may give us some insight.[26] The attention of this book is, instead, directed toward an analysis of the specific address that Behn, Manley, and Haywood make to female readers and the interpretative conflict between the genders that is the structuring feature of their amatory plots.

My analysis of three major women writers of the early eighteenth century makes no attempt to provide a teleology of romantic fiction from 1684 to the present day. As this chapter has sought to demonstrate, teleologies of narrative fiction all too frequently erase historical difference and silence complexity. Indeed, my reading of early narrative prose by women suggests that the advent of the sentimental novel in the 1740s constituted a displacement of the direct political engagements of amatory fiction into the realm of the domestic and the private (see Conclusion).

This book offers, rather, a synchronic analysis of a particular historical moment in the making of the English novel. As such, it challenges both conventional (historicist and formalist) and feminist histories of the bourgeois novel, arguing that the early woman writer was very far from the modest and amateur lady of letters most histories would have her be. She was rather a prostitute of the pen, trafficking in desire for profit and, in this respect, no different from many of her male contemporaries. Behn, Manley, and Haywood reveal themselves to be far from subjected by the imposition of an emergent philosophy of 'separate spheres' (politics and romance, masculine and feminine, the coffee-house and the boudoir). Indeed,

[26] Dorothy Osborne and later Mary Wortley Montagu were both avid readers of 'romance' fiction. See Dorothy Osborne, *The Letters of Dorothy Osborne to William Temple*, ed. G. C. Moore Smith (Oxford, 1928) and Mary Wortley Montagu, *The Complete Letters of Lady Mary Wortley Montagu*, ed. Robert Halsband (4 vols.; Oxford, 1966). Both are fascinating commentators on the French romance of the mid-seventeenth century and Montagu was a reader of a variety of early eighteenth-century English women writers. For research into twentieth-century women readers of romance see Janice Radway, *Reading the Romance: Women, Patriarchy and Popular Literature* (London, 1984).

they exploit this division in order to construct, against a short history of literary models, a specifically female writing identity for themselves. Their experimental texts dramatize the seduction of the female reader by amatory fiction, exploring alternatives that offer models for the female victim to come to 'mastery' of or resistance to the fictional text through the figure of the heroinized female writer.

2
Observing the Forms: Amatory Fiction and the Construction of a Female Reader

[W]ithout the several formalities that are us'd in it, Love would not be that which it is. . . . Ceremonies make up the principal beauties of many things; for example, separate a sacrifice from the Temple, the Altar, the Wood-pile, the holy Vessels, and Knives, the fillets of the Victims, and Garlands of Flowers which crown them, and you will see nothing but a miserable animal, which is no fairer than another of its kind.[1]

Women enjoy'd, are like Romances read, or Raree-shows, once seen, meer Tricks of the slight of hand, which, when found out, you only wonder at your selves for wondering so before at them. 'Tis Expectation endears the Blessing; Heaven would not be Heaven, could we tell what 'tis.[2]

In the quotations above, the two women who dominated the sphere of love fiction in the late seventeenth century in England, one French and one English, draw our attention to the fact that the passion of love only becomes eroticized through the workings of cultural convention. Love, it appears, is a matter of form. Indeed, for Aphra Behn's heroine, Belvira, femininity itself is, simply, an attractive fiction. The equation between the female 'form', or body, and female forms, or amatory fictions, is the subject of this chapter, which explores the established modes of love fiction available to British women novelists of the late seventeenth and early eighteenth century, and the role of the female reader inscribed in their making. The term 'amatory' is employed here as a means of distinguishing a particular body of narrative fiction by women which was explicitly erotic in its concentration on the representation of sentimental love.

[1] Madeleine de Scudéry, *Clelia: An Excellent New Romance*, trans. J. Davies and G. Havers (London, 1678), pt. 5, p. 655. First published as *Clélie* (Paris, 1654–61). (The edition used throughout unless otherwise stated is the English translation of 1678 above; pts. 1–3 trans. J. Davies (1659), pts. 4–5 trans. G. Havers (1677); cited by part since page numbering is irregular, running pts. 1–2 (pp. 1–330) and pts. 3–5 (pp. 217–736).)

[2] Aphra Behn, 'The Unfortunate Bride, or, The Blind Lady a Beauty', in *The Works of Aphra Behn*, ed. Montague Summers (London, 1915), v. 407. (All subsequent references to Behn's works are to this edition, unless otherwise indicated, cited as Behn, *Works* with volume and page numbers and included in the main body of the text.)

Defining Amatory Fiction

The fiction of Aphra Behn, Delarivier Manley, and Eliza Haywood was perceived as distinctively different both from male pornography and the didactic love fiction of other women writers of the period. Roger Thompson and David Foxon have meticulously detailed the male-centred pornography of the late seventeenth century.[3] The primarily anatomical, procreative and instructional emphasis of this literature bears little resemblance to the erotic-pathetic drive of the seduction and betrayal narratives of Behn, Manley, and Haywood.[4]

The didactic love fiction produced by female contemporaries of Behn, Manley, and Haywood bore closer formal resemblances to their writing than pornography of this kind, but emerged in reaction to their influence. Penelope Aubin, Elizabeth Singer Rowe, Jane Barker, and, to a lesser extent, Mary Davys, seek to revive moral vigour in feminocentric representations of love. The roots of their fiction lie in didactic prose, the conduct book, and the 'chaste' Platonic idealism of that early feminist polemicist, Mary Astell.[5]

Penelope Aubin, in her preface to *The Life of Charlotta du Pont*, published in 1723 when the career of Eliza Haywood was at its height, took pains to distinguish herself from other female producers of women's (fictional) histories:

My booksellers say my novels sell tolerably well. I had designed to employ my pen on something more serious and learned, but they tell me I shall meet with

---

[3] Roger Thompson, *Unfit for Modest Ears: A Study of Pornographic, Obscene and Bawdy Works Written or Published in England in the Second Half of the Seventeenth Century* (London, 1979) and David Foxon, *Libertine Literature in England 1660–1745* (New York, 1965).

[4] For discussions of male-centred pornography in the eighteenth century, dominated by *L'École des Filles* and Aretine's *La Putane Errante*, other than Foxon and Thompson, see Paul Gabriel Boucé (ed.), *Sexuality in Eighteenth Century Britain* (Manchester, 1982); Peter Wagner, *Eros Revived: Erotica of the Enlightenment in England and America* (London, 1988); Roy Porter, 'The Secrets of Generation Display'd: *Aristotle's Masterpiece*', and James G. Turner, 'The Properties of Libertinism', in Robert M. Macubbin (ed.), *'Tis Nature's Fault: Unauthorized Sexuality during the Enlightenment* (Cambridge, 1987), 1–21, 75–87. For a discussion of the evidence as to class and gender of readers, see Thompson on 'Writers and Readers', in *Unfit for Modest Ears*, 197–210.

[5] Mary Astell's *Serious Proposal to the Ladies* (1696) is probably the single most influential treatise on female education of the seventeenth and eighteenth centuries. See *The First English Feminist: Reflections on Marriage and Other Writings*, ed. Bridget Hill (Aldershot, 1986) and Ruth Perry, *The Celebrated Mary Astell: An Early English Feminist* (Chicago and London, 1986).

no encouragement and advised me to write rather more modishly, that is, less like a Christian, and in a style careless and loose, as the custom of the present age is to live. But I leave that to the other female authors, my contemporaries, whose lives and writings have, I fear, too great a resemblance.[6]

In similar vein, Jane Barker prefaced her *Exilius, or, The Banish'd Roman* (1715) with a long panegyric to 'heroic love' as the foundation for a good marriage, declaring that she 'would burn both the Copy and [her] Fingers, rather than employ them toward [her book's] Publication' if she felt it contained anything 'opposite to real Virtue'.[7] Elizabeth Singer Rowe came to represent the epitome of female piety in eighteenth-century England with the publication of her *Friendship in Death, or Letters from the Dead to the Living* (1728) and was given the honour in John Duncombe's poem, *The Feminiad* (1754), of banishing Manley, Suzannah Centilivre, and Aphra Behn from the scene of women's literature because of their immodesty.[8]

The early eighteenth century, then, saw a split between female-authored pious and didactic love fiction, stressing the virtues of chastity or sentimental marriage, and erotic fiction by women, with its voyeuristic attention to the combined pleasures and ravages of seduction. Richetti points out the links and differences between these two kinds of love fiction available in the first half of the eighteenth century, cynically concluding that Aubin, Barker, and Rowe introduced a new and 'insistent pious frame of reference' as 'a deliberate attempt to sell female fiction to a wider audience by making it impeccably respectable' (239).

Richetti's suggestion, however, seems premature. It was not until later in the century that pious polemic could be sure of the lion's share of the market. Barker, Aubin, and Rowe produced the fictional correlatives of the feminist philosophy of Mary Astell, advocating sexual control or submission in women and subscribing to her high Anglican spiritualism as the solution to female suffering in the temporal world. 'The Animal Spirits', Astell informed her readers in 1697:

must be lessen'd, or render'd more Calm and Manageable; at least they must not be unnaturally and violently mov'd, by such a Diet, or such Passions,

[6] Penelope Aubin, 'Preface', *The Life of Charlotta du Pont* (1723), repr. in *Eighteenth Century British Novelists on the Novel*, ed. George L. Barnett (New York, 1968), 35.
[7] Jane Barker, 'Preface', *Exilius: Or, the Banish'd Roman*, Garland Foundations of the Novel Ser., 25; New York and London, 1973).
[8] John Duncombe, *The Feminiad: A Poem* (1754) (Augustan Reprint Society Ser., 207; Los Angeles, 1981), 15–16.

Design, and Divertisments as are likely to put 'em in a ferment. Contemplation requires a Governable Body, a sedate and steady Mind, and the Body and
the Mind do so reciprocally influence each other, that we can scarce keep the
one in tune if the other be out of it.[9]

Beside the extravagant rhetoric of desire that marks Behn's,
Manley's, and Haywood's fictions of seduction, Astell's advocacy of
abstinence and self-control seems prim and cold. Aubin's refusal to
write more 'loosely' in order to earn more money from her fiction is,
perhaps, an indicator of the fact that the woman writer seeking to
earn her living solely by her pen faced a choice of keeping either her
body or her soul together. Behn, Manley, and Haywood appear to
have had no option but the former.

The fiction of Behn, Manley, and Haywood might then be seen as
the early modern equivalent of what Ann Barr Snitow, with reference
to twentieth-century mass-market romantic fiction, has defined as
'pornography for women'. Snitow observes that pornography is
driven by 'the universal infant desire for complete, immediate
gratification, to rule the world out of the very core of passive
helplessness' (269). Patricia Meyer Spacks in her essay 'Ev'ry Woman
Is at Heart a Rake' identifies this very quality as symptomatic of
Eliza Haywood's somatic heroines, whose inability, like dreamers, to
'wake up' and control their actions at the moment of seduction,
'enact[s] a vision of irresponsibility, expressing female sexuality
without being subject to judgment. Only under such special circumstances can sexuality be separated from the need to moralize'.[10]

Late seventeenth- and early eighteenth-century amatory fiction
does indeed subscribe to many of the conventions feminist critics
have analysed as central to twentieth-century romantic fiction.
Romantic fiction entails 'a reversal of the common view of history,
allowing the usually marginalized female sphere to dominate'.[11]
Historical events are deployed as mere proof of the eternal division of
the sexes and the eternal power of love to bridge that division. Thus,
historical specificity is dissolved, since history itself is generated
solely by the unchanging power of love. By dehistoricizing and
mythologizing the public sphere, the romantic fiction writer provides

[9] Mary Astell, *A Serious Proposal to the Ladies, Part II: Wherein a Method Is Offer'd for the Improvement of their Minds* (London, 1697), 106.

[10] Patricia Meyer Spacks, 'Ev'ry Woman is at Heart a Rake', *Eighteenth Century Studies*, 8 (1974), 33.

[11] Janet Batsleer *et al.*, *Rewriting English: Cultural Politics of Gender and Class* (London, 1985), 92.

the female reader with a sense of feminine power and agency in a world usually closed to her participation.

Romantic fiction returns repeatedly to women's 'one socially acceptable moment of transcendence', that of romance.[12] In other words, romantic fiction constantly renarrates the story of courtship, closing with marriage or betrayal, as though no other period in a woman's life held significance. The pornographic pleasures of romantic fiction are built on a process of persistent textual withholding in which the act of seduction is repeatedly deferred. As Rosalind Brunt comments, romantic fiction 'appeals to a prurient curiosity of this kind: how, and how long, can the heroine "hold out"?'[13]

As later chapters demonstrate, Behn's, Manley's, and Haywood's amatory fiction display all of these characteristics. If we choose to interpret their narratives as prototypes of romantic fiction (which, I would argue, is only one facet of the complex ideology of their philosophies of love), we must consider the reasons why at this particular point in history, a 'pornography for women' should emerge. The presence of a number of social and cultural factors are necessary for the development of romantic fiction for women. Most important, romantic fiction can only flourish in an intellectual environment in which women's needs and desires are perceived as different from men's. Under the transforming power of romantic fiction our normal 'pathological experience of sex difference' is converted into pleasure, that is, 'Distance becomes titillating'.[14] In other words, romantic fiction emerges with the development of a publishing industry that differentiates between the desires of male and female readers.

The Emergence of a Female Reader

The eighteenth century is commonly perceived as a period in which mass-market book production first becomes a possibility. As Leo Lowenthal and Margaret Fiske argue, 'If one takes the term "mass" media to mean marketable cultural goods produced for a substantial buying public, the eighteenth century in England is the

---

[12] Snitow, 'Mass Market Romance', 265
[13] Rosalind Brunt, 'A Career in Love: The Romantic World of Barbara Cartland', in Christopher Pawling (ed.), *Popular Fiction and Social Change* (London, 1984), 146.
[14] Snitow, 'Mass Market Romance', 260, 262.

first period of history where it can be meaningfully applied' (52). If the broadside, chapbook, and ballad had always been available to the common reader since the development of the printing press, the mid- to late seventeenth century saw a considerable expansion of the market in fiction and secular 'histories' in accessible forms.[15] The evidence of printing history would seem to bear out the argument that the late seventeenth and early eighteenth century saw a democratization in secular culture, providing previously debarred classes with new opportunities for reading. Bertrand Bronson notes that novels throughout the eighteenth century were, on the whole, published in the cheaper form of duodecimo.[16] It is tempting to view the duodecimo novel as the early modern equivalent of the twentieth-century 'pulp' paperback commonly associated with light fiction for women.

However, a consideration of literacy figures and wages in the late seventeenth and early eighteenth century somewhat handicaps this account. The figures of Gregory King, pioneer statistician of wages and social class, reveal massive poverty among English wage earners. Over half the families in the country in 1688, according to King, were earning less than their annual expenditure.[17] Even the comparatively cheap cost of one to three shillings a volume for a duodecimo novel in the early 1700s would have been prohibitive for the vast majority of working people in England who could command a wage of only seven to fifteen shillings a week, while the folio edition of French romances at a guinea a volume were probably only within the range of the aristocracy and upper bourgeoisie.[18]

[15] See Victor E. Neuburg, *Popular Literature: A History and Guide from the Beginning of Printing to the Year 1897* (Harmondsworth, 1977) and Margaret Spufford, *Small Books and Pleasant Histories: Popular Fiction and its Readership in Seventeenth-Century England* (London, 1981).

[16] Bertrand Bronson, *Printing as an Index of Taste in Eighteenth Century England* (New York Public Library Reprint; New York, 1958), 12. On the structure of the eighteenth-century publishing industry, see Terry Belanger, 'Publishers and Writers in Eighteenth-century England', in Isabel Rivers (ed.), *Books and their Readers in Eighteenth-Century England* (Leicester, 1982), 5–26.

[17] Gregory King, 'Natural and Political Observations and Conclusions about the State and Condition of England' (1696), in *Two Tracts*, ed. George E. Barnett (Baltimore, 1936). Gregory King's findings are discussed in Roy Porter, *English Society in the Eighteenth Century* (Pelican Social History of Britain; London, 1982), 386–7. For an outline of women's work and earnings in this period see Alice Clark, *Working Life of Women in the Seventeenth Century* (London, 1919), 80.

[18] Watt, *Rise of the Novel*, 46. Circulating libraries were not founded in Britain until later in the century. In his groundbreaking essay on the eighteenth-century reading

Economic considerations are not the only bar to an easy equation of the early book-buying public with the twentieth-century mass market. Literacy figures, particularly for women, in the late seventeenth century are especially damning. David Cressy points out that despite a tenfold increase in print publication between 1640 and 1660 in England, 'At the very time that the popular press was expanding ... the direct evidence of marks and signatures shows the literacy of the common people to have been stagnant or even deteriorating'.[19] Cressy's analysis of signatures and marks on ecclesiastical records as an index of literacy reveals a strong demographic contrast in women's literacy as opposed to that of men. While the figures for male literacy differ according to class and status, they remain proportionately the same in most areas of the country. However, women's literacy shows a rapid improvement in London over the same period in comparison with all other regions.[20] London, Cressy argues, was 'uniquely hospitable to female accomplishments' (129). It is, then, no surprise that nearly all the women writers of the late seventeenth and early eighteenth century lived, worked, and found their audience in the country's capital.

Regardless of the special status of London in women's literacy figures, the fact remains that few men, and even fewer women, in late seventeenth-century and early eighteenth-century England had the ability to read or could afford to buy the amatory fiction which is the subject of this study. In the light of this knowledge, it seems that we must turn a more sceptical eye on the 'discourses' of the literary market in this period. In other words, if there were no obvious economic gains to be made by addressing women readers, what were the ideological forces at work in the creation of a myth of a fiction-hungry mass of women seducing the commercial book trade by the temptations of profit away from the publication of more 'literary' endeavours?

public, A. S. Collins cited the Reverend Samuel Fancourt, dissenting minister, who set up a library in 1740 at the cost of one guinea a year per subscriber, as the founder of the circulating library. See A. S. Collins, 'The Growth of the Reading Public during the Eighteenth Century', *Review of English Studies*, 2 (1926), 292–3. More recently, Fancourt's first library has been dated even earlier, in Salisbury in the mid-1730s. See Monte Little, *Samuel Fancourt, 1678–1768: Pioneer Librarian* (Wiltshire Monographs 3; Trowbridge: Wiltshire Library and Museum Service, 1984).

[19] David Cressy, *Literacy and the Social Order* (Cambridge, 1980), 48.

[20] From 81% illiteracy in London amongst women for the decade 1640–9, the figure drops to 52% for the decade 1690–9. In East Anglia, by contrast, women's illiteracy dropped in the same period from 91% to 79%.

Some insight into the significance of the figure of the female reader in bourgeois letters can be gleaned from two of the most popular journals of the early eighteenth century, the *Tatler* and the *Spectator*.[21] Joseph Addison and Richard Steele were by no means the first journal writers to exploit an address to the 'fair Sex', but it is, I would argue, in these two periodicals that we find the 'figure' of the bourgeois woman reader as the signifier of a newly constituted cultural order most clearly articulated.[22] Despite some twentieth-century critics' tendency to portray Addison and Steele as the fathers of an urbane and gentlemanly literary amateurism, a cursory glance at the earliest numbers of both journals reveals their interest in the female addressee.[23]

Isaac Bickerstaff, Steele's pompous elder statesman of the coffee-house, opens his *Tatler* on Tuesday, 12 April 1709 with a promise to instruct the 'worthy and well-affected Members of the Common-wealth . . . what to think', adding that he has resolved 'also to have something which may be of Entertainment to the Fair Sex, in Honour of whom [he has] invented the Title of this Paper'. By number ten, the *Tatler* had introduced Jenny Distaff, Isaac's half sister, as an occasional editor.

Only two months after Bickerstaff had been retired from his self-appointed office, the first number of the *Spectator* appeared, to be published daily rather than thrice weekly. Here too, the first numbers were explicitly oriented toward the female reader. In number ten (12 March 1711) Addison outlined the expected market for the journal, that 'Fraternity of Spectators who live in the World without having anything to do in it', or 'the Blanks of Society'. He quickly goes on to announce that.

there are none to whom this Paper will be more useful, than to the female

---

[21] Joseph Addison and Richard Steele, *The Tatler*, ed. Donald F. Bond (3 vols.; Oxford, 1987) and *The Spectator*, ed. Donald F. Bond (5 vols.; Oxford, 1965). In his introduction to the *Spectator*, Donald F. Bond suggests that its circulation in the second year of publication stood at around three to four thousand (vol. i, p. xxvi) and notes that it was one of the few journals to survive the imposition of the Stamp tax in August 1712 (vol. i, p. lxxx).

[22] For earlier and later journal publications addressed to women, see Bertha Monica Stearns, 'The First English Periodical for Women', *Modern Philology*, 28 (1930), 45–59 and 'Early English Periodicals for Ladies', *PMLA* 48 (1933), 38–60.

[23] For readings of Addison and Steele as progenitors of the 'gentleman critic', see John Barrell, 'Introduction: Artificers and Gentleman', *English Literature in History 1730–80: An Equal, Wide Survey* (London, 1983), 17–50 and Terry Eagleton, *The Function of Criticism* (Oxford, 1984), 9–27.

World. I have often thought there has not been sufficient Pains taken in finding out proper Employments and Diversions for the Fair Ones. Their Amusements seem contrived for them rather as they are Women, than as they are reasonable Creatures; and they are more adapted to the Sex, than to the Species. The Toilet is their great Scene of Business, and the right adjusting to their Hair the principal Enjoyment of their Lives. The sorting of a Suit of Ribbons, is reckon'd a very good morning's Work; and if they make an Excursion to a Mercer's or a Toy-Shop, so great a Fatigue makes them unfit for any thing else all the Day after.

The conclusion is obvious. The *Spectator* will provide a more suitable and improving form of leisure pursuit. It will, Addison adds, 'endeavour to make an innocent if not an improving Entertainment, and by that Means at least divert the Minds of [its] female Readers'.

The *Spectator* insists on the material differences between male and female reading requirements. In number four (5 March 1711) Steele discusses the sort of language and subject-matter Mr Spectator will employ on 'Woman's Day' in his journal:

I shall endeavour at a Stile and Air suitable to their Understanding.... I shall take it for the greatest Glory of my Work, if among reasonable Women this Paper may furnish *Tea-Table Talk*. In order to it, I shall treat on Matters which relate to Females as they are concern'd to approach or fly from the other Sex, or as they are tyed to them by Blood, Interest or Affection.

Although Steele here represents women's 'interests' as distinctively different from men's (requiring a more refined language, for instance), they also exist only in relation to men. Woman remains the object or consumer of polite discourse, rather than the subject or producer of it.

Yet, if the reality of bourgeois gender division was, as Addison and Steele present it, that of entirely disjunct or 'separate spheres', the lady at her tea-table and the gentleman in his coffee-house, we must ask why these journals, whose primary aim was to provide informed political commentary, were so interested in attracting the woman's attention? Why did the *Tatler* spin its tales around, and the *Spectator* direct its gaze so obsessively upon, the figure of the early eighteenth-century lady? The answer, I suggest, lies in the importance of that figure to the creation of early modern political discourse and a new political subject following the Stuart restoration. It is, indeed, no coincidence that 'tattling' and 'spectating' are two traditionally feminine pastimes. 'Woman', defined as a category of reader in Addison and Steele's journals, comes to represent the

Actually very much it (handwritten marginal note)

boundary or margin of that sensitive and disinterested critical awareness that they sought to encourage in their (male) readers.

Like Mr Spectator himself, a gentleman living in the city on the revenue from his country rents, the leisured woman had no direct 'interest' in the contemporary political and social order. Her alienation from the political realm simultaneously qualified her for the role of the disinterested 'jury member' (the defining characteristic of the eighteenth-century reader for Ian Watt (34)), and disqualified her from an active engagement, or influence, in its making. Thus a set of characteristics explicitly associated with the 'feminine' are employed as a means of constructing the borders of proper gentlemanly behaviour. Neurosis, apathy, lethargy, and triviality, characteristics associated with the idle bourgeois lady, are also the pitfalls of the ideal of 'disinterest' for the early eighteenth-century gentleman. Repeatedly in this period of intense party political conflict we find the figure of the woman functioning as a means of constructing an ideal model of the male political agent, whether she stands as his opposite or his ideal.

I have cited the *Tatler* and *Spectator* here as representative of a turn-of-the-century 'address' to the female reader. If she functions in these journals primarily as substitutive sign for masculine subjectivity, what relation did, or could, the woman writer develop to this gendered drama of reading? Aphra Behn, Delarivier Manley, and Eliza Haywood were all metropolitan women who could expect that their audience in London would in fact comprise a fair number of women readers. Yet it is only Eliza Haywood, publishing from 1719 to the late 1750s who consistently \addresses her texts to an exclusively female audience.] In all three, however, the figure of the female reader occupies a central place.

Inscribed in these fictions is a gendered struggle over interpretation. Again and again, a dramatic conflict between men and women over the 'meaning' of the amatory sign is enacted. In other words, a competition between men and women for control of the means of seduction becomes the central theme of these love stories. Against the background of my discussion of Addison's and Steele's use of femininity it is tempting to suggest that the battle for control over sexual representation acts as an analogy for women's search for political 'representation' or agency.]

The late seventeenth- and early eighteenth-century journal or periodical did not, however, wield a very significant influence upon

Behn's, Manley's, and Haywood's fictions, although Manley and Haywood both experimented in the form.[24] The importance of a 'myth' of female readership for love narrative had already been established in prose fiction before the late 1680s, although not in a specifically 'British' context. The precursors of Behn, Manley, and Haywood in the field of love fiction were primarily French and female. French language was of course one of the few skills that girls were encouraged to acquire in what little education they were given, and Behn, Manley, and Haywood were all clearly fluent in it.[25] Indeed, Behn and Haywood themselves contributed to the flood of translations from the French on the market.[26]

There were, of course, other significant influences in the making of Behn's, Manley's, and Haywood's particular vein of amatory fiction, not least those of the Restoration heroic tragedy and comedy in which all three engaged with varying degrees of success.[27] How-

[24] Manley edited Swift's Tory paper, the *Examiner* from 14 June to 26 July 1711 (nos. 46–52) and may have been the Phoebe Crackenthorpe of the *Female Tatler*. See Paul Bunyan Anderson, 'The History and Authorship of Mrs. Crackenthorpe's *Female Tatler*', *Modern Philology*, 28 (1931), 354–60. Eliza Haywood's the *Female Spectator*, published monthly from April 1744 to May 1746 with two months omitted, was published in four volumes (London, 1745) and had gone into seven editions by 1771. The periodical did not become the major journalistic form until after Aphra Behn's death, but, interestingly, the rise to popularity of her own novels in the 1690s coincided with that of the periodical. Nevertheless, Carolyn Nelson and Matthew Seccombe locate 700 serial titles, about one-quarter of publications in Britain, for the period 1641–1700 (*British Newspapers and Periodicals 1641–1700* (New York, 1987), vii).

[25] On girl's education in this period ranging from charity schools to ladies' academies to the bluestocking, see Josephine Kamm, *Hope Deferred: Girls' Education in English History* (London, 1965), 83–136.

[26] Behn's major translations are Balthazar de Bonnecorse's *The Lover's Watch* (1686), Tallemant's *Lycidus, or The Lover in Fashion* (1688) (both in Behn, *Works*, vi), and a paraphrase of Fontenelle's *Theory of the System of Several New Inhabited Worlds* (London, 1700), which was accompanied by her own 'Essay on Translated Prose'. The essay is reprinted in Moira Ferguson (ed.), *First Feminists: British Women Writers 1578–1799* (Bloomington, Ind., 1985), 148–51. Haywood's entire œuvre could be interpreted as imitations of French fiction, but her best known and acknowledged translations are from Madeleine Poisson de Gomez, *La Belle Assemblée, or The Adventures of Six Days* (London, 1724) and from Sieur de Préchac, *The Disguis'd Prince, or The Beautiful Parisian* (London, 1728).

[27] Aphra Behn, during her lifetime, was best known for her sixteen plays, tragedy and comedy, and only took to novel writing toward the end of an already distinguished career in the theatre. Delarivier Manley wrote four plays, one comedy and three tragedies, but her major contribution was in the scandal novel. Haywood had the least success of all three, despite her history as an actress; she wrote one comedy and two tragedies in contrast with around seventy novels. The decreasing importance of dramatic writing in each successive woman's literary career is probably as much an indicator of the decline in the theatre as it is of their different gifts as writers.

ever, in the fiction of Madeleine de Scudéry, Marie de Lafayette, Marie d'Aulnoy, the mysterious 'Portuguese nun', Marie Desjardins (or Madame Villedieu), Bussy-Rabutin, all much published writers of the mid- to late seventeenth century in Britain, we find an already established feminocentric prose narrative tradition for British women writrs to exploit. The rest of this chapter provides a closer analysis of this French fiction in order to establish the aesthetic 'ground' from which Behn, Manley, and Haywood elaborated their own distinctive fiction. The three chapters that follow provide a detailed consideration of Behn's, Manley's, and Haywood's different imitations and transformations of French models in order to produce an indigenous British amatory tradition peculiarly attuned to the ideologies of gender in contemporary (party) political discourse.

I have chosen to classify French fiction, as it was imported to Britain in the seventeenth century, into four distinct narrative forms: the romance, the *petite histoire* or *nouvelle*, the *chronique scandaleuse*, and the epistolary or letter novel. Not all the major contributors to these prose fiction forms in France were women, but all of the narratives partake of what I have termed a 'feminocentric' frame, that is, they simultaneously address and construct an explicitly 'feminine' or 'feminized' realm.[28]

The French Romance

Despite the diversity in the different forms of 'romance' available to the late seventeenth century, it appears that the French heroic romance was the hegemonic form. Charlotte Morgan details seven types of romance in England in the late seventeenth century: classical, chivalric, arcadian, euphuistic, political, allegorical, and heroic.[29] Yet it is clear that most references to the 'romance', associating it with heroism, fantasy, love, and above all, female consumption, point exclusively to the heroic form. As Charlotte Morgan goes on to note it was the heroic romances, ostensibly

[28] As far as possible, I have used in each case the most popular or accessible English translation from the French in the period as the basis for discussion. Although Behn, Manley, and Haywood may well have read them in their original French, my interest is mainly in the British reception of these works and the kind of cultural hegemony they produced in the field of love fiction. Translation, precisely because it was inclined to be exceptionally 'free' in the late seventeenth and early eighteenth century, provides the best record of this reception.

[29] Charlotte E. Morgan, *The Rise of the Novel of Manners: A Study of Prose Fiction between 1600 and 1740* (New York, 1911), 3–37.

developed from classical Greek modes, that set the generic norm for romance in general in France and Britain (29–31), and it was these conventions that Bishop Huet's influential essay, 'Sur l'origine des Romans' (1670), laid out in detail.[30] Romance, according to Huet, took love as its principal subject; its story was 'feigned' though grounded in historical fact, and it aimed to inculcate the right principles by rewarding the virtuous and punishing the vicious.

The two dominant conventions of the French romance, namely *bienséance* (decorum) and vraisemblance (truth to nature) were closely identified with forms of social practice and epistemological understanding that were assumed to be 'feminine'. A closer analysis of Madeleine de Scudéry's *Clelia* (1654–61) will demonstrate the vital links that the heroic romance established between a gender (femininity) and a genre (the romance) which in the mid-eighteenth century in Britain was to be turned so effectively against the woman writer, but in the late seventeenth and early eighteenth century provided the aesthetic basis on which Behn, Manley, and Haywood were to enter the prose fiction market.

Behn, Manley, and Haywood produced fictions which were in many ways the antithesis of Scudéry's romance but their writings were consistently associated with the genre.[31] The link between early British women's fiction and the imported French heroic romance, then, must lie rather in the association of both forms with peculiarly 'feminine' modes of literary production and consumption, than in exact formal equivalences. Aphra Behn's use of the title 'Astrea', identifying herself with the eponymous heroine of Honoré d'Urfé's heroic romance, *Astrée* (1610–27) is just one indicator of the extent to which the French romances signified a link between femininity and literary creativity.[32]

[30] Huet's essay was originally prefixed to the first edition of Marie de Lafayette's *Zaïde: Histoire Espagnole* (1670–1) and was translated by Stephen Lewis as *The History of Romances* in 1715 (Ioaon Williams (ed.), *Novel and Romance*, 43–55).

[31] See Sheridan Baker, 'The Idea of the Romance in the Eighteenth Century', *Publications of the Michigan Academy of Arts, Sciences and Letters* 48 (1964), 507–22; Dieter Schulz, ' "Novel", "Romance", and Popular Fiction in the First Half of the Eighteenth Century'; Edith Kern, 'The Romance of the Novel/Novella', in Peter Dernetz, Thomas Green, and Lowry Nelson, jun. (eds.), *The Disciplines of Criticism: Essays in Literary Theory, Interpretation and History* (New Haven, Conn., 1968), 511–30; Gerald Gillespie, 'Novel, Nouvelle, Novelle, Short Novel?—A Review of Terms', *Neophilologus*, 51 (1967), 117–27.

[32] *Astrée* was licensed in Britain in 1611. An anonymous version of the first part appeared as *The History of Astrea* in 1620, and a translation of the entire work entitled *Astrea* from 1657–8. See Ernest Baker, *The History of the English Novel*, iii: *The Later Romances and the Establishment of Realism* (London, 1929), 14–15.

Madeleine de Scudéry (1607–1701), a respected member of the
Marquise de Rambouillet's Parisian salon circle in the 1640s and
1650s, published all three of her lengthy romances, *Ibrahim, où
l'Illustre Bassa* (four volumes in 1641), *Artamène, où le Grand Cyrus*
(thirty volumes between 1649 and 1653) and *Clélie* (ten volumes
between 1654 and 1661), under the name of her brother, the playwright George Scudéry.[33] Although this fiction of male authorship
was on the whole left unchallenged in Britain, Madeleine's name was
consistently linked with her 'brother's' romances.[34] The translator's
dedication to Elizabeth, Countess of Rivers, for part five of *Clelia*
also noted Madeleine's involvement in the writing of the romances,
and exploited it to make a point of the 'femininity' of the genre:
'*since it was reported it was not the illustrious* Scudery, *but that celebrated*
Vertuosa *his Sister who finish'd the Romance after his decease, I could not
make a more apt Dedication than the work of a Lady to the most Noble and
accomplish'd Person of her own Sex*' (pt. 5, p. 592)

Throughout her literary career, Scudéry strove to preserve her
reputation as a coterie writer. The lengthy 'conversations' in *Clelia*
both embody her ideal system of artistic exchange and frequently
centre around the discussion of the best means of circulating
amateur literary endeavours without incurring public notoriety. The
eponymous heroine, Clelia, is horrified when her *carte de tendre*
produced for the edification of a select group of friends is copied
and distributed more widely. She asks: 'Do you think I imagined, this
spective fancy had any thing pleasant but for our *Cabala* in
particular to become publick, and that I made to be seen but by five
or six persons which have noble spirits, should be seen by two
thousand who scarce have any, and who hardly understand the best
things?' (pt. 1, p. 43). Scudéry's picture of the amateur, secluded and
modest author catering to a small, but élite, audience is at odds with
the obvious facts of her own existence; her lengthy romances
supported her brother and their household as well as herself and,

---

[33] For biographical information and discussion of Scudéry's involvement in Fronde
politics and salon life in Paris, see Dorothy McDougall, *Madeleine de Scudéry: Her
Romantic Life and Death* (London, 1938) and Nicole Aronson, *Mademoiselle de Scudéry*,
trans. Stuart Aronson (Boston, 1978).

[34] See Osborne, in a letter of September 1653 to her lover William Temple, where
she comments with respect to a Scudéry novel, that 'the Gentleman ... has a Sister
that lives with him as a Mayde, and she furnishes him with all the little Story's that
come between, so that he only Contrives the maine designe ...' (Osborne, *Letters*,
82–3).

since the Scudérys were not aristocrats with private wealth, although they mixed with the élites of the salon, consistent literary output was probably a financial necessity.

Scudéry's artistic ethics present women as the ideal consumers and arbiters of art, but on the whole advocates that they should be prohibited from its creation. Men have control over artistic production, but their creativity is regulated and refined by the female audience. Herminius, frequently the spokesperson for salon etiquette in *Clelia*, asserts that the influence of women shapes men's crude intellectual power into art: 'as for the handsomeness of language, it is attainable only by conversation, which withal, must be a conversation of people of the World, whereof Women make the greatest part otherwise it will be too sublime and learned, dry, rude or affected . . .' (pt. 4, p. 481).

The very form of narration in Scudéry's heroic romance mirrors this gendered distribution of labour. The outer story, in this case that of the frustrated love of Clelia and Aronces, is interrupted by a series of inner stories narrating the love affairs of their friends and acquaintances. These inner stories are usually narrated by a man to a select mixed group of 'interested' parties, privileging a single woman in the audience as primary addressee. The 'sub-plots' are all left unresolved until the conclusion of the book when the main lovers are united.[35] The narratives are always tailored toward the supposed needs of the female audience. Thus, when Merigenes narrates Elismonda's story to Valeria, he cuts short a description of a duel on the grounds that 'Ladies love not very well these kind of relations, when they are too long' (pt. 4, p. 444). If women are condemned for attempting to enter the public sphere as producers in Scudéry's aesthetic, it is because this 'interest' may undermine the function of their roles as consumers and arbiters within it.

Femininity in Scudéry's romances is nothing more nor less than the organizing principle of the text. Both its primary conventions, *bienséance* and vraisemblance, can only be understood within the context of the heroic romance's valorization of 'the feminine' as the organizing agent in culture, embodied in the idealized figure of the

---

[35] On the complex formal structure of Scudéry's narratives, see René Godenne, *Les Romans de Mademoiselle de Scudéry* (Geneva, 1983). Godenne divides the 'sub-plots' into two kinds, *histoires ajoutées* which diverge from the main plot and provide moral tales not instrumental to it as such, and *histoires intégrées* which are independent but also further the main plot.

aristocratic female reader. Scudéry, in her introduction to her first heroic romance, Ibrahim, asserted that 'You shall see there, Reader, if I be not deceived, the comeliness of things and conditions exactly enough observed; neither have I put any thing into my Book, which the Ladies may not read without blushing.'[36] Thus, according to Scudéry, the aristocratic woman reader's natural *delicatesse* and sense of propriety, signified by her blush, will determine whether a text has stayed within the bounds of convention.

Scudéry's representations of villainy always centre around the refusal to accord femininity a proper respect. Most interestingly, perhaps, in her representation of evil in women, Scudéry locates its source in the rejection of heroic femininity for a debased identification with the aggression and brutality of the 'masculine' world. In *Clelia*, the traditional contrast between two sisters is expressed through a dispute over heroic 'models'. While the 'Princess' aspires to be a Vestal, since 'it is only in them, that our Sex is held in any Rank and Consideration, since in all other conditions, they do not hold their own rank, but only that of their Parents', her sister Tullia craves the opportunity to be a soldier, 'so little satisfied' is she 'with [her] own Sex' (pt. 1, p. 87). Both of these 'heroic' models are, then, rejections of patriarchal power, the father's law, but the former rests on a valorization of female community, the latter on a negation of it. Tullia, we are told, 'did extremely slight all Women, and would not admit of any conversation but men' (pt. 1, p. 99).

Scudéry's romance, then, repeatedly inverts conventional value systems. True heroism is founded in 'feminine' love. Vice is the property of the masculine and it is the influence of women that regulates it into 'propriety'. This inversion operates also on the level of vraisemblance, where fictionalized 'feminine' accounts of history repeatedly substitute for conventional 'masculine' fact. Scudéry's aristocratic conversationalists insist that 'invention' in love histories is more probable than truth itself. As Herminius puts it at one point, 'fiction ... has greater verisimilitude, than truth it self. When the purpose is to bring about extraordinary events it is no question handsomer to introduce love in them than any other cause' (pt. 4, p. 540).

Scudéry takes real historical events and filters them through her all-powerful rationale of love. Love is perceived as the sole

[36] Madeleine de Scudéry, 'Preface', *Ibrahim, or The Illustrious Bassa, written in French by Monsieur de Scudery, and now Englished by Henry Cogan, Gent* (London, 1674).

motivating force of history and our only means of understanding its processes. Sentimental identification, presented as the special capacity of the woman, is the ideal method of comprehending past ages. As Clelia puts it: 'there is no distance of places which takes away the sensibility of the heart, no Age so remote, but the fancy becomes near enough to it to excite compassion: for 'tis the things themselves we are moved with, and not so much the places or the persons' (pt. 4, p. 496). Sentimental identification is also the key to Dorothy Osborne's response to the heroic romance. Writing to her lover William Temple, with reference to a sub-plot in Scudéry's *The Grand Cyrus* in 1653, she comments: 'I know you will pitty Poore Amestris strangely when you have read her Story. i'le swear I cryed for her when I read it at first though shee were but an imaginary person' (85).

If Osborne had no difficulties in exercising her sympathy regardless of the factual or fictional basis to the story, her contemporaries were less flexible. Samuel Pepys recorded a meeting with Sir Edward Walker whilst attending an audience with the Committee of Lords for the Navy in 1664, in which Sir Edward, a noted collector of heraldry, 'among other things did much enveigh against the writing of Romances; that five hundred years hence, being wrote of matters generally true, ... the world will not know which is the true and which is the false'.[37]

The romance's corruption of history lay in its insistence on placing the heroine at its centre. The importance of the heroine is paralleled by the inversion of values on the level of narrative form. Scudéry's minor, private, and invented 'histories' continually disrupt the 'master' narrative which makes up the ostensible matter of the book. Wars are conveniently halted while her characters collect to hear the 'true history' of a new acquaintance. Romance, then, absorbs the master narrative of 'history' into the privatized discourse of 'love'. Historical difference is erased by the totalizing power of love and the diachronic processes and changes of history flattened out by its universalizing mythology. In other words, textuality comes to supplant the 'real'.

The struggle over definitions of fact and fiction, then, in relation to the romance, is revealed to be a gendered conflict over the nature of the 'real', in which the female 'reality' of a world of love,

---

[37] Samuel Pepys, *The Diary of Samuel Pepys* (1660–1669), ed. Robert Latham and Robert Matthews (London, 1970–83), v. 319.

reproduction, and art is privileged over the male 'reality' of a world of war and production. Domna Stanton has argued that male anxiety over female inversion of truth, history, and language is most commonly articulated in mid-seventeenth-century France through the much satirized figure of *la précieuse*.[38] As we have seen, Scudéry's heroic romance places the entire labour of cultural regulation upon the shoulders of an educated and discriminating woman reader. The figure of *la précieuse* comes to embody masculine anxiety about this valorization of the 'feminine' in satires of the period. Above all else *la précieuse* is a corrupter of language. Molière's 'affected ladies' in his 1659 play, *Les Précieuses Ridicules*, refer to a mirror as 'le conseiller des grâces' and chairs as 'les commodités de la conversation'.[39] The *précieuse*'s linguistic irregularities are a measure of her disruption of history and the 'real'. In other words, she substitutes fiction for fact.

Early in the eighteenth century, Addison, in his description of a 'ladies library' had made similar links between the feminine imagination and fictional travesties of the real. On Thursday, 12 April 1711, Mr Spectator describes a visit to a country lady named Leonora. Attending her presence in the library, he is fascinated by its organization and aesthetics. Leonora's library is a monument to conventional stereotypes of the feminine, an altar to artifice, trivia, and minutiae. One of the few books that shows signs of reading is Scudéry's *The Grand Cyrus* 'with a pin stuck on one of the middle leaves'. Addison's description is as follows:

At the end of the *Folio's* (which were finely bound and gilt) were great jars of *China* placed one above another in a very noble piece of Architecture. The *Quarto's* were separated from the *Octavo's* by a pile of smaller Vessels, which rose in a delightful Pyramid. The *Octavo's* were bounded by Tea Dishes of all Shapes, Colours and Sizes, which were so disposed on a wooden Frame, that they looked like one continued Pillar indented with the finest Strokes of Sculpture and stained with the greatest Variety of Dyes. That part of the Library which was designed for the Reception of Plays and Pamphlets, and other loose Papers was enclosed in a kind of Square, consisting of one of the prettiest Grotesque Works that ever I saw, and made up of Scaramouches, Lions, Monkies, Mandarines, Trees, Shells, and a thousand other odd Figures in *China* Ware. In the midst of the Room was a little Japan Table,

---

[38] Domna C. Stanton, 'The Fiction of Préciosité and the Fear of Women', *Yale French Studies*, 62 (1981), 107–34.

[39] Jean Baptiste Molière, *Les Précieuses Ridicules* (1659), in *The Plays of Molière in French and English*, ed. A. R. Waller (Edinburgh, 1907), ii. 18, 23.

with a Quire of gilt Paper upon it, and on the Paper a Silver Snuff-box made in the shape of a little Book. I found there were several other Counterfeit Books upon the upper Shelves, which were carved in Wood, and served only to fill up the Number, like Faggots in the Muster of a Regiment.

Leonora's library is in and of itself an elaborate 'fiction', as well as a shrine to the book as commodity. Her books are arranged by size rather than subject-matter, and, indeed, some of them are counterfeits deployed merely for aesthetic effect. Ultimately, then, female reading is revealed to be nothing more than a form of conspicuous consumption, form without matter.

This analysis has demonstrated the means by which the French heroic romance and the critical machinery that was elaborated from it in England, established an ideological equivalence between fictionality and femininity. However, as the example of Leonora shows, the French romance remained wedded to an aristocratic ideal that, by the late seventeenth century in England, may well have appeared outmoded. Much of the comedy in satirical representations of preciosity lay in the pretentiousness of the bourgeois woman's aspirations to an aristocratic lifestyle. Moreover, this aristocratic ideal demanded a high price for its valorization of femininity. Heroism, or female agency in the public sphere, was only achieved in these fictions, through the absolute renunciation of female desire.

The advent of the *histoire* or *nouvelle* in France was to challenge this tradition of women's desireless rationalism in love fiction. The 1670s in France saw the emergence of the short romance of passion which, without undermining the link between femininity and fiction that the romance had forged, turned its attention to the representation of female desire as opposed to female heroism.

The Petite Histoire, Histoire Galante, *or* Nouvelle

English commentators on the French romance in the late seventeenth and early eighteenth century expressed their impatience with its protracted niceties and complex narrative strategies, as well as its aristocratic idealism. In 1677 a parody of the heroic romance entitled *Zelinda* and supposedly written by 'Monsieur de Scudéry', drew the reader's attention to the improbabilities of the romance's representations of male chastity. The hero, Alicidalis, duped by a double of his virtuous mistress, Zelinda, finds himself with the opportunity to make love to her in her husband's absence. The author addresses his reader directly:

But let the ingenious Reader imagine, after a long and passionate Courtship of so Beautiful a Lady as *Zelinda*, if he was kneeling by her Bed (the Altar of Love) pressing her soft Palm, laying his amorous Head on her panting Breast, in the height of exstasie, just at the Minute of Fruition ... how it would stir him to be disappointed. ... Here some Romantic Zealots may perhaps accuse me of a gross mistake, in supposing a Prince so sublimely Virtuous as *Alcidalis* is Characteriz'd could be guilty of the common Failings of meaner persons; But I refer my self to the impartial Judgement of this ripe-witted Age, whether that Lover is not most perfect, whose Passion has no limits.[40]

Zelinda mocks the perversely titillatory aspect of the French romance's persistent deferral of erotic fulfillment, and here calls on readers to recognize in the hero's sexual frustrations, their own frustrations with a form that refuses to represent sexual desire.

Delarivier Manley took up a similar argument with respect to the impossibility of the female chastity represented in the French romance. Her famous preface to *The Secret History of Queen Zarah* (1705) is one of the most fully developed critical manifestos of the early eighteenth century. Manley criticizes the romance for its prolixity and its idealism, opening her argument with the assertion that '*Little Histories* ... have taken place of *Romances*, whose Prodigious Number of Volumes were sufficient to tire and satiate such whose Heads were most fill'd with these Notions', since they are 'much more agreeable to the Brisk and Impetuous Humour of the *English*'. Manley labels this new form of prose narrative, the 'Historical Novel' and congratulates it on restoring the 'feisable' to fiction.

In her critique of the romance's improbability, Manley pays particular attention to the romance heroine: 'It wou'd in no wise be probable that a Young Woman fondly beloved by a Man of great Merit, and for whom she had a Reciprocal Tenderness, finding her self at all Times alone with him in Places which favour'd their Loves, cou'd always resist his Addresses; there are too Nice Occasions'. Although, as other critics have pointed out, Delarivier Manley's own fiction rarely lives up to the programme she outlines in the preface, being given itself to the very sins of prolixity, idealiza-

---

[40] *Zelinda, an Excellent New Romance*, trans. 'T. D.' (London, 1677), 81–2.

tion, and improbability she cites, her statement does mark a shift in the theorization of the nature of prose fiction. Her preface is by no means an early manifestation of a new drive toward realism in prose fiction. It rather signifies an important change in the conceptualization of textual pleasure in love fiction. The French romance gave its delight by a constant withholding of stasis, introducing narrative after unresolved narrative, until it rapidly tied them up in its few final pages. In contrast, Manley tells us that

'Tis an indispensible Necessity to end a Story to satisfie the Disquiets of the Reader, who is engag'd to the Fortunes of those People whose Adventures are described to him; 'tis depriving him of a most delicate Pleasure, when he is hindered from seeing the Event of an Intrigue, which has caused some Emotion in him, whose Discovery he expects, be it either Happy or Unhappy.[41]

The 'history' or 'novel' rejected the romance's 'chinese box' method of narration, narrating its love stories chronologically rather than commencing them *in medias res*. Thus Manley's own long novel *The New Atalantis* (1709) takes the form of a repetitious series of completed amatory tales presented in a contiguous chain. Her comments above imply the link between textual and sexual gratification. If the French romance teased by providing the reader with mere glimpses of future erotic possibilities in the narrative, the fictional 'history' provided a more immediate form of gratification. The necessary result of the removal of formal narrative suspense was the provision of a newly eroticized content. This brand of French fiction of the late 1660s and early 1670s, variously called the *nouvelle*, *histoire*, or *petite histoire* was rapidly imported and translated in England and it is this new form of 'historical novel' to which Manley was doubtless referring.

By the late 1660s in France the romance appears to have been on the wane. Madeleine de Scudéry herself turned to shorter fiction in the shape of her three *nouvelles*, *Célinte* (1661), *Mathilde d'Aguilar* (1667), and *La Promenade de Versailles* (1669). The high 'heroinism' of the 'Fronde' years (1648–53) which had seen a woman regent, women's active engagement in political decision-making and the flourishing of the 'salon', was dampened by the reinstitution of Mazarin as regent in 1653 and eventually King Louis XIV's coming of age. Domna Stanton has noted that the female-centred political

---

[41] Ioaon Williams (ed.), *Novel and Romance*, 33, 35, 38.

life of the salons came to be replaced by a more patriarchal organization with Louis's removal of the court to Versailles (123).

The shorter love fictions of the late 1660s and 1670s in France register this changed political and cultural climate by the reversal of a number of romance conventions. The heroic romance's depiction of ideal and rational love was replaced by a vision of the rapacious and destructive power of sexual passion. This prose fiction laid claim to the status of pure historical 'fact', where the romance had called attention to its own skill in 'feigning'. The most influential writers in the evolution of the new 'psychological' novel were two women, Marie Catherine Hortense de Desjardins (or Madame de Villedieu) and Marie Madeleine de la Vergne, comtesse de Lafayette. In the former, we see the advent of the professional woman of letters in France. Reputed to have obtained one hundred sous from her publisher, Barbin, for her *Annales Galantes* (1669), Villedieu produced a novel a year from 1668 to 1671, usually under her own name (rather than under a male pseudonym or anonymously).[42]

One of the major departures of the *histoire galante* from the romance was its preference for modern history over ancient. Lafayette and Villedieu both elaborated their largely fictional plots from the historical basis of the early to mid-sixteenth-century French court.[43] Yet the preoccupation with the amorous lives of aristocrats, which had been the focus of the romance, remained, with the major difference that these stories were more concerned with illicit than legitimate love.

No less fictional than the love stories in the heroic romance, these *nouvelles* abandoned the conventions of vraisemblance and *bienséance*, adhering instead to spurious claims to historicity. Thus, Villedieu went so far as to introduce a 'table' prefixed to her *Annales Galantes* (1669), which purportedly provided irrefutable truth of the verity of her stories, on the grounds that

The Age we live in, pretending to so much subtilty, and the liberty of writing Intrigues, being grown so common; to prevent publick mistakes, I have thought good to premise this Advertisement; that these Annals of Love are really History, whose

---

[42] For the story of Villedieu's commercial success, see F. C. Green, *French Novelists, Manners and Ideas from the Renaissance to the Revolution* (Toronto and London, 1928), 58.

[43] See Madame de Villedieu, *Les Désordres de l'Amour* (1677), ed. Micheline Cuénin (Geneva, 1970), p. xxiii. Cuénin points out that most of Villedieu's information came from the work of the far from respectable French historian, François-Eudes de Mezeray and, in particular, his *Histoire de France depuis Pharamond jusqu'à maintenant* (1598).

Foundations and Originals, I have on purpose inserted in the ensuing Table. They are no witty and facetious Inventions, exhibited under true Names . . . but faithful touches taken out of History in general.[44]

This insistence on the verity of the tale was to become a familiar trope in Aphra Behn's variations on the 'little history'. Her dedication to *The Fair Jilt* (1688) announces that 'this little History . . . has but this Merit to recommend it, that it is the Truth' (*Works*, v. 70), while *Oroonoko* (1688) scorned to 'entertain [the] Reader with the adventures of a feign'd *Hero*, whose Life and Fortunes Fancy may manage at the Poet's Pleasure' (*Works*, v. 129).

Whereas the ostentatiously fictional devices of the heroic romance had demanded that the author maintain a high moral tone, since the only defence for producing a fiction was that it could convey some higher truth, the claim to reproduce fact ostensibly liberated the author from such strictures. By this logic, if fiction pleased by creating visions of moral order and justice to which the reader should aspire, fact surprised by disclosing the irrationality, decadence, and unpredictability of real life which the reader should shun. Madame de Villedieu's apologia for the warmth and explicitness of her representations of vice stands in direct contrast to Scudéry's promise never to make her women readers blush:

If I drive on the Immodesty of Women even to Impudence, 'tis but to represent that Vice in its more natural Colours. Indeed it is many times dangerous to give a feeble and imperfect description; in some cases a Woman may be overcome by a temptation, which (had she known all the consequences of the History) she would probaly have master'd. And that I might interlace, and inlay my Examples with profitable Precepts, I observe this Maxime in all of them, to punish Vice, and reward Vertue. With this Caution it is lawful to bring the most detestable action upon the Stage.[45]

Villedieu's comments here mark a significant shift in the address to a female reader. Whereas the heroic romance encouraged the female reader to believe in the invincibility of women's power through their capacity to inspire ideal love, the *histoire galante* warned them that sexual desire might well engulf and destroy them.

The third part of Villedieu's collection of *histoires galantes* of the courts of Henri III and IV, *Les Désordres de l'Amour* (1675) was translated into English in 1677 under the title *The Disorders of Love*.

---

[44] Madame de Villedieu, *The Annals of Love, Containing Select Histories of the Amours Of Divers Princes' Courts, Pleasantly Related* (London, 1672), A2ʳ.

[45] Ibid. A3ʳ.

This narrative of the young Marquis d'Anglure's rejection of his first mistress, the widow Madame Maugiron, due to a hopeless passion for the imperious Mademoiselle de Guise, is concluded with a typical invocation against amorous passion. The marquis, known as Givry, is described as an able commander of King Henri IV's forces against the aristocratic League of the 1590s in France, but when Mlle de Guise prefers his friend, the Marquis de Bellegarde, over himself, he becomes reckless in battle and is killed. His slighted but still devoted mistress, Mme Maugiron, sickens and dies on receipt of the news. Villedieu concludes:

> What Example more proper to make out the malignity of Love, and inspire into us that horrour against it, it deserves? . . . An amorous despair destroy'd all [Givry's] hopes, and robb'd the Kingdom of one of its finest Ornaments. The same Passion disorder'd, and at last destroy'd a Lady, whose constancy and sincerity deserved better fortune. The like end commonly make all those, who absolutely abandon themselves to this fatal folly: if it makes but light impression, it is an inexhaustible sourse [sic] of perfideousness and ingratitude: if it be submitted to in great earnest, it leads into an excess of disorder and despair.[46]

As this quotation suggests, Villedieu's novels present a litany of disaster, reducing history to the wreckage of criminal and destructive sexual passions. From the romance's presentation of love as a form of elaborate artifice, we have moved to the depiction of love as an uncontrollable and entropic effect of nature.

Madame de Lafayette's *Princesse de Clèves* (1678) is perhaps the best known early French *nouvelle* in the twentieth century. Like Villedieu, Lafayette turned to sixteenth-century French court history and aristocratic intrigue to provide the source or backdrop to her fictional narrative. Peggy Kamuf alerts us to Lafayette's most innovative technique, the introduction of an impersonal, third person narration, whereby 'obfuscation of the origin of . . . knowledge, instead of arousing the reader's suspicion, casts the narration in the incontrovertible form of an omniscient given, that which, in other words, is itself the origin of other, contingent modes of knowing.'[47] It is precisely the omniscient capacity of the narration which enables

---

[46] Madame de Villedieu, *The Disorders of Love Truly Expressed in the Unfortunate Amours of Givry with Mademoiselle de Guise* (London, 1677), 147–8.

[47] Peggy Kamuf, *Fictions of Feminine Desire: Disclosures of Heloise* (Lincoln, Nebr. and London, 1982), 68. See also Arnold Weinstein on 'Public Intimacy: *La Princesse de Clèves*', in his *Fictions of the Self: 1550–1800* (Princeton, NJ, 1981), 66–83.

the text to dwell in such exquisite and enraptured detail on the psychological conflicts that love generates, particularly in the psyche of her heroine.[48] The distinctive characteristic of Madame de Cleves is her un(self)consciousness. Her mother, husband, and readers, the narrator tells us, can always see what her heroine cannot or will not recognize in herself. Thus, when she obtains a letter she believes to be from a discarded mistress to Nemours, the man she loves, Madame de Cleves is thrown into a confusion which the narrator interprets on her readers' behalf:

Madam *de Cleve* read the Letter again and again, yet knew not what she read: she perceived only, Monsieur *de Nemours* was not so in love with her as she had thought, but lov'd others, who were no less deceiv'd in him than she. What a Discovery was this for a Person of her humour, who had a violent Passion, who had newly given Evidence of it to a Man she judg'd unworthy of it; and to another she us'd ill for love of him. Never was grief so cutting as hers; she imputed the sharpness of it to that day's adventures; and that if Monsieur *de Nemours* had not had occasion to believe she lov'd him, she would not have car'd for his loving another: Yet she did but deceive herself, the Disease she was sick of and thought so intollerable, was Jealousie, with all its horrible Attendants.[49]

Not only is Madame de Cleves one of the first married heroines in seventeenth-century fiction, she also represents the beginning of a long line of somatic and hysterical female victims of passion. With this figure, a radical disjunction between knowing reader and unselfconscious heroine is introduced.

Beyond desire, Scudéry's heroines experience no such confusion, serving rather as ideal models of virtue and rationality to which the reader is encouraged to aspire. In *Clelia*, Herminius informs the listening audience that the reading of heroic romance by 'the Ladies' 'would rather hinder them from admitting of Gallants, than induce them to entertain them; for ... they would compare the love pretended to them, with what they found describ'd ... [and] they would never suffer themselves to be moved with it' (pt. 4, p. 543). In contrast, the careful moral instruction into the dangers and duplicities of love by her mother prove no preparation for Madame

---

[48] Tania Modleski in her book, *Loving with a Vengeance*, comments on the use of an impersonal third-person narration in women's romantic fiction of the twentieth century, a device which allows the text to expose the heroine's 'forbidden desires' to the reader without making the heroine appear conscious, and thus guilty, of her own sexual passion as she would in a first-person narrative (55–6).

[49] Marie de Lafayette, *The Princess of Cleves* (London, 1679), 122–3.

de Cleves for the force of 'genuine' desire when she is introduced to Nemours. In the case of romance, then, the representation of desire, the fiction, is figured as exceeding the empirical world, while in that of the *nouvelle*, the representation is figured as a poor shadow of what it seeks to signify.

In conclusion, then, the *histoire galante* or *nouvelle* maintained a feminocentric tradition in prose narrative but introduced a reversal in many romance conventions. The feminocentric world of love remains the structural centre and motivating force of history, but the female libido substitutes for the desireless heroinism of the romance as the dynamic force in historical process. In other words, femininity comes to be aligned with nature, as opposed to culture. Death, ruin, and renunciation become the limited options of the romantic heroine, as opposed to the fantasy of unlimited power that the romance had extended.

The Chronique Scandaleuse

Like the *nouvelle* or *histoire galante*, the *chronique scandaleuse* provided narratives of the sexual intrigues of French aristocracy, but its heroines were very far removed from the tragic Princess of Cleves, and its interest was in contemporary rather than historical events. The formal origins of the *chronique scandaleuse* are notoriously difficult to determine. Peter Wagner describes it as a 'hybrid form, with literary, semi-literary, and sub-literary branches offering many degrees of fact and fiction', while Ronald Paulson concludes that 'At its best, [it] represents another form of anti-romance, a conscious effort to attain to the real in reaction to romance'.[50]

Unlike the romance and the *nouvelle*, the scandal chronicle had a directly political and often incendiary purpose, and its authors display an attendant wariness with regard to their claims to veracity, in order to avoid legal reprisals or ostracism from the court.[51] Roger de Rabutin, Count de Bussy's *Histoire Amoureuse des Gaules* (1665) became the model for many scandal fictions in France and England,

---

[50] Wagner, *Eros Revived*, 89; Ronald Paulson, *Satire and the Novel in Eighteenth-Century England* (London and New Haven, Conn., 1967), 221.

[51] C. R. Kropf draws attention to the importance of the libel laws in late seventeenth- and early eighteenth-century Britain to the construction of convoluted satirical forms, such as the scandal chronicle, developed in order to avoid prosecution. See his 'Libel and Satire in the Eighteenth Century', *Eighteenth Century Studies*, 8 (1974–5), 153–68.

while his experiences as a result of its publication also acted as a warning to later authors. Bussy-Rabutin was imprisoned for fifteen months in the Bastille as a punishment for ridiculing King Louis XIV in his representation of the king's affair with Louise de la Vallière. Later editions of the novel were accompanied by a letter from Bussy-Rabutin to the Duke de St Agnan which constructed an elaborate history of the theft of the original manuscript by a lady friend of whom he was enamoured and the subsequent publication and corruption of the text at her hands.

In his letter, Bussy-Rabutin presents himself in the role of a Scudéryan wit whose 'spective Fancy', like Clelia's *carte de tendre*, fell into the wrong hands:

it is now Five Years since, not knowing how to divert my self in the Country where I then was, I verified the Proverb, that *Idleness is the Mother of all Vice*; for I sate my self to writing a History, or rather a Satyrical Romance, in reality without intending to make any ill use of it against the Persons introduced in it, but only to employ my self at that time; or, at the most, to show it a few of my most intimate Friends to please them with it, and to gain some Applause from them for writing well.[52]

He goes on to claim that as 'true Events are never extraordinary enough to give any great Interest, [he] had recourse to Invention, which [he] thought would be more pleasing' (A5^v). As a result, he took as 'the principal heroines of [his] Romance' two women 'to whom no good Qualities were wanting, nay who were indeed Mistresses of so many, that Envy might serve to make the ill [he] said of them more easily believed' (A5^v). He goes on to swear his absolute loyalty to the king and intention to produce a biography of the great man.

Bussy-Rabutin's letter, then, supposedly establishes that the entire text is an 'invention'. The truth about the text is its falsity. A further level of inversion is introduced in Bussy-Rabutin's claim that his lady friend edited the text to make it even more scandalous and 'as everybody is most pleas'd with the highest Satyr, the true Copies were thought flat, and suppress'd as false' (A5^v). Once again, Bussy-Rabutin employs a familiar romance convention to construct his own fiction of the text's invention. Fiction is more 'pleasing' than fact. Its readers are more willing to believe it because it fulfills their own fantasies (the female reader's desire for power over the

---

[52] Roger de Rabutin, Count de Bussy, *The Amorous History of the Gauls* (London, 1725), A4^v–A5^r.

processes of history and the male world, or the female reader's
desire to believe all other women 'false').

Bussy-Rabutin's scandalous history about the duplicities of power-
hungry court ladies is put into circulation by just such another
ambitious lady who exploited the author's amorous disposition so
that he would not believe her 'false'. Femininity is associated with
art but female art is in turn associated with artifice and employed to
inflame rather than regulate the passions. *The Amorous History of the
Gauls* is indeed an anti-romance in that it exposes the 'will to power'
at the heart of the romance narrative's feminized world of love and
condemns it as self-interest.

Bussy-Rabutin's court ladies, like Scudéry's, are virtually free of
the disorders of sexual desire, but they are instead slaves to the
passions of avarice and ambition. The description of Madame de
Châtillon, in the form of a conventional romance 'portrait', highlights this identification of femininity with artifice and the lust for
power:

She was of a sweet, affable, fawning Temper, and full of Contrivance; but
however she was prepossess'd by these ill Qualities, when she had a mind to
please, it was impossible to help loving her; She had some ways that
charmed, and others that drew on her the Contempt of the whole World. For
Money or Honours she would have dishonour'd her self, and sacrificed
Father, Mother and Lover. (102)

The two 'heroines' of the novel, Madame d'Olonne and Madame
de Châtillon, manipulate and manœuvre their way to wealth, power,
and influence by the discriminating surrender of their bodies to men
of power. Bussy-Rabutin, meanwhile, presents himself as a 'ladies'
man', maligned by the world due to his weakness for the female sex
but still gallant in their cause. He even presents a fictionalized
version of himself as further vindication; the Count de Bussy, we are
told,'was gallant with the Ladies, and very well bred, and his
Familiarity with those that were his best Friends amongst them,
never made him lose that Respect he ow'd them: This manner of
Behaviour made the World believe he had a Passion for them; and it
is certain there was a little in all his greatest Intimacies' (187). Under
the cloak of gallantry, Bussy-Rabutin introduces the familiar
misogyny of the satiric tradition. As author, character and man of
gallantry, he mediates between the gender dichotomies of his own
text in which men figure as dupes and women as seductresses. Only
Bussy-Rabutin himself, it appears, can take up both positions, at one

moment the victim of female artifice, at another, able to turn the trick back upon the trickster.

Misogyny was not, however, the only means of identifying the tangled power relations of scandal narratives with 'feminine' art. Marie Catherine La Motte, Baronne d'Aulnoy introduced a different frame for the narration of intrigues in the European courts, that of the female gossip. D'Aulnoy built her reputation as a writer on her 'travel' narratives about Europe. Forced to leave the country following the discovery of a conspiracy with her mother to instigate a prosecution for treason against her husband in the late 1660s, she was finally allowed to return to France in recognition for her assistance to the French secret service in Europe.[53] On her return, she published a series of narratives detailing the intrigues of the aristocracy of the European courts.[54] D'Aulnoy frequently addresses herself to a female cousin in France, on whose behalf she acts as 'spy'. She underpins her narratives throughout with a claim to absolute veracity. Having no 'interest' to protect in her wanderings beyond that of providing a faithful account to her correspondents, d'Aulnoy presents herself as uniquely positioned to provide an impartial account.

However, d'Aulnoy's apparent candour conceals political intent. The fiction of the innocent dispatch of diverting love stories to another woman cloaks the 'truth', that d'Aulnoy was acting as a government spy. Thus, the *naiveté* of her preface to her *Memoirs of the Court of England* must surely be interpreted as disingenuous: 'The Acquaintance of so many Persons of Distinction gave me opportunity of knowing a thousand diverting Stories, of which I have composed these *Memoirs*, and, according to your Desire, put them

---

[53] The facts of d'Aulnoy's biography are still unclear. A supposed autobiography published in France in 1697 and translated as *The Memoirs of the Countess of Dunois, Author of The Lady's Travels into Spain* . . . (London, 1699), was in fact the fictional creation of one Madame de Murat. See Melvin D. Palmer, 'Madame d'Aulnoy in England', *Comparative Literature*, 27 (1975), 239. The 'memoir' is a defence of d'Aulnoy that claims she and her mother were mortal enemies throughout their lives, and presents its subject as a martyr to gossip and scandal. D'Aulnoy's twentieth-century biographer, Raymond Foulché-Delbosc, claims that d'Aulnoy never went to Spain and her 'travels' are literary hoaxes. See Foulché-Delbosc, 'Madame D'Aulnoy et l'Espagne', *Révue hispanique*, 67 (1926), 1–151 and James Rush Beeler, 'Madame d'Aulnoy: Historical Novelist of the Late Seventeenth Century' (Univ. of North Carolina, Ph.D. diss., 1964).

[54] *Mémoires de la cour d'Éspagne* (1679–81), *Mémoires sur la cour de France* (1692) and *Mémoires de la cour d'Angleterre* (1695). Most of her novels appeared in translation in Britain in the 1690s.

into as regular a Method as I could.'[55] So too, in her *Travels into Spain* (1691), a letter novel as opposed to memoir, d'Aulnoy explains her curiosity by virtue of her cousin's demand for detail: 'The Exactness I observe in giving you an Account of things which I judge worthy of your Curiosity, puts me often times on Enquiries into several Particulars which I should otherwise have omitted, had you not perswaded me that you are a great Lover of Novelties, and that you love to travel without going out of your closet.'[56] In one sentence, d'Aulnoy excuses both the sexual explicitness of some of her narratives and the curiosity that prompts her investigation of them.

D'Aulnoy's scandal narratives bring us closer to the 'erotic-bathetic' cliches of scandal fiction in England in the late seventeenth and early eighteenth century. Unlike Bussy-Rabutin, d'Aulnoy presents the male aristocrat as the duplicitous villain, seducing and corrupting innocent ladies. Thus her heroines owe more to Lafayette and Villedieu than to her more obvious predecessor, Bussy-Rabutin. Women tend to be presented as innocent 'readers' of masculine fiction-making, unable to judge the verity of their lovers' claims to fidelity and passion.

In contrast to their faithless seducers, d'Aulnoy undertakes to act as guardian for women's secrets. She has no qualms about naming her male characters, but she introduces this same volume with the explanation that she has 'concealed some of the Ladies Names . . . while [she has] nam'd others, hoping that what [she] speak[s] in their Favour, will counterballance what the Malice of their Enemies should say against them' (2). Women, it appears, are less guilty than men in affairs of sexual intrigue, and thus more deserving of protection. D'Aulnoy's early use of the seduction and betrayal motif of the *histoire galante* was to be developed by her female followers in Britain into a full-blown use of gender polarities to signify political conflict.

The Love-Letter

If the scandal chronicle took the epistemological play between fact

---

[55] Marie d'Aulnoy, *Memoirs of the Court of England* (London, 1707), 2.

[56] Marie d'Aulnoy, *The Ingenious and Diverting Letters of the Lady—Travels into Spain*, 2nd edn. (London, 1692), pt. 2, p. 30. All subsequent references are to this edition, cited as *Travels into Spain* with part and page number (two parts numbered separately), and included in the main body of the text.

and fiction to new heights of ambiguity, the fictional love-letter became the trope of absolute sincerity. The love-letter was perhaps the most popular and ubiquitous fictional device of the late seventeenth and early eighteenth century in both England and France.[57] Whereas the traditional links between scandal and misogyny can be traced back to the classical models of Juvenal and Horace, Ovid's *Heroides* were the classical precedent for the association of women's writing with the love-letter.[58] The letter appears as fictional device in virtually every amatory narrative in Britain in the period 1680 to 1740, both as a means of seduction and an expression of complaint, reaching, of course, its apotheosis in Richardson's *Pamela* (1740) and *Clarissa* (1747–8).

However, in the heroic romance, little history, and scandal chronicle in France the letter was mainly employed as a plot device. The loss, discovery, theft, forging, or exchange of love letters function as a means of 'witnessing' (the letter, obtained by the author, supposedly proves the verity of his or her story), as a means of disclosing a secret, or as the source of a misunderstanding or misinterpretation between lovers. One of the earliest characters to be introduced in Scudéry's *Clelia* is a compulsive letter-opener, Statilia, who informs the noble Aronces when he refuses to open a letter to his mistress from another, that 'there is nothing fuller of delight than to make ones self Mistress of anothers secrets unperceivedly, and never be beholding to them for it: ... there is always some kind of pleasure in knowing that which others know not, and which they do not know, that others know it, be the thing of what nature it will' (pt. 1, p. 68). Statilia sees the illicit viewing of others' letters as providing access to secret knowledge, without incurring responsibility. She goes on to add that 'it is more easie to open Letters than hearts, and ... sometimes opening the one, the other is discovered' (pt. 1, p. 68).

Ruth Perry, in her analysis of early modern letter fiction in Britain has noted the fact that the letter frequently acts as signifier

[57] See Robert Adams Day, *Told in Letters: Epistolary Fiction before Richardson* (Ann Arbor, 1966). Day estimates that between 1660 and 1740 200 in every 500 editions and issues were works of letter fiction (2) and that about a third of the latter were translations (29).

[58] Ovid, *'Heroides' and 'Amores'* trans. Grant Shaverman (Loeb Classical Library; Cambridge, Mass., 1914). For an illuminating reading of Ovid, Sappho, and the letter, see Linda S. Kaufmann, *Discourses of Desire: Gender, Genre and Epistolary Fictions* (Ithaca, NY, and London, 1986), 29–62. Ovid's 15 heroines all write to a silent lover who has seduced, betrayed, or left them behind.

for the woman's body, through its function of providing an opening into consciousness for the reader.[59] 'Breaking open' the woman's letter is an act of 'mind-rape'; persuading her to enter into correspondence is the first step in seduction. As I suggested earlier, d'Aulnoy's epistolary travelogues make significant associations between the letter form and the act of 'spying'. The unsolicited reader is, then, above all a voyeur, getting pleasure from invading another's consciousness, and thus by analogy the body, without taking any of the risks of an actual encounter. The novel reader by this logic is, of course, the voyeur *par excellence*, provided with the opportunity to enter, explore, and abandon the letter fiction as he or she pleases.

It was the publication of the anonymous *Lettres Portugaises* (1669) by Barbin in Paris that re-established the Ovidian convention of the letter of complaint from the victim of seduction in seventeenth-century prose fiction. Although the French heroic romance had privileged women's relation to the letter, it had done so for quite opposite reasons than that of the Portuguese letters. One of Scudéry's liveliest heroines, Plotina, distinguishing between letters of 'love' and letters of 'gallantry', explains women's superiority in the epistolary form as follows:

I have it from a very virtuous person, that ordinarily women are more exquisite at Love-letters than men. . . . For when a Lover is resolved to make a full discovery of his passion, there is no need of Art, to say *I am still under the Martyrdom of your Love*; but for a woman, in regard she never absolutely acknowledges her love, but doth all things with a greater Mystery, this Love, whereof there can only be a glympse [*sic*], causes a greater pleasure than that which is apparent, and without ceremony. (Pt. 2, p. 284)

The woman's letter/body is then more erotic because more concealed than that of the man. Like clothing, the letter's cloaking devices serve to enhance the appeal of the body by the very act of concealment. Even in the private realm of the letter the romance heroine cannot afford to express her desire directly.

If the French romance represented women's letter-writing as superior because of its artful strategies of concealment, the *Lettres Portugaises* reversed the equation.[60] These five letters from a

---

[59] Ruth Perry, *Women, Letters and the Novel* (New York, 1980), 130–1.

[60] The letters first appeared in Britain in translation as *Five Love-Letters from a Nun to a Cavalier*, trans. Roger L'Estrange (London, 1678). Repr. in Natascha Würzbach (ed.), *The Novel in Letters: Epistolary Fiction in the Early English Novel 1678–1740* (London, 1969), 1–23. All subsequent references, unless otherwise noted, are from this edition, cited as *Five Love-Letters*, and included in the main body of the text.

Portuguese nun to a French army officer, the lover who has seduced and abandoned her, flout virtually every convention of the heroic romance and articulate the woman's prerogative in amatory discourse in an entirely 'novel' way for the seventeenth century at least. Mariane is the very opposite of the traditional romance heroine. She admits: 'I had a kindness for your Person, before you ever told me anything of your Love; and you no sooner declar'd it, but with all the joy imaginable I receiv'd it, and gave my self up wholly to that Inclination' (*Five Love-Letters*, 12). Dorothy Osborne's stricture that a romance heroine should 'neither love when she is not first Loved', nor 'have the face to own it' if she should, is here flagrantly broken.

Where love in the romance is a stimulus to heroic denial, refinement of sensibility, and moral sensitivity, in the Portuguese letters it encourages 'Licentious Idolatry' (20). Mariane is paralysed by her love, both physically and mentally. The first letter informs her lover that his last missive 'laid [her] three hours senseless' (5) and in the second she states that '[her] Honour and Religion are brought only to serve the Turn of [her] Love' (8). Mariane refuses to listen to anything in her lover's letters that she describes as 'Unprofitable and Impertinent to [their] Affair' (6). Love in both the romance and the *nouvelle* was the cause of a variety of events from abductions to major wars. The *Portuguese Letters*, ostensibly at least, dedicate twenty-odd pages to a solitary woman's struggle to elicit an epistolary response from her absent lover.

Most important, the *Portuguese Letters* and their English translation introduced a new language to amatory fiction, a language that was ostentatiously 'natural' and implicitly associated with female desire. Amatory passion in the letters is signified typographically, through the use of parentheses, exclamation marks, the ubiquitous dash; syntactically, through the rhetorical question, inverted word order, abbreviated sentences; and finally lexically. This latter is perhaps the most important in that the romance vocabulary epitomized in Clelia's *carte de tendre* was superseded. The euphemism and periphrasis of the *précieuse*, Clelia's lexicon of 'amity', 'recognizance', 'inclination', 'tenderness', 'esteem', was substituted by the 'Portuguese' vocabulary of the 'heart', 'soul', 'sigh', 'tear', and 'torment' (*Five Love-Letters*, 4). The language of religious experience, and spiritual autobiography, peculiarly appropriate to the nun, is profanely employed in the service of sexual passion.

Desire in the Portuguese style is registered by linguistic disorder and logical inconsistency on the part of the writer. Mariane confesses that 'I do not know what I am, or what I do, or what I would be at. I am torn to pieces by a Thousand contrary Motions, and am in a Condition deplorable beyond Imagination' (10). It is this 'beyond' that is the key to the *Portuguese Letters'* representation of desire. Again and again, Mariane calls attention to the poverty of available amatory discourse. 'There is so great a difference', she writes at the beginning of her second letter 'betwixt the Love I write and That which I feel, that if you measure the One by the Other, I have undone my self' (7).

Love, the peculiar province of the woman, is now associated with 'excess'. Through its linguistic disruptions the female letter attempts to transgress the boundaries of language, to substitute signified for signifier. Hence Mariane's desire to 'convey [her] self in the Place' of her first letter (6). Linda Kaufmann views amatory discourse, and the epistolary fiction in particular, as an attempt to figure this transgressive marginality, associated with the woman writer's struggle in and against the restrictions of a patriarchal order of language: 'Love is the ultimate transgression, and therefore love is relegated to the realms of myth and utopia. Yet the aim of all amorous discourse is to inscribe what has been relegated to the margins in the conceptual universe, to explore a theory of knowledge based on the senses—loving as a form of knowing.'[61] It was, I would argue, this transgressive impulse that made the *Portuguese Letters* an object of such fascination and imitation for so many of their readers in England and France.

From their publication onwards it became a commonplace for amatory fiction to present the letter as the privileged site of passionate expression, and the woman writer as the nonpareil in its production. Aphra Behn in her own original combination of Portuguese epistolary style with the scandal novel, *Love-Letters between a Nobleman and his Sister* (1685–7), wrote that 'when a Lover is insupportably afflicted, there is no ease like that of writing to the person loved; and that, all that comes uppermost in the soul: for true love is all unthinking artless speaking, incorrect disorder, and without method, as 'tis without bounds and rules.'[62] In similar vein, Delarivier Manley's *Court Intrigues* (1711) instructs an absent lover in the art of letter writing: '*take my Example, I write unartfully, without*

    [61] Kaufmann, *Discourses of Desire*, 60.
    [62] Aphra Behn, *Love-Letters between a Nobleman and his Sister*, ed. Maureen Duffy (London, 1987), 184. All subsequent references, unless otherwise indicated, are to this edition, cited as *Love-Letters* and included in the main body of the text.

Method, or perhaps Coherence; my Thoughts naturally (as they arise in my Mind) fall from my Pen, not polished by Art, nor better'd by Study.' [63]

Mariane's rhetoric insistently distinguishes between her lover's 'Artificial disguise' (9) and her own 'Integrity of . . . Soul' (13). In her final letter she bitterly concludes that 'it is not Love alone that begets Love; there must be Skill, and Address; for it is Artifice, and not Passion, that creates Affection' (2). The male seducer, then, feigns love and the woman is trapped by his art, but the sincere passion he has created only alienates him. Thus, the *Portuguese Letters* establish a system of gender opposition whereby women are subjects of and subjected to nature, while men command culture. This dramatic conflict between male artist and guileless woman (reader) was the founding structure of seduction fiction in late seventeenth- and early eighteenth-century Britain.

This same gender conflict has remained moreover the basis for most discussions of the authorship of the letters themselves. The *Portuguese Letters*, it appears, set the terms for their own debate. In brief, the dispute over authorship has polarized between those who accept the text's own claim to be the work of a Portuguese nun, and those who trace its composition to the well known French raconteur, Gabriel Joseph de Laverne de Guilleragues (1628–85).[64] A number of feminist critics of epistolary narrative have noted that questions of gender and of genre come to be inextricably associated in this debate.[65] If we accept the ascription to a woman, the argument has run, then they are indeed the spontaneous and untutored out-

[63] Delarivier Manley, *Court Intrigues,* in *A Collection of Original Letters from the Island of New Atalantis, & Co.* (London, 1711), 136–7.

[64] The ascription to Maria Ana Alcoforada, a Portuguese nun at the Convent of Notre-Dame-de-la-Conception at Béja is based largely on the note of a bibliographer named Boissonade under the pseudonym of 'Omega' to the *Journal de l'Empire* (5 January 1810), who cited Guilleragues as the translator and based his argument on a handwritten note attached to a 1669 edition of the text referring to a 'Mariana Alcaforada'. The ascription to Guilleragues was first made convincingly by F. C. Green in an article entitled 'Who was the author of the "Lettres Portugaises"?' *Modern Language Review,* 21 (1926), 159–65. Green's argument rested on the evidence of the manuscript version of the manuscript 'privilège du roi' for the 1669 letters, which refers to a book entitled *Les Valentins lettres portugaises, Epigrammes et Madrigaux de Guilleraques.* I am indebted for my own information here to an unpublished article by Ron Hammond entitled, 'Why "Who wrote the Portuguese Letters?" Matters'.

[65] See Kaufmann, *Discourses of Desire,* 94; Peggy Kamuf, 'Writing like a Woman', in Sally McConnel-Ginet, Ruth Borker, and Nelly Furman (eds.), *Women and Language in Literature and Society* (New York, 1980); Katharine A. Jensen, 'Male Models of Feminine Epistolarity, or, How to Write Like a Woman in Seventeenth-Century France', in Elizabeth C. Goldsmith (ed.), *Writing the Female Voice: Essays on Epistolary Literature* (Boston, 1989), 25–45.

pourings of a wounded heart and should be considered as occupying a sub- or non-literary provenance. If we advance the claim of Guilleragues, they must be assumed to be an example of a sophisticated artistic sensibility. In other words, female authorship here signifies naturalness; male authorship signifies artifice. The letters, depending on the sex of the author, are either fact or fiction.

French Texts/English Contexts

It is this alienation of the woman writer from the realm of art and representation, dramatized in the *Portuguese Letters* reversal of the gender ideologies of the romance, which Behn, Manley, and Haywood sought to address and subvert in their amatory fiction. I will return in the following chapters to the French precedents I have discussed here in order to demonstrate the ways in which English amatory fiction simultaneously exploited and challenged them. The following chapters look, in particular, at Behn's transformations of the 'little history' and the letter, Manley's reworking of the 'scandal chronicle', and Haywood's adaptations of the romance and the *histoire galante.*

Literary criticism and history, in the rare moments when it has considered early love fiction by English women, has largely ignored or denigrated French influence. Behn, Manley, and Haywood are most commonly seen as drawing on indigenous traditions in popular culture and the drama, such as the ballad, the rogue narrative, the Restoration comedy, and heroic tragedy. Their work is presented either as sub-literary, or scoured for signs of incipient realism and judged wanting. All three writers, however, were instrumental in popularizing the almost exclusively aristocratic forms of French love fiction. With few models in women's writing, particularly in prose fiction, upon which to draw in England, they looked to France. More important perhaps than the fact of female authorship in these French narratives is what I have termed their 'feminocentrism'. Across a variety of forms, and reaching a variety of conclusions, French love fiction addressed repeatedly the question of women's role in the production and consumption of art. It is these links between gender and genre, and, in particular, the search for a specifically female amatory form, which the fiction of Behn, Manley, and Haywood elaborates.

II

Women Writers

3

'A Devil on't, the Woman Damns the Poet': Aphra Behn's Fictions of Feminine Identity

Though I scorn to guard my Tongue as hoping 'twill never offend willingly, yet I can, with much adoe, hold it, when I have a great mind to say a Thousand Things, I know will be taken in an ill sense. Possibly, you will wonder what compels me to write, what moves me to send where I find so little welcome; nay, where I meet with such Returns, it may be a wonder too.[1]

A supposedly private letter to an unknown lover by Aphra Behn unexpectedly reveals some of the most important preoccupations and contradictions of her public literary career. She commences with the moral imperative that the author/lover must 'scorn to guard [her] Tongue', only to recognize that honesty, though the best, may not always be the most successful, policy. Words are inevitably subject to interpretation over which the author/lover can have no absolute control. The reader/beloved can wilfully misinterpret, take her words 'in an ill sense'. Interpretation, it appears, is an amorous struggle, despite the writer's desire to 'author' absolute meaning, or to have authority over meaning.

That a 'private' love letter should demonstrate the struggle to produce an authoritative 'public' female voice is peculiarly appropriate in the case of Aphra Behn. Behn's narrative voice, as this chapter will argue, is precisely that of the lover addressing his or her absent object, the beloved or reader. The telling of a story of seduction, as noted in Chapter 1, is also an act of seduction. Behn repeatedly inscribes herself into her tales of love, compulsively turning her reader's gaze from the amorous couple to the amatory narrator, who then uncannily retreats or withholds herself from view, in order to set the pursuit in train again.

It is perhaps not surprising that the first professional woman's writing in Britain should take the shape of a profound act of

[1] Aphra Behn, 'Love-Letters to a Gentleman', in *The Histories and Novels of the Late Ingenious Mrs. Behn* (London, 1696), 405.

narcissism.[2] Luce Irigaray, in an essay entitled 'Any Theory Of The "Subject" Has Always Been Appropriated By The "Masculine"', has pointed to the crisis of articulation that faces the woman writer:

Stifled beneath . . . eulogistic or denigratory metaphors, she is unable to pick the seam of her disguise and indeed takes a certain pleasure in them, even gilding the lily further at times. Yet even more hemmed in, cathected by tropes, how could she articulate any sound beneath this cheap chivalric finery? How find a voice, make a choice, strong enough to cut through these layers of ornamental style, that decorative sepulchre, where even her breath is lost. Stifled under all those airs.[3]

If the woman writer finds 'so little Welcome' from the object of her desires, the reading other that she seeks to effect, why, we must ask ourselves, does she write at all?

In 1929, Virginia Woolf's *A Room of One's Own* ambiguously restored Behn to a significant place in literary history, insisting on her importance as a model for the professional woman writer, while quietly dismissing the works themselves as without literary value: 'She made by working very hard, enough to live on. The importance of that fact outweighs anything that she actually wrote, . . . for here begins the freedom of the mind, or the possibility that in the course of time the mind will be free to write what it likes.'[4] Woolf's conflation of the writing subject, Aphra Behn, and the actual historical figure, Aphra Behn, is by no means a wilful misreading of Behn's texts. Behn frequently presents herself to her readers as an erotic object, a seductive hieroglyph, or more mundanely, a fascinating eccentric, whose personality and personal history can be deciphered between the lines of her amatory narratives. Woolf's comments may well have been indebted to the analysis of Vita Sackville-West who, only two years before *A Room of One's Own*,

[2] I am employing the concept of narcissism here as a rejection of any external means of judging the self. See Sigmund Freud, 'On Narcissism: An Introduction', in *Essential Papers on Narcissism*, ed. Andrew P. Morrison (New York and London, 1986), 17–43. Freud asserts that in the narcissist the 'libido that has been withdrawn from the external world has been directed to the ego', resulting in 'a belief in the thaumaturgic force of words, and a technique for dealing with the external world—"magic"—which appears to be a logical application of these grandiose premises' (19).
[3] Luce Irigaray, 'Any Theory of The "Subject" Has Always Been Appropriated By The "Masculine"', in *Speculum of the Other Woman*, trans. Catherine Porter (New York, 1985), 142–3.
[4] Virginia Woolf, 'Aphra Behn', in *Virginia Woolf: Women and Writing*, ed. Michèle Barrett (London, 1979), 89. See also, George Woodcock, *The Incomparable Aphra* (London and New York, 1948) and Frederick Link, *Aphra Behn* (New York, 1968).

published a biography of Behn. Woolf, it appears, was merely reiterating Sackville-West's assertion that: 'The fact that she wrote is much more important than the quality of what she wrote. The importance of Aphra Behn is that she was the first woman in England to earn her living by her pen'.[5] Thus, both Sackville-West and Woolf succeed in substituting the woman for the writing; the reality of Behn's existence is the only proof we need of her achievement. Behn's biography, in these two early feminist commentaries, has finally come to stand in for her text, a move she repeatedly invites from her readers and yet, as I will go on to argue in more detail, also frustrates.

A properly historicist and feminist account of Behn's prose writing must cease to view Behn's texts as mere sources for biographical investigation, and recognize the fictional nature of the figure of the female writer, Aphra/Astrea, who surfaces repeatedly in her narratives. Throughout her varied literary career, in drama, poetry, and prose, Behn was fascinated by the possibilities of the female writing subject, what she might be, and how she might survive within a masculine literary history. The narcissistic inscription of the figure of the female writer into her fiction, however, serves specific political and literary ends, and should not be reduced, as it has been in the main, to random insertions of biographical evidence. The figure of the female artist in Behn's writing releases a meditation upon, and an unsettling of, the nature of poetic and authorial identity. This in turn leads to an exploration of the woman writer's capacity to produce meaning against the interpretative will of the reader, as well as the potential to capitalize upon the erotic and seductive effects of the text upon the reader for political purposes. The reduction of the study of Behn's texts to biographical history serves only as a further example of taking her 'in an ill sense', closing down the 'Thousand Things' she has 'a great mind to say'. Behn's fictions, in this critical 'recovering', become mere vehicles for the discovery of the 'facts' of her biography, where they might be employed to undo the very opposition between fact and fiction, body and text, self and other.

The 'Masculine Part'

Behn's best-known attempt at self definition is her vindication of herself as poet in the preface to a late play, *The Lucky Chance* (1687).

[5] Vita Sackville-West, *Aphra Behn: The Incomparable Astrea* (New York, 1927), 12.

Her writings on her writing, habitually triggered by the hostility of male 'wits', turn on the question of gender attribution. The preface to *The Lucky Chance*, a comedy of manners performed at the Theatre Royal in 1687, defines 'masculine' writing in two ways. The first definition refers solely to the question of content, and the double standard employed with regard to a woman playwright. Sexual explicitness is only permissible, she notes, for the male author. Addressing her female audience, Behn writes: 'Had I a Day or two's time, . . . I would sum up all your Beloved Plays, and all the Things in them that are past with such Silence by; because written by Men: Such Masculine Strokes in me, must not be allow'd' (*Works*, iii. 186). Behn's second definition of 'masculine' writing raises, however, more complex issues. This time addressing her male peers in the theatre, she writes:

All I ask is the Priviledge for my Masculine Part the Poet in me, (if any such you will allow me) to tread in those successful Paths my Predecessors have so long thrived in, to take those Measures that both the Ancient and Modern Writers have set me, and by which they have pleas'd the World so well; If I must not, because of my Sex, have this Freedom, but that you will usurp all to your selves; I lay down my Quill, and you shall hear no more of me, no not so much as to make Comparisons, because I will be kinder to my Brothers of the Pen, than they have been to a defenceless Woman; for I am not content to write for a Third Day only. I value Fame as much as I had been born a *Hero*; and if you rob me of that, I can retire from the ungrateful World and scorn its fickle favours. (*Works*, iii. 187)[6]

Poetic genius is here firmly identified with 'masculinity', and 'heroic' male adventurism. If Behn rejects the pertinence of the double standard with regard to poetic content, these remarks suggest that she saw excellence in poetic form as an exclusively masculine quality. As a woman poet, she presents herself a divided subject, one of the female sex but with access to a 'masculine' power of poetry.

Judith Kegan Gardiner employs this difficult passage to shed light on Behn's conception of authorial identity as a whole, arguing that 'To enable herself to write, Behn created a poetic identity for herself

---

[6] Behn's reference to 'the third day' is to the common method of payment for playwrights. The author received the profits from the third day of the play's performance and authors would try to 'pack' the audience in order to receive a good return. A failed play would not reach the third day. This method could result in a playwright receiving between £50 and £100 per play, whereas a long poem might earn about 10 guineas outright payment from a publisher, and a novel from 1 to 10 guineas (see Day, *Epistolary Fiction before Richardson*, 79).

as Astrea, muse of a lost golden age who could combine 'Female Sweetness and a Manly Grace'. More fundamentally, to avoid becoming the disdainful lady or the disdained whore of male polarization, she identified with the male role while modifying its view of women.'[7] Gardiner does not differentiate, however, between Behn's strategies of gender identification in the different genres in which she wrote. Behn only uses this language of the 'masculine part' to refer to the writing she classifies as poetry, and to discuss her interest in poetic *form*. Although her comments are made in a preface to a play the demand to 'take those Measures' literary traditions have made available to her suggests that we read them in the context of notions of creative power in metred verse. Behn, it is clear, was all too aware of the conventional polarization of the 'female' in Restoration poetry. Here, woman appears either as the ideal Petrarchan mistress, to be slavishly worshipped and anatomized from her eyebrows to her toes, or as the engulfing, destructive whore of libertine poetry.[8] The only response to these rigid dichotomies in Restoration love poetry seems to be precisely that which Behn adopted in her poetry, that of lifting the female poet into a position which supposedly transcends the enclosures of ideologies of the 'feminine', by casting her as the possessor of a male poetic gift, or as a muse or goddess.

This is not, however, Behn's only strategy in her writing as a whole. In her preface to her first play, *The Dutch Lover*, produced at the Theatre Royal in 1673, she makes very bold claims indeed for women's literary abilities, insisting that 'Plays have no great room for that which is men's great advantage over women, that is Learning' (*Works*, i. 224). Noting that neither Shakespeare nor Jonson were respected for their intellectual breadth, she adds of her male contemporaries, that, with the exception of Dryden, there are 'none that write at such a formidable rate, but that a woman may well hope to reach their greatest heights' (224). The drama and fiction appeared far more accessible genres to Behn than poetry, since neither necessarily required a classical training. Behn consistently identifies poetry as a heroic masculine preserve. Thus, she

---

[7] Judith Kegan Gardiner, 'Aphra Behn: Sexuality and Self-Respect', *Women's Studies*, 7 (1980), 67.

[8] Behn mockingly reworks the Petrarchan tradition in the male lover's response to his mistress's address in *The Lover's Watch*, entitled *The Lady's Looking Glass, to Dress Her Self by, or The Art of Charming* (*Works*, vi. 94–111). Here, the mistress's bodily parts are anatomized ad absurdum.

most frequently adopts a Sapphic or oracular poetic voice in her poetry, in sharp contrast to the intimate and confiding persona of her novelistic prose, and the incisive wit of her dramatic prefaces.

This is not to say, however, that Behn's poetry is not equally inclined to exploration and subversion of gender dichotomies. Her utopian poem, 'The Golden Age', in many ways a conventional piece of Tory pastoral nostalgia, is also a remarkable exercise in female self-creation. Behn's pastoral idyll is a world in which a female Nature cannot be constrained by the power of man:

> The stubborn Plough had then,
> Made no rude Rapes upon the Virgin Earth;
> Who yielded of her own accord her plentious Birth,
> Without the Aids of men;
> As if within her Teeming Womb,
> All Nature, and all Sexes lay,
> Whence new Creations every day
> Into the happy World did come:
> The Roses fill'd with Morning Dew
> Bent down their loaded heads,
> T'adorn the careless Shepherds Grassy Beds
> While still young opening Buds each moment grew,
> And as those withered, drest his shaded Couch anew.
> (*Works*, vi. 139)

In this female economy, earth/woman contains all sexual difference within herself. Both virgin and mother, Nature has the power of sexual emission and generation. She impregnates and reproduces herself, as the roses filled with morning dew dispel their liquid, die, and replenish autonomously. Once again it is the female who has access to both sides of the sexual divide. Behn's 'The Golden Age', in the context of her other work, can be read as a further contribution to her narcissistic exercise in female self-creation.

It is in the ambiguous poem, 'To the fair Clarinda, who made Love to me, imagin'd more than Woman', appended to her translation of *Lycidus*, that this narcissistic challenge to masculine exclusions reaches its height:

> Fair lovely Maid, or if that Title be
> Too weak, too Feminine for Nobler thee,
> Permit a Name that more Approaches Truth:
> And let me call thee, Lovely Charming Youth.
> This last will justifie my soft complaint;
> While that may serve to lessen my constraint;

And without Blushes I the Youth persue,
When so much beauteous Woman is in view.
Against thy Charms we struggle but in vain
With thy deluding Form thou giv'st us pain,
While the bright Nymph betrays us to the Swain.
In pity to our Sex sure thou wer't sent,
That we might Love, and yet be Innocent:
For sure no Crime with thee we can commit;
Or if we shou'd—thy Form excuses it.
For who, that gathers fairest Flowers believes
A Snake lies hid beneath the Fragrant Leaves.

Thou beauteous Wonder of a different kind,
Soft *Cloris* with the dear *Alexis* join'd;
When e'er the Manly part of thee, wou'd plead
Thou tempts us with the Image of the Maid,
While we the noblest Passions do extend
The Love to *Hermes*, *Aphrodite* the Friend.
(*Works*, vi. 363)

This twenty-four line poem, like so much of Behn's work, has largely prompted biographical investigation. What, her critics ask, is the (sexual) identity of the lover?

The poem is most frequently interpreted as a panacea to lesbian desire. Thus, George Woodcock sees 'Clarinda' as proof that Behn was 'not uninterested in the predilections of the original Sappho', Angeline Goreau describes it as a 'playful tribute to her own sex' but devoid of the 'consuming passion' of the *Love-Letters to a Gentleman*, and Cora Kaplan sums it up as 'a witty poem about a lesbian attraction'.[9] Under the protection of the disguise of idealized female friendship, supporters of this interpretation argue, the lovers are safe from recognition of their lesbian practices ('For sure no Crime with thee we can commit; | Or if we shou'd—thy Form excuses it').

Another possible reading, however, is that the lover is a cross-dressing or transvestite man. Disguised as a woman, the male lover gains easy access to his mistress ('For who that gathers fairest Flowers believes | A Snake lies hid beneath the Fragrant Leaves'). This reading might lead us back to John Hoyle, the supposed

[9] Woodcock, *The Incomparable Aphra*, 114; Angeline Goreau, *Reconstructing Aphra: A Social Biography of Aphra Behn* (Oxford, 1980), 206; Cora Kaplan (ed.), *Salt and Bitter and Good: Three Centuries of English and American Women Poets* (London, 1975), 50.

'Lycidus' of the *Love-Letters to a Gentleman*, for whom there is some evidence of homosexuality, although none of transvestitism.[10]

Behn allows us no easy solution to this riddle, but rather encourages her reader to enjoy the play across both sexes and the subversive power of the image of the hermaphrodite. The rhyming couplet provides the ideal structure for the undercutting of each successive clue, and a reversal of the beloved's sexual identity ('And without Blushes I the Youth persue, | When so much beauteous Woman is in view', and 'When e'er the Manly part of thee wou'd plead | Thou tempts us with the Image of the Maid').

'To Fair Clarinda' is, I would argue, best illuminated within the context of Behn's narcissistic contemplation of her own poetic practice. The concluding line, a splitting of the term Hermaphrodite, the figure who contains both sexual morphologies, also contains an embedded pun. Aphrodite is both the goddess of love, and the lover of Aphra. Aphra is then both subject and object of her own poem. The riddling tautologies of the poet are a seductive plea to her reader to abandon the search for a unitary identity behind the writing, whether that of the lover or the beloved. The reader, like Behn's fictional lovers, is encouraged to take his or her pleasure from the pursuit of (sexual) meaning, rather than in its definitive resolution.

The complex play of gendered subjectivity to which 'Clarinda' points us is more fully developed as the specific property of the female writer, however, in Behn's use of narrative as opposed to lyric form. Behn abandons the oracular, mythic persona of Astrea in her prose writings for a more familiar feminine subject position, that of the 'gossip' or story-teller.

The Female Plot

Aphra Behn turned to fiction writing late in her literary career, and only when she could no longer support herself by drama.[11] Until

---

[10] Hoyle was accused of buggering a poulterer, one William Bistow of Gracechurch Street, and appeared before the grand jury on 26 February 1687. The jury returned a verdict of 'ignoramus', a not unusual decision in cases of this kind since the penalty for sodomy was execution. See Goreau, *Reconstructing Aphra*, 203. Whitelocke Bulstrode's description of Hoyle as 'an atheist, a sodomite professed, a corrupter of youth, and a blasphemer of Christ' is quoted by Goreau (192).

[11] Vita Sackville-West, (*Aphra Behn*, 62) and Goreau (*Reconstructing Aphra*, 251) argue that Behn abandoned her playwrighting for four years due to the political

1682, dramatic writing had proved the most accessible and most lucrative genre for a woman writer. It was, after all, the only truly profitable literary genre that relied on public rather than private patronage. By the 1680s, however, the London theatres were in financial straits and ideological confusion. The mass paranoia that followed the discovery of the Popish plot (a supposed Catholic plot engineered by Pope Innocent XI, the King of France, the Archbishop of Dublin, and the Jesuits to murder Charles and crown the Catholic Duke of York in his stead 'exposed' by a Jesuit priest, Titus Oates), resulted in the King's departure to Newmarket, a succession of executions and purges of suspected Catholics, and, more important for Behn perhaps, a general decline in theatre-going. Between 1678 and 1679, the King's Company closed down due to internal disputes and the Duke's Company staged only six new plays where in the two years preceding it had staged eighteen a season.[12] Behn abandoned the stage for the novel.

Her success in this new medium was remarkable. Robert Adams Day lists six books that went into more than ten editions between 1660 and 1740. Among them are both Behn's *Love-Letters between a Nobleman and his Sister* and her *Histories and Novels* and all but one of the remainder are translations from the French. Four of the six are by, or purported to be by, women, and the same four are amatory fictions.[13] In the light of my discussion in Chapter 2 of literacy levels and financial differentials, it would seem that it is not enough to explain this phenomenon as the simple effect of the fact that early fiction was almost exclusively read by and written for women. Rather, I would suggest, the figure of the woman, and in particular the female love victim, had a larger ideological significance than the appeal to women readers alone.

The execution of a king in 1649 was no easy event to purge from the public memory even with the restoration of his son to the throne

---

disfavour she incurred in August 1682. Behn had contributed a prologue and epilogue attacking the Duke of Monmouth for an anonymous play, *Romulus and Hersilia, or, The Sabine War* (1682). On 12 August 1682 Charles II had Behn and the actress, Lady Slingsby, who had delivered the offending lines taken into custody by Arlington, the Lord Chamberlain. A broadside of the epilogue and prologue was promptly published, entitled *Prologue to Romulus* (London, 1682).

[12] Goreau, *Reconstructing Aphra*, 237–41.

[13] Day, *Epistolary Fiction before Richardson*, 78. The six are the *Turkish Spy*, Marie d'Aulnoy's *Ingenious and Diverting Letters*, John Reynold's *God's Revenge against Murther*, the *Portuguese Letters*, and Behn's two works.

in 1660, and the hysteria that resulted from Oates's revelation of the Popish plot was doubtless the result of renewed anxiety about the dangers of Catholic 'tyranny' in England. In particular, the dynastic struggles of the Stuart sovereigns from Charles I's execution until the Hanoverian succession in 1714 seems to have thrown philosophical, literary, and political discourses into a profound crisis about the nature of authority and the means of its legitimation. Aphra Behn, a confirmed royalist, was no exception to this rule and her location of authorial legitimation in a female narrative voice might be ascribed to a larger cultural movement towards locating moral value, law and order in the individual, rather than directly 'feminist' sentiment on her part.

As Susan Staves argues in her *Players' Scepters: Fictions of Authority in the Restoration*, a clear social consensus against the exercise of violence, whether manifested in the arbitrary tyranny of a king or the lawless behaviour of 'the mob', seems to have emerged following Charles II's 'restoration' in 1660. This ideological consensus generated a search for new models for social behaviour in contemporary literature, to which the representation of heroic resistance through passivity in the figure of the sexually beleaguered woman seemed a particularly apposite response.[14] Ellen Pollak both reinforces the argument and notes the tensions it produced in contemporary accounts of the position of women. The feminocentric focus of much fiction in this period, she argues, did not produce an easy transition into the according of a full subjectivity and autonomy to women in general. Rather, artists, philosophers, and political theorists, Locke not least among them, sought to deploy the figure of the woman as a means of evolving a new concept of the masculine subject, while simultaneously maintaining a theory of 'natural' female subordination to familial hierarchy and patriarchal rule.[15] Seen in this light, Behn's narrative strategies, whereby woman is represented as simultaneously subject (the female writer) and subjected (the female character) within the social order, are a register of this confusion, as well as an attempt to resolve it.

It is a critical commonplace to view Behn's feminist and party politics as deeply at odds. George Woodcock refers to her 'radical

---

[14] See Susan Staves, *Players' Scepters: Fictions of Authority in the Restoration* (Lincoln, Nebr. and London, 1979), 186.

[15] Ellen Pollak, *The Poetics of Sexual Myth: Gender and Ideology in the Verse of Swift and Pope* (Women in Culture and Society Series; Chicago, 1985) 2.

and even revolutionary tendencies' and explains her 'rather foolish loyalty to the reactionary Stuarts' as mere evidence of 'the confusion of social ideas in that age' (151). Angeline Goreau asserts at one point in her 'social biography' of Behn that 'no two philosophical systems could be more opposed than Aphra's revolutionary [i.e. feminist] and Tory thinking' (268). According to these critics, Behn's commitment to 'authorizing' a female narrative voice and her devotion to the authority of the king constitute an unresolvable contradiction in her writing. However, the correlation of Whig politics with bourgeois individualism and Tory politics with anti-quated notions of hierarchy and patriarchy in the late seventeenth century is to a large extent a twentieth-century fiction.[16] Like Manley and Haywood, her successors in amatory fiction, Behn found a specific and progressive form of individualism in Tory myth and ideology in contrast with the repression and egoism she commonly identified with the Whig politician. Following the Restoration in 1660, as Judith Kegan Gardiner argues, the sexual libertarianism and cosmopolitan outlook of Tory royalism seemed to offer new hopes for the revival of 'heroic' individualism in contrast with the supposedly worn-out dogmatism of the old Commonwealth (69). It appears, then, that both Behn's and her readers' interest in giving public validation to the 'authority' of private female experience may have been due to general political concerns, rather than specific feminist ones. Behn's success lay in her dual articulation of Tory myth and feminocentric individualism.

Behn recognized at an early stage in her literary career that the roles of woman writer and political commentator were incompatible in the public mind, and that if she was to make her living by her writing and succeed in scoring political points for the Tory camp, she would not be able to do so directly. An interesting anecdote from one of her earliest biographers, known only as 'One of the Fair Sex', illustrates the restrictions Behn faced and the strategies of deceit she employed to escape them. In the summer of 1666, Behn was commissioned on the advice of her friend the playwright Thomas Killigrew, by Arlington, then Secretary of State, to act as a spy on the activities of British insurrectionaries exiled in Antwerp during the second Anglo-Dutch wars. Her friendship and possible romance with William Scot, the son of a regicide, and a somewhat unreliable

---

[16] Staves, *Players' Scepters*, 77.

double agent for the British government, made her an ideal choice for this sensitive mission.[17] 'One of the Fair Sex', in her 1698 'The History of the Life and Memoirs of Mrs Behn', claims that Behn sent information of a planned attack by the Dutch up the Thames in order to destroy the English harboured fleet, which was ignored. Clearly her spying role was to be solely that of the woman behind the man, William Scot (who is satirized as the Dutchman Vander Albert in the 'Memoir'), since:

all the Encouragement she met with, was to be laugh'd at by the Minister she wrote to; and her Letter shew'd by way of Contempt, to some who ought not to have been let into the Secret, and so bandy'd about, till it came to the Ears of a particular Friend of hers, who gave her an Account of what Reward she was to expect for her Service, since that was so little valu'd; and desir'd her therefore to lay aside her politick Negotiation, and divert her Friends with some pleasant Adventures of *Antwerp*, either as to her Lovers, or those of any other Lady of her Acquaintance; that in this she wou'd be more successful than in her Pretences of State, since here she wou'd not fail of pleasing those she writ to.[18]

Here then, Behn is taught an important lesson about the woman writer's relation to audience, and appropriate 'forms'. A woman may write pleasant accounts of love affairs to her friends, but she will receive only contempt if she attempts to narrate political affairs to men of state.

Women's only political instrumentality was to be achieved by playing the role of seductress. Not only does the woman writer

[17] For Behn's activities in Holland, see William J. Cameron, *New Light on Aphra Behn* (Auckland, 1961). Cameron reproduces nineteen documents preserved among Williamson's State Papers kept in the Public Record Office from and to Aphra Behn between July and December 1666 (34–86). Behn's letters are largely taken up by her financial concerns, since Arlington at no point provided her with any money for her spying activities. A letter from Byam to Sir Robert Harley in March 1664 makes it clear that Scot and Behn were friends in Surinam, and suggests a romantic interest between them (see Cameron, p. 12).
[18] 'The History of the Life and Memoirs of Mrs Behn By One of the Fair Sex', *All the Histories and Novels of the Late Ingenious Mrs Behn*, 5th edn. (London, 1705), 7. This version first appeared in the 3rd edn. of *All the Histories and Novels of the Late Ingenious Mrs Behn* (London, 1698), but was in fact a much expanded version of the biographical sketch entitled 'Memoirs on the Life of Mrs Behn Written By a Gentle-woman of her Acquaintance' in *The Histories and Novels* (London, 1696). For details of the Dutch victory, when the Thames was blocked for three days, the 'Royal James' at Chatham sunk, and the 'Royal Charles' towed away, see Goreau, *Reconstructing Aphra*, 108.

receive approval rather than scorn for her confinement of her 'interest' to the sphere of love, she also receives financial remuneration. On her return from Antwerp, Behn's biographer tells us, the 'rest of her Life was entirely dedicated to Pleasure and Poetry' (28). In fact on her immediate return, Behn faced imprisonment for debts she had incurred in the king's service as a passionate begging letter to Killigrew demonstrates.[19] This experience alone was doubtless enough to teach her that she could better make money by veiling her political interest in the appropriate female form of amatory fiction.

Closer study of Behn's fictions reveals that these seemingly harmless and escapist fictions of seduction and betrayal and tragic love do indeed address and rework a number of urgent ideological dilemmas in the period from the Restoration to the Glorious Revolution of 1688. *Oroonoko* (*Works*, v. 125–209), is the story of the life, romance, and death of an African prince who is tricked onto a slave ship, sold into slavery in the English colony of Surinam, bitterly humiliated and tortured by the white male colonists following his attempt to lead a slave rebellion, and finally executed having taken the life of his pregnant wife.

The pathetic story of an African prince is 'framed' within a specific debate on the nature of kingly authority and passive valour. Oroonoko himself is presented as a natural prince. His enslavement is an indignity to his class rather than his race. Renamed Caesar by his considerate master, Trefry, Oroonoko is indeed the modern equivalent of a Roman hero. Behn's description of him places him firmly within the Roman analogy: 'His Face was not of that brown rusty Black which most of that Nation are, but a perfect Ebony, or polished Jet.... His Nose was rising and *Roman*, instead of *African* and flat: His Mouth the finest shaped that could be seen; far from those great turn'd Lips, which are so natural to the rest of the Negroes' (136). Behn's description of her hero has generated a critical controversy about the extent of her anti-racism and/or

---

[19] See *Calendar of State Papers*, Domestic Series, Public Record Office (London, 1668–9), 172. Behn had borrowed £150 from one Edward Butler. When Arlington refused to pay it he had her thrown into prison. Behn wrote two petitions asking for an order for payment of the money due, the second accompanied by a covering letter to Killigrew the day before she was taken to prison, saying that she has 'cried [herself] dead' and is 'sick and weak and ill' with worry. There is no record of how Behn obtained her release from prison.

abolitionist sympathies.[20] However, Behn goes out of her way to stress Oroonoko/Caesar's distinctive difference from his fellow slaves. When they agree to a cowardly surrender following the slave rebellion he has led, Oroonoko declares himself 'ashamed of what he had done in endeavouring to make those free, who were by Nature Slaves, poor wretched Rogues, fit to be used as Christian Tools; Dogs, treacherous and cowardly, fit for such Masters' (196).

It would seem that Oroonoko serves less as a symbol of ethnic superiority than as a model of absolute virtue isolated in a politically and socially corrupt environment, and in this respect he has strong symbolic links with the suffering heroines of her other histories and novels. Behn's black hero is above all else a 'suffering king', like the Caesar he is named after, a victim of political corruption, abandoned by his own people and his enemies. Maureen Duffy suggests the novel might be read as a 'key novel', in which the exiled Duke of York, his wife Mary of Modena, and their son are cast as Oroonoko, Imoinda, and their unborn child, while Laura Brown identifies Oroonoko as the 'martyred' Chares I.[21] Whatever specific identification with the Stuart kings we choose to locate in the story of Oroonoko, it seems evident that the novel is deeply involved with contemporary political controversies, despite its claims to 'romance'.

A number of Aphra Behn's heroines, Philadelphia in *The Unfortunate Happy Lady* (1698), Agnes de Castro in *Agnes de Castro* (1688), Arabella in *The Wandering Beauty* (1698) and Atlante in *The Lucky Mistake* (1698) (*Works*, v), share Oroonoko's symbolic function of representing virtuous merit which resists social or domestic tyranny by exhibiting a passive, and even self-martyring, heroism.

---

[20] For early critiques of Behn's palliation of anti-slavery discourse through her use of heroic romance conventions to depict her hero, see Hoxie Neale Fairchild, *The Noble Savage: A Study in Romantic Naturalism* (New York, 1928) 34–41 and Wylie Sypher, *Guinea's Captive Kings: British Anti-Slavery Literature of the XVIIIth Century* (Chapel Hill, NC, 1942), 108–22. Laura Brown makes the reverse argument, that Behn's appropriation of her hero to Western ideals is a means of negotiating racial difference for the purposes of anti-racist polemic, in her essay, 'The Romance of Empire: *Oroonoko* and the Trade in Slaves', in Laura Brown and Felicity Nussbaum (eds.), *The New Eighteenth Century: Theory, Politics, English Literature* (London, 1987), 41–62. Finally Jerry C. Beasley has argued that Behn's novel is a subversive political allegory of British government with no interest in denouncing the slave trade. See Jerry C. Beasley, 'Politics and Moral Idealism: The Achievement of Some Early Women Novelists', in Cecilia Macheski and Mary Anne Schofield (eds.), *Fetter'd or Free? British Women Novelists 1670–1815* (Athens, Ohio, 1985), 222.

[21] Maureen Duffy, *The Passionate Shepherdess: Aphra Behn 1640–89* (London, 1977), 267; Brown, 'Romance of Empire', 59–60.

Like her other fictions, *Oroonoko* takes the form of a sentimentalized romance; its political message is more evident only because of the masculine gender of its protagonist, which has inclined readers and critics to dismiss it less readily as a mere derivative of the French romance's feminocentrism (the common fate of its fellows).

The representation of passive heroism, embodied in the marginal figure of the slave or woman, is not the only covert means by which Behn allegorizes political agency. Susan Staves points out that several of the novels Behn wrote between the Exclusion Crisis and her death in 1689 address the acutely felt political dilemma over the value of oath-taking following the Popish plot. Perjurers, Catholics forced to disavow their church in order to escape persecution, became the recipients of public sympathy in this period. Thus, absolute moral justice became a problem, rather than a given, or, in Staves's words, the 'Restoration understanding of oaths offers a particularly focused and elegant example of how a nominalist universe of force and passion triumphs over an idealist universe of words'.[22]

With this ethical and epistemological contradiction in mind (whether to break a vow to the Church or to the State in order to avoid political repression), Behn's frequent use of the plot convention of a heroine torn between vows (to a religious life and to a lover, or to an old lover and a new) take on a newly political light. This is an acute psychological dilemma in *The Fair Jilt*, *The Perjur'd Beauty*, *The Impious Vow Punish'd*, and *The Fair Vow-Breaker* but particularly evident in the last. In this novel, the heroine's progress toward the desperate decision to murder both husbands when the first, presumed dead, suddenly returns is seen as the result of unresolvable conflicts of loyalty and presaged in her first act of 'vow-breaking', when she elopes from a convent in order to marry her first husband. Behn informs us that her passion for this first lover was such that, unless gratified, 'nothing but Death would put an end to her Griefs, and her Infamy' (*Works*, v. 281). Vow-breaking becomes in this novel an inevitability rather than a choice. There can be little doubt that Behn's dramatization of the destructive confrontation between a concept of absolute moral justice (the inherent truth-telling capacities of the word) and the contingencies of political and social survival (in the form of a feminocentric tale of love) was one of the major causes of her popularity as a fiction-writer in the late seventeenth century.

It has, then, become evident that the almost exclusive interest in feminine subjectivity in Behn's short novels of the late 1680s is, in many ways, a serviceable fiction. These novels provide rather a means of articulating party politics through the mirror of sexual politics, in which the feminine acts as substitute for the masculine, signifier to his signified. Embattled virginity, virtue rewarded or ravished, what we might call the female plot, serve to reflect and refract male plotting, in other words, the party, dynastic, and ideological conflicts of late Stuart government.

'Little Histories': Mirroring Masculinity

Shoshana Felman, in a different context, has pointed out the metaphorical status of woman as love-object in the rhetorical hierarchy of masculine and feminine that governs the amatory plot.

Defined by man, the conventional polarity of masculine and feminine names woman as a *metaphor of man*. Sexuality, in other words, functions . . . as the sign of a rhetorical convention, of woman as the *signifier* and man the *signified*. Man alone has thus the privilege of proper meaning, or *literal identity*: femininity, as signifier, cannot signify *itself*; it is but a metaphor, a figurative substitute; it can but refer to man, to the phallus, as its proper meaning, as its signified. The rhetorical hierarchization of the very opposition between the sexes is then such that women's *difference* is suppressed, being totally subsumed by the reference of feminine to masculine identity.[23]

In the romantic plot, then, femininity serves to reflect masculine desire. Behn's plots are no exception to this rule, although her self-conscious and self-reflective deployment of the persona of the female narrator habitually questions the rhetorical function of femininity in relation to masculinity within her fiction.

Not surprisingly, then, sexual attraction in Behn's fiction is fundamentally narcissistic and frequently incestuous. Imoinda is the female mirror to Oroonoko, 'Female to the noble Male; the beautiful black Venus to our young Mars' (*Works*, v. 137). She reflects, and indeed accentuates, Oroonoko's strangeness and eroticism in the white colonists' eyes. Behn tells us that the people of Coramantien practise carving upon the body; whilst Oroonoko has only 'a little

---

[23] Shoshana Felman, 'Rereading Femininity', *Yale French Studies*, 62 (1981), 25.

Flower, or Bird, at the Sides of the Temples', Imoinda is 'carved in fine Flowers and Birds all over her Body' (174). The lovers' sibling likeness is reinforced by the fact that Imoinda's father, an army commander, has acted as a substitute father to the orphaned Oroonoko. In fact the lovers first meet in Coramantien due to Oroonoko's filial loyalty. On the general's death we are told that Oroonoko 'thought in Honour he ought to make a Visit to *Imoinda*, the Daughter of his Foster-Father, the dead General' (137).

Jean Hagstrum has drawn attention to the proximity between narcissistic and incestuous desire in *Oroonoko*, viewing Southerne's dramatic adaptation of the novel (produced at Drury Lane in 1696) as an attempt to temper its transgressive view of sexual desire. Southerne breaks the mirror effect by making Imoinda white (perhaps because it would have been considered improper for a white actress to 'black up') and introduces a comic sub-plot involving a hermaphrodite, and a cross-dressing woman who marries another woman. Thus, what Hagstrum terms the 'morbidity' of the narcissistic and incestuous relation between Behn's central lovers is displaced into comic farce and role-playing in another area of the plot, leaving the tragic love affair of the main plot thoroughly sentimental and heterosexual.[24]

The incestuous innuendo of *Oroonoko* is not an isolated example in Behn's fiction. Sibling relations positively encourage love affairs in these novels, it appears, because they are not bound by the usual social separations and constraints enforced upon men and women. The most striking example occurs in a letter from Sylvia to Philander in the first part of the *Love-Letters between a Nobleman and his Sister* (1684), where she details her unwitting seduction through sibling closeness. Philander is Sylvia's brother-in-law, the husband of her sister Myrtilla, but Sylvia unequivocally condemns their liaison as incestuous. In what she calls 'a fit of virtue', Sylvia chastises her lover for exploiting sibling familiarity in order to encourage incestuous desire:

Why did you take advantage of those freedoms I gave you as a brother? I smil'd on you; and sometimes kiss'd you too;—but for my sister's sake, I play'd with you, suffer'd your hands and lips to wander where I dare not now; all which I thought a sister might allow a brother, and knew not all the while the treachery of love: oh none, but under the intimate title of a

[24] See Jean Hagstrum, *Sex and Sensibility: Ideal and Erotic Love from Milton to Mozart* (Chicago, 1980), 81–2 and Thomas Southerne, *Oroonoko: A Tragedy* (London, 1696).

brother, could have had the opportunity to have ruin'd me; that, that betray'd me; I play'd away my heart at a game I did not understand. (*Love Letters*, 14–15)

Philander's incestuous desire for his sister-in-law is represented as part and parcel of his Whiggish politics. Sylvia is, as Behn puts it, 'a true Tory in every part',[25] seduced away from her respect for her own father's authority, but also, by implication, from that for her king's.

The siblings' 'unnatural' rebellion against paternal authority is thus presented as analogous to the Earl of Monmouth's disloyalty to his 'natural' father and later to his uncle in successive rebellions. In indicting Cesario's (Monmouth's) behaviour, Sylvia unwittingly condemns herself and foresees her own fate, for, like him, once she has broken her contract with paternal authority, she will embark on a steady decline into vice and manipulation. Seeking to persuade her lover to abandon Cesario's cabal, she warns:

let the world judge what he must prove to his servants, who has dealt so ill with his lord and master; how he must reward those who present him with a crown, who deals so ungraciously with him who gave him life, and who set him up a happier object than a monarch: no, no, *Philander*; he that can cabal, and contrive to dethrone a father, will find it easy to discard the wicked and hated instruments, that assisted him to mount it. (36)

Sylvia's moral decline acts as a mirror to Cesario's increasing political corruption. Thus, Behn's novel doubly articulates the political and the sexual, eroticizing the former while it politicizes the latter.

Behn's self-conscious use of femininity as a mirror to the masculine self and a register of both psychic and social disturbance is nowhere more evident than in the novella, *The Dumb Virgin, or, The Force of Imagination* (1700; *Works*, v. 415–44). The story is a tragic one of unwitting incestuous desire between brother and sister. The hero, Dangerfield, is separated as a baby from his mother in a frustrated pirate attack upon a pleasure barge off the coast of Venice. Subsequently, she bears two girl children, one physically handicapped, the other dumb. Dangerfield is symbolically the father of his own sisters, in that his loss produces her sickness during both pregnancies and births. Upon her death we are told she 'left the most beautiful Daughter to the World that ever adorn'd *Venice*, but

---

[25] Aphra Behn, 'Dedication to Tho. Condon', *Love-Letters between a Nobleman and his Sister* (London, 1684), A7^r.

naturally and unfortunately Dumb, which defect the learn'd attributed to the Silence and Melancholy of the Mother, as the Deformity of the other was to the Extravagance of her Frights [following the pirate raid]' (*Works*, v. 424). The two sisters, Belvideera and Maria, meet Dangerfield once they have all reached young adulthood. He comes to Venice having been raised as an English cavalier. Both sisters feel an instant attraction to him, and he is in turn captivated by the deformed Belvideera's wit and the dumb Maria's beauty.

Behn leaves us in no doubt that this sudden love for and from both women is mutually narcissistic and implicitly incestuous:

Maria . . . found something so Sweet in the Mien, Person and Discourse of this Stranger, that her Eyes felt a dazling Pleasure in beholding him, and like flattering Mirrours represented every Action and Feature, with some heightning Advantage to her Imagination: *Belvideera* also had some secret Impulses of Spirit, which drew her insensibly into a great Esteem of the Gentleman. (429)

For Dangerfield, the two sisters act as twin distorting mirrors necessary to the erection of the perfect masculine self: 'his Love was divided between the Beauty of one Lady, and the Wit of another, either of which he loved passionately, yet nothing cou'd satisfy him, but the Possibility of enjoying both' (431).

Not surprisingly perhaps, it is the dumb sister, Maria, whom he finally seduces. Maria is the consummate female object, the immaculate mirror to the masculine self since she cannot speak and therefore, to the male gazer, has no autonomy, no separate subjectivity. Behn explains why Dangerfield cannot resist temptation once he has gained access to Maria's bedroom: 'he knew they were alone in the Dark, in a Bed-chamber, he knew the Lady young and melting, he knew besides she cou'd not tell, and he was conscious of his Power in moving' (440).

Behn provides us with one of her most highly eroticized depictions of femininity perceived through the male gaze when she describes Dangerfield's 'reading' of the sight of Maria at her window in a nightgown just previous to the seduction. Maria's body is her only means of signification, since she cannot herself speak, and the passage reveals that she has no control over its messages. Like the pre-Oedipal child of psychoanalytic theory, Maria is not a subject, but rather a mere agglomeration of bodily impulses. She simply mirrors the 'desire' of her figurative 'author', Dangerfield. Without speech, locked in her pre-Oedipal world of pulsions and needs, Maria can have no autonomous desire, but only mirror or mimic that of her lover, who

> saw her in all her native Beauties, free from the Incumbrance of Dress, her Hair black as Ebony, hung flowing in careless Curls over her Shoulders, it hung link'd in amorous Twinings, as if in Love with its own Beauties; her Eyes not yet freed from the Dulness of the late Sleep, cast a languishing Pleasure in their Aspect, which heaviness of Sight added the greatest Beauties to those Suns, because under the Shade of such a Cloud, their Lustre cou'd only be view'd; . . . her Night-gown hanging loose, discover'd her charming Bosom, which cou'd bear no Name, but Transport, Wonder and Extasy, all which struck his Soul, as soon as the Object hit his Eye; her Breasts with an easy Heaving, show'd the Smoothness of her Soul and of her Skin; their Motions were so languishingly soft, that they cou'd not be said to rise and fall, but rather to swell up towards Love, the Heat of which seem'd to melt them down again; some scatter'd jetty Hairs, which hung confus'dly over her Breasts, made her Bosom show like *Venus* caught in *Vulcan's* Net, but 'twas the Spectator, not she, was captivated. (433)

Maria's hair, eyes, clothing, and body itself all conspire to present her as an object to be possessed in order to complete the male gazer's selfhood by perfectly mirroring his desire. The non-subject, the dumb virgin, simultaneously empty and whole (without speech she cannot enter subjectivity and thus does not 'know' desire and, hence, the 'lack' or separation that engenders desire), offers the possibility of 'wholeness' to the Oedipal lover. Expenditure of desire need not be loss because the 'smooth' mirror will restore that same desire replete with selfhood to the lover.

Luce Irigaray, in theorizing the sexual economy of what she describes as a homosocial male imaginary, cites the virgin as the most valuable of all commodities in the masculine use of women for social exchange between men. It is this value which Maria, as her name (Mary the virgin) implies, quite literally embodies: '*The virginal woman . . . is pure exchange value*. She is nothing but the possibility, the place, the sign of relations among men. In and of herself, she does not exist: she is a simple envelope veiling what is really at stake in social exchange. In this sense, her natural body disappears into its representative function.'[26] Dangerfield is on his way to visit with Rinaldo, his real father, when he is arrested by the sight of Maria. Rinaldo is called away on business, leaving the lovers in the same

---

[26] Luce Irigaray, 'Women on the Market', *This Sex Which Is Not One*, trans. Catherine Porter (London, 1985), 186.

house. The sexual encounter between brother and sister defers the acquaintanceship between the two men but also creates the conditions in which the encounter becomes one of recognition of their 'true' relation to each other, that of father and son. Dangerfield's two rivals for Maria fight with him over his reported presence at the window of her bedroom; his father intervenes in the fight, and both father and son are mortally wounded. Dangerfield's wig falls off to reveal a birthmark and Rinaldo dies recognizing his long-lost son. Maria promptly commits suicide, speaking her first and last words: 'Oh! Incest, Incest ... O my Brother, O my Love' (444). Maria's entry to subjectivity/speech is then coterminous with her death and her recognition of her desire as incestuous.

The plot of *The Dumb Virgin* is revealed to be constructed wholly in pursuit of the real identity of the male lover. It leaves, however, one loose end, precisely that of the speaking woman in the shape of Belvideera and, further, the figure of Aphra Behn herself, who is both narrator and character in this text. After the deaths of both men and the dumb virgin who mediates their mutual recognition, the second sister Belvideera 'consign'd all her Father's Estate over to her Uncle, reserving only a Competency to maintain her a Recluse all the rest of her Life' (444). Belvideera thus metaphorically substitutes for her dead sister, both virgin and dumb, but withdraws from society handing over her newly conferred economic power to the 'legitimate' male line. Belvideera's withdrawal appears to be both a gesture of submission to patriarchal power, by mediating the passage of familial wealth between her father and uncle, and of resistance, by refusing to participate any longer in a specularizing and objectifying male homosocial economy. Where she previously used voice and wit to negotiate that world, she now uses silence and virginity to deny it. Behn does, however, leave us with the presence of a speaking, autonomous woman in the shape of her own character. Dangerfield dies trying to tell the narrator his real name in order that she may tell his and her countrymen in England his tragic fate. He produces only the first three letters of his name, 'Cla—', and 'His Voice there fail'd him, and he presently dy'd; Death seeming more favourable than himself, concealing the fatal Author of so many Misfortunes, for I cou'd never since learn out his Name; but have done him the Justice, I hope, to make him be pity'd for his Misfortunes, not hated for his Crimes' (444). If all other voices 'fail' in this narrative, that of its female 'teller' survives to bear witness and to transform hatred into pity. It is, it appears, only from this contradictory position of the female subject, the woman who escapes the male subject/woman object dichotomy, that the story can be told. Although the ideology of the text seems to argue that the role of specularizer and speaker is only available to the masculine subject—that men make 'plots' and women suffer under them—the emergence of the female narrator as closing character projects the possibility of occupying both sides of the dichotomy in the figure of the female artist.

The space that Behn negotiates for her female narrator is, however, not the transcendent one of muse or goddess that marks her poetic voice. It is rather a negotiation between masculine and feminine positions. Like the other women in the text, Behn as narrator still mediates or mirrors masculine identity to other men, in this case Dangerfield's history to his 'countrymen', converting criminal seduction into a tragic story of unwitting incest. However, the project of mirroring masculine heroism is to a certain extent ironized by the very associations of the name Dangerfield in the late 1680s in England. 'Duke Dangerfield' was a famous agent of anti-Catholic persecution in the years of the Popish plot, who posed first as an ardent Catholic named Willoughby in order to gain information to prosecute Mary Cellier, a Catholic midwife, for treason in 1680. In 1685, when in Sheffield, he posed as the Duke of Monmouth during the latter's exile in Brussels in order to pass fake coin. Dangerfield produced his own 'romance' version of his biography entitled *Don Tomazo* in 1680 in which he described his exploits as a mercenary in Spain, making much of his sophisticated use of disguise.[27] In the light of this history, Behn's seemingly innocent desire to clear her countryman's reputation becomes an ironic subversion of a political enemy's attempts at heroic self-representation and aggrandizement.

In *The Unfortunate Bride, or, The Blind Lady a Beauty*, published in the same year as *The Dumb Virgin*, Behn once again presents physical disability in a woman as a means of dramatizing masculine specularity and narcissism (*Works*, v. 401–14). Here too Behn appears as an actor in the plot as well as narrator, but is incapable

---

[27] On Dangerfield, see Philip W. Sergeant, 'Duke Dangerfield', in *Liars and Fakers* (London, 1926), 133–98; John Kenyon, *The Popish Plot* (London, 1972), 179–80; and Dangerfield's 'biography', *Don Tomazo, or The Juvenile Rambles of Thomas Dangerfield* (London, 1680).

of averting the tragic denouement. The female narrator was, we are told, a 'particularly intimate Acquaintance' of the heroine, Belvira. She obtains some letters that reveal a plot to separate Belvira from her lover but they arrive too late to prevent Belvira from marrying his best friend. The female narrator's power lies not in her actions within the plot, but in her writing of it. Indeed it is her very lack of instrumentality in the 'real' world she supposedly represents that gives her power and authority in the 'imaginary' realm of art.

The Unfortunate Bride is a short romantic fiction which is dominated by tropes of vision and economic exchange. The hero, Frankwit, falls in love with Belvira whose very name sets the symbolic language in motion; she is 'a beautiful vision'. '[E]ven from their Childhood', Behn tells us, 'they felt mutual Love, as if their Eyes, at their first meeting, had struck out such Glances, as had kindled into amorous Flames' (403). When Belvira admits her love they do not exchange words but loving looks: 'Eager they looked, as if there were Pulses beating in their Eyes' (403–4). Frankwit indeed is so obsessed with his love that he neglects his financial concerns: 'he fancied little of Heaven dwelt in his yellow Angels, but let them fly away, as it were on their own golden Wings; he only valued the smiling Babies in *Belvira's* Eyes' (404). Women's 'value' then lies in their capacity to reflect and enlarge male desire.

Belvira's cousin, Celesia, is also in love with Frankwit, but it is clear that her love cannot be reciprocated because, as the blind lady of the narrative's title, she is incapable of reflecting his desire. Celesia is 'the only child of a rich *Turkey* merchant, who, when he died, left her Fifty thousand Pound in Money, and some Estate in Land; but, poor Creature, she was blind to all these Riches, having been born without the use of Sight, though in all other Respects charming to a wonder' (405). Her financial 'value', then, is meaningless because she lacks the only thing that Frankwit values, the capacity to mirror masculine desire. Her attempts to break in on the narcissistic closure of the lovers' looks are futile. When Belvira pities her cousin for her inability to see Frankwit she challenges their equation of desire and vision with the question: 'if I fancy I see him, sure I do see him, for Sight is Fancy, is it not? or do you feel my Cousin with your Eyes?' (406).

Belvira shrewdly recognizes the nature and provisionality of her 'value' in her lover's eyes. She is unwilling to marry him, arguing that 'her Desires could live in their own longings, like Misers wealth-devouring Eyes' (405). A move out of the purely specular economy of love which they have previously inhabited into the legal and financial contract of marriage is a risk for the woman-mirror. 'Marriage Enjoyments', she insists, 'does but wake you from your sweet golden Dreams' (406). The possession, as opposed to viewing of the image of desire, may shatter the mirror, and deprive the woman of her power.

Frankwit succeeds in persuading his mistress of the impossibility of living paralysed in their specular economy and promptly breaks it by departing for Cambridge to set his financial affairs in order before their marriage. In his absence, Celesia's sight is providentially restored and Belvira informs her lover in a poem: 'And yet, beyond her Eyes, she values thee, | 'Tis for thy Sake alone she's glad to see' (409). The only 'value', of Celesia's newly found sight is that it provides her with an opportunity to enter the sexual economy from which she was previously debarred. Meanwhile Frankwit falls ill and a woman at his lodging house, Moorea, being infatuated with him, keeps back his letters to Belvira, and writes anonymously to inform the latter of his death. In her grief, Belvira consents to be courted by Frankwit's best friend, Wildvil. On the wedding day, following the ceremony, both Frankwit and the letters the female narrator has retrieved and forwarded to their proper recipient, arrive. The two men fight, Belvira seeks to intervene and she and her new husband are killed. On her deathbed, Belvira instructs Frankwit to marry Celesia to whom she also leaves her fortune.

Through her complex and sometimes laboured play with images of sight, expanding upon the well-tried metaphor of love's blindness, Behn sets up a tension between the power of vision and the power of writing. While the lovers can see each other, their love is inviolable, but the fixity of this mirroring relation is also revealed to be impossible to maintain. In psychoanalytic terms, the lovers move from the nonverbal dyadic bonding that children experience with their mothers in the pre-Oedipal imaginary, to the symbolic world of paternal law and language as represented by the contract of marriage.[28] Belvira's consent to marry entails a separation; the

[28] Jacques Lacan's theory of the 'mirror-stage' as a transitional moment in the pre-Oedipal child's development toward the entry into paternal law and language that he terms the 'symbolic' is particularly suggestive in this context. See his 'The Mirror Stage as Formative of the Function of I', in *Écrits*, 1–7. Lacan writes: 'The jubilant assumption of his specular image by the child at the *infans* stage, still sunk in his motor incapacity and nursling dependence, would seem to exhibit in an exemplary

symbolic rupture of their non-verbal visual exchange is accompanied by a literal separation with Frankwit's departure to Cambridge. From this point on, they have to rely on the much more perilous relation of writing. The letter is, it appears, a far more unstable means of communication than the eye; it can be lost, mislaid, mis-interpreted, or suppressed. The lovers have to move out of the field of vision, but the substitution of writing is ultimately unsatisfactory.

As the figure of Celesia proves, both vision and writing are vital to subjectivity. Deprived of her capacity for both because of her blindness from birth, Celesia accounts for nothing. Without sight and without writing, Celesia lacks the precondition and the capacity to signify meaningfully in the social order.

'Little Histories': Feigning Femininity

Behn represents her own creative function in relation to the stories she tells as a complex interplay of these two poles of vision and writing. She not only narrates the stories, but insists *she was there*. This narrative strategy is, of course, by no means unique to Aphra Behn in late seventeenth-century fiction.[29] However, as I will argue, it is explicitly associated with the gender of her narrator in a formulation that is indeed novel in English prose fiction of the period. Behn's authority as narrator rests, then, on the authority of her presence at the scene itself; she both looks and tells. In her prefatory remarks to *Oroonoko* she insists, 'I was myself an Eye-witness to a great Part of what you will find here set down; and what I could not be Witness of, I receiv'd from the Mouth of the chief Actor in this History, the *Hero* himself' (*Works*, v. 129). Almost exactly the same formulation appears in her dedication to Henry Pain prefixed to *The Fair Jilt*, the story of Prince Tarquin's fatal obsession with the manipulative Miranda, 'Part of which [she] had from the Mouth of this unhappy great Man, and was an Eye-Witness

---

situation, the symbolic matrix in which the I is precipitated in a primordial form, before it is objectified in the dialectic of identification with the other, and before language restores to it, in the universal, its function as object' (2).

[29] Michael McKeon notes the recurrence of 'authenticating' strategies such as Behn's 'see and tell' claim in narratives in this period (particularly improbable tales of foreign lands or behaviour) in order to distinguish them from the devalued 'old Romance'. He notes too the ultimate instability of such strategies in that they come to function as rhetorical tropes in their own right, thus undermining their own claims to truth as opposed to art (see McKeon, *Origins of the English Novel*, 105–14).

to the rest' (*Works*, v. 70).   Behn's stories, then, are supposedly a
form of 'bearing witness', ensuring the posterity of her hero or
heroine. If she does not claim to have been an eye-witness, her
'authorities' are always those with special access to the subject-
matter. Thus, Philadelphia's story in *The Unfortunate Happy Lady* was
delivered to her by 'one who liv'd in the Family, and from whom
[she] had the whole Truth of the Story' (*Works*, v. 37), while that of
Arabella in *The Wandering Beauty* was rendered by 'a Lady of [her]
Acquaintance, who was particularly concern'd in many of the
Passages' (*Works*, v. 447). By this means, Behn successfully denies
her own 'authorship' of her stories. They are not, she claims,
imaginative fiction but bare facts to which she simply testifies.

Whereas Scudéry's romances give priority to fiction over history
as a means of rendering dull fact more interesting, Behn's 'little
histories' represent fiction as a corruption or distortion of the fact. It
is interesting to speculate what particular advantages Behn found in
the novelistic strategy she so doggedly pursues. There could be no
more definitive statement than that in the dedication to *The Fair Jilt*,
where she writes: 'however it may be imagin'd that Poetry (my
Talent) has so greatly the Ascendant over me, that all I write must
pass for Fiction, I now desire to have it understood that this is
Reality, and Matter of Fact, and acted in this our latter Age' (70).
Here Behn distinguishes her poetic from her prose writing,
representing herself as a scribe rather than artist, writer rather than
author. By figuring herself as mere teller of tales Behn presumably
makes herself more acceptable to male critics, at least within the
terms of her own fictional economy.

Behn's truth-claims function as more than a protective cover from
masculinist abuse to which she was by this late stage in her literary
career, after all, well accustomed. Behn's female narrator claims not
only to be the author (imaginative creator) of her plots by virtue of
her femininity, but also excuses her lack of power as author of
events in the plot by the same means. The lack of social power
accorded to women excuses her lack of activity and intervention in
the tragic stories she tells. It is this very inactivity that endows her
with a privileged position as writer. Her only 'power' lies in her
testificatory writing. In *Oroonoko*, the turn to writing as a result of
practical impotence in the events she sees becomes a seizure of
power, converting the enforced role of spectator into positive value
in the scene of writing. Jane Spencer comments, 'her gender is an

important part of her authority; what she knows, and the comments she is able to make, depend on it. The female pen is vindicated'.[30] Despite the claim to simply mirror or 'represent', writing comes to transform vision.

It is in *Oroonoko* that Behn is at the greatest pains to analyse the position of the narrator in relation to the tragic action of which she is both part and not part. Despite her statement that it was her hero's 'Misfortune . . . to fall in an obscure World, that afforded only a Female Pen to celebrate his Fame' (169), Behn's narrator constantly calls her reader's attention to her status in the contemporary literary culture. Of another 'hero' she also encountered in Surinam, one Colonel Martin, she comments in passing that she has 'celebrated' him 'in a Character of [her] new Comedy, by his own Name' (198).[31] Describing the English trading with native Indians in Surinam she slips in that she presented a set of feathers to the King's Theater which were used in a production of *The Indian Queen* and 'infinitely admir'd by Persons of Quality' (130).[32] Behn's 'Female Pen', then, as she makes perfectly clear, is by no means as 'obscure' as her deprecatory comment might suggest. Her female pen is precisely the agent of her power.

The female narrator wins the affection and confidence of the proud and aristocratic slaves, Oroonoko and Imoinda, by her story-telling, tailoring her narratives towards their specific gendered interests: 'I entertained them with the Lives of the *Romans*, and great Men, which charmed him to my Company; and her, with teaching her all the pretty Works that I was Mistress of, and telling her Stories of Nuns' (175). Oroonoko and Imoinda are thus inscribed as readers in relation to the female author, as the former terms her, of the heroic and amatory plot, and have a suitably eroticized and subjected relationship to her as writer. Oroonoko, who only comes to understand the concept of the lie through painful experience at the hands of hypocritical white slave traders and colonists, is on one level the 'ideal reader' of Behn's texts. He believes her claims to tell

---

[30] Spencer, *Rise of the Woman Novelist*, 48.

[31] The comedy was *The Younger Brother*, not performed until February 1696 at Drury Lane and published in the same year, adapted by Charles Gildon and accompanied by his 'Memoir' of the author.

[32] Sir Robert Howard's *The Indian Queen* was first produced by the King's Company in January 1664, while Behn, if she was there at all, must still have been in Surinam. The feathers would have had to have been used in one of the many revivals of this popular play.

the truth and is won to her service by the seductive power of her fictions and the heroic models they offer. Oroonoko, she tells us, prefers the company of the white women to the drunken debauchery of their male counterparts, so that 'obliging him to love [them] very well, [they] had all the Liberty of Speech with him, especially [her] self, whom he call'd his *Great Mistress*; and indeed [her] Word would go a great Way with him . . .' (175–6).

However, Oroonoko's inability to move outside of a simple dichotomy of truth and lies is ultimately his downfall. He believes the promises of the corrupt governor of Surinam, Byam, and also of his 'Great Mistress' who persuades him not to rebel and allow his white friends to work for his release from slavery. While Behn claims to be an influential figure in the government of the colony, she never acts on his behalf. She herself is clearly sceptical of the status of the 'promise'. When Oroonoko eventually leads a slave rebellion, Behn, like the other women of the settlement, flees upriver, 'possess'd with extreme Fear, which no Persuasions could dissipate, that he would secure himself till Night, and then would come down and cut all our Throats' (198). Her absence explains away the fact that Oroonoko is brutally whipped as punishment on the grounds that she had 'Authority and Interest enough there, had [she] suspected any such Thing, to have prevented it' (198). Again, Behn's femaleness is her alibi for her inactivity.

The full extent of Behn's authority both inside and outside the text, then, lies in her authority as a fiction-maker, a role which is, in turn, intimately connected with her femaleness. Her relegation to the margins by the white male colonists, despite her claims to authority, puts her in an analogous position to her hero, whose voice is also powerless. She is only useful to the white establishment, as she was in Antwerp, as a seductress, influencing an aberrant and politically dangerous man into co-operation with their political needs. Since Oroonoko only has eyes for his beautiful wife, Imoinda, Behn seduces him into the position of courtly lover through her stories. By telling his story after his death and elevating him to the status of hero, Behn claims, she is repaying her 'promise' to him, exercising the power on his behalf that she was denied as an observer at the time.

Yet Behn is more than an observer in *Oroonoko*. She is, in the fullest sense of the word, a spectator, or rather, a specularizer. As noted earlier, Behn customarily formulates sexual desire as a narcissistic investment in the other as mirror to the ego. She is thus as ambiguous about the Surinam natives' ignorance of the erotic joys of specularity, the scene of vision, as she is about the advantages of Oroonoko's inability to comprehend the ambivalent status of fiction, the scene of writing. Like her hero, the natives of Surinam are at first idealized for their 'natural innocence', which differentiates them from the corrupt and dissolute behavior of the white colonists.

However, two passages in *Oroonoko* bring into question any interpretation of the novel as a nostalgic idealization of African and Indian cultures. In the first, with reference to their uninhibited nakedness, Behn explicitly identifies the Surinam Indian natives with prelapsarian innocence but appears to question the desirability of this quality, commenting that 'They are extreme modest and bashful, very shy, and nice of being touch'd ... and being continually us'd to see one another so unadorn'd, so like our first Parents before the Fall, it seems as if they had no Wishes, there being nothing to heighten Curiosity; but all you can see, you see at once, and every Moment see; and where there is no Novelty, there can be no Curiosity' (131). In courtship, the young man simply gazes on his love object 'and sighs [are] all his language', while his mistress looks down 'with all the blushing modesty ... seen in the most Severe and Cautious of our World' (131). This is not, then, a world without sexual difference, but it is one in which no attempt is made to heighten sexual curiosity by exaggeration of that difference.

The importance of clothing in the business of erotic pleasure is highlighted in a second passage that sets about contrasting native Indian and white European culture. When an expedition visits a native Surinam community deep inland and as yet unexposed to white people, Behn insists on going ahead with her woman and brother, leaving Oroonoko and the others to hide in the reeds and observe the reaction to them. It is the white European's clothing, and particularly that of the women, that fascinates the Indians:

By Degrees they grew more bold, and from gazing upon us round, they touch'd us, laying their Hands upon all the Features of our Faces, feeling our Breasts, and Arms, taking up one Petticoat, then wondering to see another; admiring our Shoes and Stockings, but more our Garters.... In fine, we suffer'd 'em to survey us as they pleas'd, and we thought they would never have done admiring us. (185)

In this passage, clothes are a means of enhancing difference, in this case, racial difference, by curiosity. And as in the sexual economy it appears that it is femininity that is the signifier of difference. The women's clothing, the petticoat, stocking, garter, all provide a means of prolonging (sexual) interest by withholding the discovery of the body beneath. Deferral brings pleasure. The pleasure is not solely, or even primarily, that of the gazer, however. It is Behn the story-teller who has engineered this particular narrative scene in order to make herself the object of the gaze. The eroticism of these looks is doubled in that she has placed Oroonoko and the other companions to watch her being watched.

Thus, while the position of viewer is habitually a powerless one for the narrator in the plot of *Oroonoko*, the position of the viewed provides an opportunity for power. Just as she insists on Oroonoko concealing himself behind the reeds in order to display herself first, in her writing she repeatedly turns her reader's eye away from the royal slave to herself. The (erotic) centre of this text is the female writer. The clothing that conceals her body, the writing that obscures the woman, only heightens the reader's pleasure, keeping possession out of reach and sustaining the libidinous drive of the text. Ultimately, *Oroonoko* 'bears witness' to its author, rather than its eponymous hero. The compulsion to consider *Oroonoko* simply in terms of biography, a compulsion that has marked criticism of the novel until recently is, perhaps, simply a register of the effectivity of Behn's narcissistic narrative strategy.

Aphra Behn's teasing play with authorial presence, identified as a specifically feminine and fictional strategy is, of course, intensely problematic in this early text of white colonialism. Artistic play and specularizing power seem to be won for the white woman writer at the expense of the black slave and the native who are positioned, like Behn's female characters elsewhere, as naïve victims. The knowledge of superior moral integrity or rectitude are little compensation for lack of political control and denial of self-representation. That *Oroonoko* is a tale of racial difference and conflict allows us to see perhaps more clearly than in Behn's narratives of sexual difference and conflict the cost of her seizure of representational power on behalf of the woman artist. It was for Manley and Haywood later in the history of women's amatory fiction to bring the woman writer, female character, and female reader into closer alliance. In Behn's texts, it appears that the female writing subject can only 'create herself' by means of differentiation from the other subject positions her text produces, and in particular those accorded her female characters.

With this in mind, however, Behn's foregrounding of the woman writer at the very inception of the novel was clearly a unique and sophisticated challenge to masculine dominance of the field of representation. Behn's troubled enquiry into the woman writer's relation to the amatory plot writes new questions of gender into the development of a new genre. At one point in her study, Vita Sackville-West complains that Behn allowed romance conventions to limit her explorations in realism, bewailing the fact that 'We might have had the mother of Moll Flanders, and all we get is the bastard of Mademoiselle de Scudéry'.[33] The contrast between Behn and Defoe, as co-founders of the early modern novel, is by no means a spurious one, but we might consider Behn's continued investment in the romance as more than a vestigial allegiance to a spent form. As argued earlier, Scudéry's artistic theory identified femininity with formal control of culture at every stage. It is this vital bond between femininity and the elusive and seductive power of fiction that Behn re-creates in her narratives. Defoe, while he shares with Behn the trope of claiming verity, and an interest in converting the 'private history' into new models of public heroism, all too often presents himself as cultural policeman of female discourse. Thus in his preface to *Moll Flanders* (1722), the 'editor' informs us that he has placed an organizing structure and a moral awareness onto the anarchy and immodesty of the female narrator:

All possible Care however has been taken to give no leud Ideas, no immodest Turns in the new dressing up of this Story, no not to the worst parts of her Expressions; to this Purpose some of the vicious Part of her Life, which cou'd not be modestly told, is quite left out, and several other Parts, are very much shortn'd; what is left 'tis hoped will not offend the chastest Reader, or the modestest Hearer.[34]

Thus the editor metaphorically holds up his coat in order to conceal the blatant eroticism of the naked body of his heroine's text. Behn's narrator, in contrast, overtly addresses the seductive nature of the *clothed* body or form. Her rhetoric seduces by a complex system of concealment and display. The fascination with the female body lies precisely in seductive dress, not the body beneath.

[33] Sackville-West, *Aphra Behn*, 73.
[34] Daniel Defoe, *The Fortunes and Misfortunes of the Famous Moll Flanders, &c.* (1722), ed. G. A. Starr (London and New York, 1971), 1–2.

Indeed, her text warns us, strip the woman and you find precisely nothing (visible) beneath, just as the attempt to strip away Behn's veils of writing to 'find out' the real woman inevitably draws a blank. Sarah Kofman, in her rereading of Freud, has succinctly described the redundancy of the pursuit of 'true' femininity:

> to speak of a riddle of femininity and to try to solve that riddle are a strictly masculine enterprise; women are not concerned with Truth, they are profoundly skeptical; they know perfectly well that there is no such thing as 'truth', that behind their veils there is yet another veil, and that try as one may to remove them, one after another, truth in its nudity, like a goddess, will never appear. Women who are truly women are perfectly 'flat'. ... For 'truth', the metaphysical lure of depth, of a phallus concealed behind the veils, that lure is a fetishist illusion of man. ...[35]

Love-Letters: Engendering Desire

The relationship between the female writing subject and truth-telling is differently articulated in Behn's epistolary fiction from the 'little histories' we have been considering. Behn's fiction owes as much to the *Five Love-Letters from a Nun to a Cavalier* as it does to Madeleine de Scudéry's romances, on the level of plot and form. The challenge of Mariane's love-letters to social taboo is double: first, in that they are an explicit expression of female desire, and second, in that they are written by a woman who is supposed to have repressed her desire in favour of the love of God. Behn, never slow to recognize popular trends, must have realized the potential of the figure of the nun in amatory fiction following the publication of Sir Roger l'Estrange's translation of the *Portuguese letters* in 1678. Many of her 'little histories' exploit the topos of the desiring nun, and her claim to have told Imoinda stories of nuns in Surinam as early as the mid-1660s might be seen as an artful piece of self-aggrandizement. The heroines of *The Fair Jilt, The History of the Nun, or, The Fair Vow-Breaker*, and *The Nun, or, The Perjur'd Beauty* (*Works*, v) all break their vows in order to gratify their sexual passion for a lover who courts them at the grate.

The nun represents an erotic challenge. The veil dresses the woman up as an enigma for the lover/reader who pursues her. Behn comments of the order to which her 'Fair Jilt', Miranda, belongs: 'as

---

[35] Sarah Kofman, *The Enigma of Woman: Woman in Freud's Writings*, trans. Catherine Porter (Ithaca, NY, and London, 1985), 105.

these Women are ... of the best Quality, and live with the
Reputation of being retir'd from the World a little more than
ordinary, and because there is a sort of Difficulty to approach 'em,
they are the People the most courted, and liable to the greatest
Temptations' (75). The attraction of the nun does not lie in her
sexual innocence, but rather in her propensity for excessive passion.
Her capacity for inordinate and single-minded devotion, evidenced
in her religious vows, may be converted to a sexual object. Mariane,
the Portuguese nun, in her final letter upbraids her lover on
precisely this point:

methinks, if a body might be allow'd to reason upon the Actions of Love, a
man should rather fix upon a Mistress in a Convent than any where else. For
they have nothing there to hinder them from being perpetually Intent upon
their Passion; Whereas in the World, there are a thousand fooleries, and
Amusements, that either take up their Thoughts entirely, or at least divert
them. (*Five Love-Letters*, 19)

The nuns in Behn's *The Fair Jilt* turn their religious retirement to
their advantage. The nuns' hours are taken up with gallantry and
flirting. The veil, far from concealing sexual innocence, is a cover for
knowing manipulation of the power of enigmatic femininity: 'there is
no sort of Female Arts they are not practis'd in, no Intrigue they are
ignorant of, and no Management of which they are not capable'
(76). The convent provides a shelter from social and parental
observance and censure.

Typically, Behn cannot resist heightening her persona by referring
to her own choice not to become a nun, implying that the sexual
abstinence prescribed by most convents would be beyond her own
powers of endurance. In *The History of the Nun, or, The Fair Vow-
Breaker* she comments on the folly of women entering convents
before they had reached sexual maturity by referring to her own
'case': 'I once was design'd an humble Votary in the House of
Devotion, but fancying my self not endu'd with an obstinacy of
Mind, great enough to secure me from the Efforts and Vanities of
the World, I rather chose to deny myself that Content I could not
certainly promise my self, than to languish (as I have seen some do)
in a certain Affliction' (265). Despite the introduction of a first-
person commentary here, *The Fair Vow-Breaker* is written largely in
an impersonal third person voice, a strategy which separates all
Behn's 'stories of nuns' from their model, the *Portuguese letters*.
The psychological intensity of the *Portuguese letters* is not only

produced by the plot device of a convent setting. The sense of enclosure provided by the 'frame' of the convent is reinforced by the claustrophobia of an individual psyche struggling to articulate its desire, conveyed by the innovation of the use of a direct first-person narrative.

Despite the insistent presence of a narrative 'I' in Behn's novels, it is an 'I', that can only watch and tell, rather than one that conveys immediacy in sexual passion. Behn habitually employs indirect speech to recount dialogue, but interestingly she shifts into direct speech and an inserted first-person narrative in *The Fair Vow-Breaker* to tell the seduction story of her heroine's friend and fellow-nun, Katteriena. Whereas Isabella is a sexual innocent, Katteriena has been exiled to the convent following a shameful love affair with her father's page. When Isabella finds herself obsessed with Henault, Katteriena's brother, Katteriena recounts her own story in order to persuade her friend that passion can be conquered by separation from the love object. By telling the story in Katteriena's own voice, Behn creates an illusion of immediacy that reported speech generally lacks. Katteriena spares Isabella no details of her psychological and physiological torment: 'my Heart would heave, when e're he came in view; and my disorder'd Breath came doubly from my Bosom; a Shivering seiz'd me, and my Face grew wan; my Thought was at a stand and Sense it self, for that short moment, lost its Faculties' (278). Far from convincing Isabella to abandon her illicit desires, Katteriena's narrative further inflames her. 'No more, no more, (reply'd *Isabella*, throwing her Arms again about the Neck of the transported *Katteriena*) thou blow'st my Flame by thy soft Words, and mak'st me know my Weakness, and my Shame' (279). The seduction narrative offered to the reader, then, as a moral warning, teaches her sexual knowledge, and provides surrogate erotic pleasure.

In her prose writing Behn effectively employs two kinds of narrative voice, the first the objectifying, specularizing Astrea who (like Scheherezade) accrues power over her audience through her story-telling (*Histories and Novels*); the second, a desirous, subjective, first-person narration put into the mouths of the central actors and providing an intense psychological display (*Love-Letters from a Nobleman to his Sister, The Lover's Watch*). Although the nun stories of the *Histories and Novels* incorporate the thematic concerns of the *Portuguese letters*, it is Behn's epistolary fiction which is their true heir. Like the *Five Love-Letters*, Behn's epistolary fiction is centrally concerned with the attempt to inscribe and engender sexual desire. These epistolary writings seek both to stimulate desire in the other, lover or reader, and to represent the specific 'difference' of female desire.

As Tania Modleski notes in her analysis of twentieth-century amatory fiction, first-person narrative produces a crisis of authenticity in relation to the speaker's discourse.[36] Without the external 'frame' of an observing narrator, which epistolary form precisely abandons, the reader remains unsure of the integrity of the central protagonist. No third person assures us of the heroine's 'truthfulness' and 'innocence'. We have only her word that she was a victim rather than a manipulator in the game of love.

The *Portuguese Letters* illustrate this dilemma over authenticating or authorizing the truth of first-person discourse. As Peggy Kamuf cogently argues in her *Fictions of Feminine Desire*, Mariane's five love-letters document the hysterical woman's coming-to-language as a means of escaping the silent pain of her 'symptomatically convulsed and contorted body' (49). Mariane's first letter expresses the desire to 'convey [her] self in the Place' of the letter (*Five Love-Letters*, 6). At this stage, Mariane finds her writing a poor substitute for the totalizing mirror function of the language of the gaze, 'Those Eyes that were ten thousand Worlds to [her], and all that [she] desir'd' (5). Her desire to substitute for the letter is not simply one of desire to be in her lover's presence. It signifies a desire to have the rhetorical capacity to put her 'self' down on the page, to convey her subjectivity through writing. The physical symptom becomes her only means of signifying desire.

Mariane repeatedly questions why and for whom she writes, gradually recognizing that the real 'addressee' is her self, not her lover. Ultimately her self-analysis allows her to re-enact her own scene of seduction, speak her desire, and liberate herself from her hysteria. In her fourth letter she ceases to construct herself as victim and finds a place in her discourse for the expression of her active desire: ''twas my own precipitate Inclination that seduc'd me', she declares (12). By the end of the fifth letter Mariane can quit her self-created analyst's couch: 'Now do I begin to Phansie that I shall not write to you again for all This; for what Necessity is there that I must be telling of you at every turn how my Pulse beats?' (21).

[36] Modleski, *Loving with a Vengeance*, 54–5.

Doubtless, one of the attractions of the Portuguese style for writers and readers of the late seventeenth century lay in the opportunity that a first-person female narrative voice offered to explore women's relation to writing and the self. As I have argued, Behn's heroines in her *Histories and Novels* are 'written upon', in that they are employed as signifiers of male desire. The epistolary style of the Portuguese letters enacts a woman's successful endeavours to write her self, rather than reflect an 'other'.

However, there is a paradox at the heart of the Portuguese style, which Aphra Behn was not slow to recognize. Mariane's discourse authenticates itself by its claims to naturalness and spontaneity, by contrast with the supposed artifice and paraphrases of the French romance's amatory language. Yet there is nothing integral to Mariane's language that makes it more authentic than that of the romance. Imitations of the Portuguese letters appear to reduce an originary moment of self-production to a series of rhetorical tropes, different in form from that of the romance to be sure, but no less a 'fiction'. The *Seven Portuguese Letters*, proclaiming themselves 'a Second Part to the Five Love-Letters from a Nun to a Cavalier', repeat tragedy as farce.[37] Supposedly written by 'a Woman of the World, whose Style is very different from that of a Cloystered NUN' (A2), these letters run the whole gamut of Portuguese sentiment as a series of rhetorical poses to the point where the heroine self-consciously directs her reader to her supposed lack of artifice. In her third letter, she comically insists that he 'may be able to judge what disorder [her] mind is in, by the irregularity of this letter' (33).

Whether parody or poor imitation, the *Seven Portuguese Letters* highlight the fact that Mariane's seemingly authentic 'discourse of desire' is indeed nothing more than a fiction of identity, as accessible to the self-interested seducer as the sincere lover. Imitating the *Portuguese Letters* only undermines their integrity. That they can be imitated is the sign of their rhetorical status. By anxiously pointing to the signs of authenticity—narrative disorder, syntactic and semantic disturbance—Mariane's imitators incriminate rather than vindicate themselves, proving that their language is not 'all artless

---

[37] *Seven Portuguese Letters, being a Second Part to the Five Love-Letters from a Nun to a Cavalier, One of the most Passionate Pieces, That Possibly Ever Has Been Extant* (London, 1681). The letters were published in France by Barbin in 1669, a few months after he had produced the *Lettres Portugaises*, to capitalize on the latter's success.

speaking, incorrect disorder, and without method' (*Love-Letters*, 184), but is, rather, self-regarding, a consciously rhetorical exercise.

Peggy Kamuf observes that Mariane's text relies on the imaginative construction of 'the interlocutor as the silent pole through which passes the invention of the writing subject'.[38] It is Aphra Behn, amongst the *Portuguese letters'* innumerable imitators, who recognized that the key to the crisis of authenticity inscribed in Mariane's self-generating narrative lay precisely in the role of the interlocutor. The effectiveness of Mariane's 'cure' (her invention of herself as female writing subject) is predicated on the absence of her lover and the irrelevance of his interpretation of the letters to her project. The self is created in relation to the word, not the other. *Reading* and the interpretative damage it may do to the claims to authenticity generated by the female writing subject do not enter the equation.

In contrast, Behn's epistolary narratives judge their efficacy by the extent to which they affect their imagined reader. Behn conceives of writing, it seems, as narrative act rather than narrative identity. In the fourth letter of her *Love-Letters to a Gentleman*, the woman concludes: 'Why I write them, I can give no account; 'tis but fooling my self, perhaps, into an Undoing. I do but (by this soft Entertainment) rook in my Heart, like a young Gamester, to make it venture its last Stake' (*Histories and Novels*, 406). The economic metaphor is significant here. Amatory discourse is repeatedly metaphorized in these letters as a form of economic exchange in which the writer trades, seeking to 'profit' by eliciting a response from her reader.[39]

Through the course of her eight letters Astrea comes to realize that language is not a vehicle for desire, but rather that which constitutes it. In letter eight she determines: 'I will never be wise more; never make any Vows against my Inclinations, or the little-wing'd Deity. I do not only see 'tis all in vain, but I really believe they serve only to augment my Passion' (414). Expanding a metaphor of economic exchange in letter four she accuses her lover

[38] Kamuf, *Fictions of Feminine Desire*, 56.

[39] At this stage in the history of the postal service, moreover, receivers rather than senders were required to pay the duty on letters mailed within the city. The return of an unopened letter by an unresponsive mistress or lover takes on a peculiarly economic motive under these circumstances. See Perry, *Women, Letters and the Novel*, 63–4 and R. W. Chapman, 'The Course of the Post in the Eighteenth Century', *Notes and Queries*, 183 (1942), 67–9.

with the words: 'you would have me give, and you, like a Miser, wou'd distribute nothing' (406). While her lover commands her to speak and write, he remains silent.

Silence is the only signifier of lack of desire in epistolary fiction. Philander's declining affection for Sylvia in *Love-Letters between a Nobleman and his Sister* is indicated by the brevity of his letters and the increasingly long silences that punctuate an enforced separation. Sylvia 'reads' his silence correctly, signifying her own continued passion by presenting a lengthy complaint in response to a cursory note: 'Where is thy heart? And what has it been doing since it begun my fate? How can it justify thy coldness, and thou this cruel absence without accounting with me for every parting hour? My charming dear was wont to find me business for all my lonely absent ones; and writ the softest letters—loading the paper with fond vows and wishes' (139). Philander meanwhile writes to Octavio, the couple's Dutch friend who is infatuated with Sylvia, and tells him the story of his new love, Calista (who, unbeknownst to Philander is Octavio's married sister). He too recognizes that writing stimulates desire, in this case on the *writer*'s part, when he apologizes: 'Pardon this long history, for it is a sort of acting all one's joys again, to be telling them to a friend so dear' (246). The lengthy letter of seduction, or the letter narrating seduction to a friend, is a psychological necessity for the rake, since it is only writing that transforms compulsive appetite, or need, into the more complex and sophisticated delights of desire.

In the second part of the *Love-Letters*, Behn shifts her narrative voice from a purely epistolary form to a combination of third person narrative and transcribed letters. Rather than indicating an inability to sustain the epistolary mode on her part, I would argue, this change is a response to the problem of authenticating voice in first-person epistolary writing. Further, it provides a means of drawing attention to the duplicitous ends to which the Portuguese style can be put. The first part of the *Love-Letters* consists of an intense exchange of letters between Philander and Sylvia interrupted only by four letters from other actors in the affair (one from Sylvia's sister and Philander's wife, Myrtilla, another from Sylvia's maid, Melinda, a note from Cesario to Philander, and a proposal of marriage to Sylvia from Philander's rival, Foscario).

The lack of third-person commentary on the nature of the lovers' passion means that the reader has no information about the motivations of the two lovers, other than the accounts they offer, nor the eventual results of the affair. The suspense of this circumstance is in keeping with the history of the novel's writing, in that Behn herself did not know its outcome when she wrote it. The first part was written less than two years after an advertisement appeared in the *London Gazette* (late September 1682) stating that 'Lady Henrietta Berkeley has been absent from her father's house since 20th August last past and is not known where she is or whether she is alive or dead' (quoted in *Love-Letters*, p. v). Lord Grey of Werke eloped with his sister-in-law and married her to his factotum, one Mr Turner (who appears as Brilliard in the novel). When her father took him to court at the King's Bench on 23 November 1682, Grey was found guilty of debauching the Earl of Berkeley's daughter. However, no sentence was ever passed on Grey since the Earl decided not to press charges, although Henrietta was imprisoned for a night. Less than six months later, the lovers fled to the continent. Grey's flight seems to have been motivated largely by the disclosure of the Rye House Plot to assassinate King Charles in Oxford in late March 1683, in which he had been involved. One of his conspirators, Algernon Sidney, was executed.[40]

Thus, at the time of writing the first part of what amounted to a contemporary scandal novel, Behn could have no resolution to the love 'plot'. On the basis of her known Tory political allegiances, however, it is safe to assume that she would have been unwilling to imply anything good could come out of a Whig rebel absconding with a Tory heiress. The choice of name for her 'hero' is our only clue to his insincerity. His rhetoric is that of the quintessential 'Portuguese' lover.

A letter of proposal from the 'old-fashioned' lover, Foscario, is inserted to highlight the attractions of Philander's language of seduction. Foscario employs the conventions of the French romance. Sylvia's eyes are 'triumphant stars', her mouth 'a storehouse of perfection' from which she can 'pronounce [his] doom'; he will receive her decision 'with that reverence and awe' suited to 'the sentence of the gods', 'the thunderbolts of *Jove*', or 'the revenge of angry *Juno*' (82). In contrast to Foscario's use of martial and classical romantic metaphor, Philander's images echo the eroticized pastoral of Behn's own 'Golden Age'. Secreted in the woods around

[40]Goreau, *Reconstructing Aphra*, 274–8.

Sylvia's house, his traditional rakish invocation to the indulgence of 'natural appetite' is couched in a description of pastoral idyll: 'the woods around me blow soft, and mixing with wanton boughs, continually play and kiss; while those, like a coy maid in love, resist, and comply by terms' (28).

Having brought his mistress to the point of submission through the eroticized language of his letters, however, Philander finds himself impotent at their late-night rendezvous. In the letter that follows, Philander seeks to explain his failure. Once again, it is the opposition between writing and vision that functions here. An excess of visual stimulus is located as the cause, and it is only through writing that Philander can regain his desire:

I saw the ravishing maid as much inflamed as I, she burnt with equal fire, with equal languishment: ... a languishment I never saw till then dwelt in her charming eyes, that contradicted all her little vows ... till quite forgetting all I had faintly promised, and wholly abandoning my soul to joy, I rushed upon her, who, all fainting, lay beneath my useless weight, for on a sudden all my power was fled, swifter than lightning hurried through my enfeebled veins, and vanished all: not the dear lovely beauty which I pressed, the dying charms of that fair face and eyes, the clasps of those soft arms, nor the bewitching accent of her voice, that murmured half love, half smothered in her sighs, nor all my love, my vast, my mighty passion, could call my fugitive passion back again: oh no, the more I looked—the more I touched and saw, the more I was undone. (53–4)

As in *The Blind Lady*, if the look is the first stage of desire it is ultimately the cause of its death unless writing intervenes to break the totalizing unity of lovers conjoined. Writing brings about the separation necessary to the creation of desire.

The lovers' elopement presents Behn with a narrative problem. Once united, it is implausible that they will continue to write to each other. Part 2 opens with the introduction of new characters, and takes a new narrative direction by combining an anonymous third-person narrative with letters, both of which serve to alleviate this difficulty. By the time Behn came to write this second part, both love story and political plot that provided its source had to some extent been resolved. It was published in the same year as Charles II's death (February 1685), James II's accession, and Monmouth's rebellion (the battle of Sedgmoor took place on 5–6 July 1685). However, it makes little or no reference to these events. The only historical event to which it refers is Lord Grey's documented trip to

Cologne, adding the probably fictional account of Philander's infidelity with Calista, Sylvia's courtship by a young prince of the House of Orange, Octavio, and the attempts of her titular husband, Brilliard, to win her sexual favours by impersonation and disguise.

This kind of action, which comes close to the bedroom farce of Restoration comedy in which Behn had already proved herself adept, seems to require a more diverse narrative structure than the psychological intensity of the Portuguese style could offer. The narrative voices and perspectives multiply, introducing contributions from Brilliard, Octavio, Sylvia's maid Antonet, Calista, and her husband Count Clarinau. Not all write letters and many are given in synopsis. Increasingly, the specularizing and objectifying narrative persona of *Histories and Novels* takes control of the interpretation of events.

By the time she published the third part in 1687, Behn had seen her story reach a suitably dramatic end with Monmouth's plot defeated and himself executed, James seemingly restored to power, and Lord Grey, consummate hypocrite as ever, escaping retribution for his involvement in the uprising. In the full knowledge of hindsight, Behn has a free hand to draw out the symbolic implications of Sylvia's moral decline and education in rakehood in contrast with Cesario/Monmouth's increasing emasculation and dotage under the influence of his mistress, Hermione/Lady Wentworth and her cronies. While Sylvia is educated out of the illusory mirror of romantic love into social power through manipulation of, rather than subjection to, the rhetoric of desire, Cesario loses his political advantages and his 'masculine' honour by falling prey to that same romantic illusion.

Behn's *Love-Letters* produce a version of the invention of the female writing subject which simultaneously imitates and critiques that of the *Portuguese Letters*. In this text, Behn, through her shifts of narrative voice, obliges her reader to recognize that the female writing subject emerges in and through the process of learning to *feign* authenticity as consummately as the male rake. By no other means can she survive in the world of discourse. Sylvia's history is a female version of the rake's progress. Behn leads her heroine through a variety of narratorial positions, from naïve reader (in her affair with Philander) to Portuguese lover (in her response to his desertion of her) to French romance writer (in her seduction of Octavio) to 'feigned' Portuguese lover (in her manipulation of her affair with both men). By the third part, Sylvia has graduated to the narratorial complexity of Behn herself, drawing upon multiple fictional identities and languages in order to secure her control over a lover/reader as sophisticated and cynical as herself (in her affair with the rakish Spaniard Alonzo).

The three parts of the *Love-Letters* effectively cover three of Sylvia's affairs. The first presents her as victim of Philander's seductive rhetoric, deceived by her belief in the absolute correspondence between word and feeling, signifier and signified. The letter, for Sylvia, is a transparent mediator of emotion between lovers, a token of an a priori desire. As she puts it, 'to him I venture to say any thing, whose kind and soft imaginations can supply all my wants in the description of the soul' (31).

In the second part, when she discovers her lover's infidelity, Sylvia is at first in despair, convulsed by the hysterical symptoms of a Mariane: 'she many times fainted over the paper, and as she has since said, it was a wonder she ever recovered' (215). However, Sylvia's 'pride and scorn' overcome her 'fits of softness, weeping, raving and tearing' (221). She now turns to 'managing' her new suitor, Octavio, in order to be revenged on Philander. In this case the artifice of the French romance enables Sylvia to escape the hysteria of the Portuguese lover. Sylvia summons Octavio to her presence, carefully preparing a seductive frame suffused with the images habitually associated with the French romance:

Sylvia adorns herself for an absolute conquest, and disposing herself in the most charming, careless, and tempting manner she could devise, she lay expecting her coming lover on a repose of rich embroidery of gold on blue satin, hung within-side with little amorous pictures of *Venus* descending in her chariot naked to *Adonis*, she embracing, while the youth, more eager of his rural sports, turns half from her in a posture of pursuing his dogs, who are on their chase: another of *Armida*, who is dressing the sleeping warrior up in wreaths of flowers, while a hundred little Loves are playing with his gilded armour; this puts on his helmet too big for his little head, that hides his whole face; another makes a hobby-horse of his sword and lance; another fits on his breast piece, while three or four little *Cupids* are seeming to heave and help him to hold it an end, and all turning the emblems of the hero into ridicule.... [T]he languishing fair one, ... lay carelessly on her side, her arm leaning on little pillows of point of *Venice*, and a book of amours in her other hand. Every noise alarmed her with trembling hope that her lover was come, and I have heard she says, she verily believed, that acting and feigning the lover possessed her with a tenderness against her knowledge and will. (200–1)

In preparing for conquest, Sylvia learns new narcissistic pleasures; like the narrator of *Oroonoko*, Sylvia gains a self-reflexive pleasure by framing herself for the sexually curious gaze. Narcissism here provides an effective means of negotiating hysteria, in which symptoms of repressed desire register on the woman's body, beyond her conscious control.

Sylvia's experiments with amorous representation are, at this stage, unsophisticated, relying on classical pictorial devices rather than the 'artificial naturalness' of the new realism of the Portuguese style. Sylvia's narrative frame, the unmanning of a military hero by the agents of love, clearly inscribes her lover's doom. She is, however, shrewd in her choice of object. In Octavio she finds a reader who wilfully interprets her language according to his own desire.

Octavio does not arrive for this rendezvous. Brilliard's stratagems to bring himself to Sylvia's bed by impersonating Octavio result in a disagreement between the prospective lovers. Sylvia's attempt to conceal her anger in a written response to Octavio's accusation that she is a 'common mistress' is unsuccessful. Behn provides us with a close analysis of Octavio's interpretation of this letter, deftly demonstrating the tension in epistolary exchange between the writer's endeavour to 'effect' the reader, to arouse his sympathy and his passions, and the reader's struggle to discover the writer's 'real' meaning:

He, reading this letter, finished with tears of tender love; but considering it all over, he fancied she had put great constraint upon her natural high spirit to write in this calm manner to him, and through all he found dissembled rage, which yet was visible in the middle of the letter.... In fine, however calm it was, and however designed, he found, and at least he thought he found the charming jilt all over; ... yet, in spite of all this appearing reason, he wishes, and has a secret hope, either that she is not in fault, or that she will so cozen him into a belief she is not, that it may serve as well to soothe his willing heart.... (248–9)

It is, then, the desire of the reader that gives writing meaning. The power of the writer lies in her ability to interpret and manipulate the reader's desire, and it is this lesson that Behn's Sylvia must learn if she is to prosper.

By the third part of the novel, Behn is dealing with two pairs of brother and sister in opposition to each other. Octavio and Calista follow the only other course open to the deserted lover. Both, like

Sylvia, are victims of seduction, duped into sacrificing their honour, but their response is retreat into holy orders, here viewed as a voluntary abnegation of discursive power. Sylvia rejects this option, choosing to assume the cynicism of the rake, rather than submit to a regime of silence and exile from social, personal, and political agency.

Sylvia succeeds for a while in maintaining relations with both Philander and Octavio, as well as stringing along Octavio's besotted elderly uncle. She elopes with Philander for a second time but soon leaves him when he attempts to immure her away in a rustic retreat. She comes to Brussels and, in need of money, writes to Octavio, who is now established in a nearby monastery. He is willing to offer her a pension if she abandons her life of shame. Sylvia's answer is a deft imitation of the style of Heloise and her Portuguese successor, Mariane. She writes 'as an humble penitent would write to a ghostly Father . . . and if ever she mentioned love, it was as if her heart had violently, and against her will, burst out into softness, as she still retained there' (433).

In her pursuit of Don Alonzo, Sylvia's new facility in amatory representation is fully tried and tested. Travelling to Brussels disguised as a man, she is obliged to pass a night in the same bed as Alonzo. During their late night conversation, Alonzo freely admits to his 'male' companion the rakish nature of his desire: 'I have burnt and raved an hour and two, or so; pursued, and gazed, and laid seiges, till I had overcome; but, what is this to love? Did I ever make a second visit, unless upon necessity, or gratitude?' (411). Sylvia sets about winning this coveted second visit by laying siege to the young Spaniard in Brussels, providing tantalizing glimpses of herself in the guise of two different women at public events. Finally, she arranges for him to visit her lodgings and fascinates him with a series of quick changes: 'he sees, he hears, this is the same lovely youth, who lay in bed with him at the village *cabaret*; and then no longer thinks her woman: he hears and sees it is the same face, and voice, and hands he saw on the *Tour*, and in the park, and then believes her woman' (441).

Sylvia's strategies appear on one level to be a simple imitation of those of her first lover, Philander, and his ability to manipulate amatory language in pursuit of sexual gratification. However, she introduces a new twist to this linguistic facility by her peculiarly feminine exploitation of enigmatic identity. Sylvia's feigned identities allow her to retain her male lover's interest and constantly renew her own. In brief, Sylvia learns the tricks of the professional woman writer of amatory fiction, generating fictions around the figure of the woman that withhold identity while they appear to reveal it. In contrast, Mariane's epistolary struggles might be interpreted as those of the amateur woman writer learning to speak her desires through the device of the absent lover. Mariane's history begins and ends in silence; Sylvia's moves on to another fiction. Behn informs us that, despite being expelled from Brussels by the governor for 'ruin[ing] the fortune' of Alonzo, Sylvia continues to roam the continent 'and daily makes considerable conquests wherever she shews the charmer' (461).

Like all Behn's prose fiction, the *Love-Letters* are a heady compound of sexual and party politics. From this and her other works, Behn emerges as a mistress of the art of disguise. Like her author, Sylvia is an anti-heroine, a survivor who in her ceaseless pursuit of social, sexual, and linguistic agency adapts every available resource to hand. Behn presents her readers with a critique of women's enslavement to a variety of fictions of feminine identity, and offers an escape route beyond retreat into silence and spurious claims to authenticity. The novelty of the novel seems to have provided Behn with the ideal platform for the elaboration of a new relationship of the female writing subject to feminine identity. It is not insignificant that Behn's earliest experiments in literature were in the drama, another literary genre in which women, in the shape of Restoration actresses, had obtained a new means of turning amatory representation to profit.

The refusal on the part of Aphra Behn critics to forsake the hermeneutic endeavour to discover her authentic voice has deflected attention from her literary complexities to the thin and unsatisfactory threads of her biography. Her fictions are indeed 'imagin'd more than Woman' in their challenge to the amatory forms traditionally associated with the woman writer. In the attempt to carve out a place for the woman writer in the newly competitive literary market, Behn's fiction turns to a radical questioning of the relationship between gender identity and fiction. These amatory narratives appropriate for the woman writer the power of representation by exposing gender identity, the dichotomy of masculine and feminine, as in itself a fiction. Like her own Clarinda, Behn poses herself to her readers as an erotic enigma in order to maintain her representational power: 'When e'er the Manly part of [her] would plead | She tempts us with the Image of the Maid' (*Works*, vi. 363).

4

'A Genius for Love': Sex as Politics in Delarivier Manley's Scandal Fiction

Watching Women: Aphra/Astrea

Delarivier Manley's first major scandal novel, *The New Atalantis* (1709) reincarnates the figure of Aphra Behn's fictional and poetic persona, Astrea, in order to authorize her own position of female satirist.[1] The opening pages of Manley's scandal novel invoke the maternal body figured in Behn's poem, 'The Golden Age'. When Astrea, self-exiled goddess of justice returns to the terrestrial world, she is at first sensuously delighted with its forgotten beauty, imagined as a fecund female body:

> How Enchanting are thy Prospects? How Generous is the Earth? How Charming her Fruits? How flowing the Waters? How cooling, how limpid the Streams? How Refreshing to the Taste and Limbs of Mortals? How pleasingly they wind to make fruitful the Neighbouring Meads? Those grassy Pastures, the aspiring shady Groves, and the whole ample Bosom of the Terrestrial Globe. (*Novels*, i. 273)

However, for mortals, this generous and self-generating female body extends only the tempting possibility of defilement. Astrea rhetorically chides Jupiter with the question 'to what a Race has thou deliver'd these Enjoyments? How Corrupt, how unworthy of Benefits so Sweet, and of Possessions so ravishing?' (274). The representation of the earth as a female body teeming with life and erotic potential is, of course, a conventional trope of pastoral idyll, but its deployment by the figure of Astrea, whose name simultaneously conjures the memory of Aphra Behn and Honoré d'Urfé's romance heroine, surely

---

[1] Delarivier Manley, *Secret Memoirs and Manners of several Persons of Quality, of Both Sexes, from the New Atalantis, An Island in the Mediteranean* (London, 1709). Repr. *The Novels of Mary Delariviere Manley 1705–1714*, ed. Patricia Köster (2 vols.; Scholars' Facsimiles and Reprints; Gainesville, Fla., 1971), 267–804. All subsequent references to Manley's works, unless otherwise stated, are to this edition, cited as *Novels* and included in the main body of the text.

invites the reader to seek the trace of a feminocentric tradition in Manley's work.[2]

Moreover, Manley, like Behn, presents her satirical powers as both female and heroic. In her introduction to the second volume of her *New Atalantis*, published in the same year as the first, Manley comments on the unexpected success of the novel. She describes herself as '*like a Hero who has gain'd an almost impossible* Victory', and who '*still trembling look[s] back with* Wonder, *at [her] own Ambition*' (i. 524).

Astrea's symbolic role is double. She is both the goddess of justice and Behn the woman writer, classical and modern precedent for the woman's moral privilege in the social and political order. Astrea has come to earth in order to review its present state on behalf of the young prince she has made her charge. The childless Princess of Inverness (Queen Anne) currently reigns over Atalantis, and Astrea is rearing the next heir (the Elector of Hanover, later to be George I) for his succession. 'I will go to the Courts', she declares:

where *Justice*, is profess'd, to view the Magistrate, who presumes to hold the Scales in my Name, to see how remote their profession is from their Practice; thence to the *Courts* and *Cabinets* of *Princes*, to mark their *Cabal* and *disingenuity*, to the *Assemblies* and *Alcoves* of the Young and Fair to discover their Disorders, and the height of their Temptations, the better to teach my young *Prince* how to avoid them, and accomplish him. (i. 280–1)

Astrea plans to visit regal and legal courts, observing both the public (political) and private (sexual) world of 'courtship'. Through the figure of Astrea, the transformation of a disempowered observer's perspective into a written 'witness' that seeks to bring about social and political change in order to influence the 'masculine' sphere, is re-enacted.

Astrea's ability to make herself and her companions invisible so that they may gain access to every particular of the world she seeks to observe and judge, is, of course, significant in this context. The lack of social and political recognition afforded to women is, in the sphere of art, converted into an asset by the female satirist's watchful pen. The enforced invisibility of women in the world of politics is now presented through the figure of Astrea as a super-

---

[2] See Rosalind Delmar, 'Eighteenth Century Amazons', *Feminist Review*, 26 (Summer, 1987), 105–16. Delmar describes Behn as serving as an 'iconic mediator between the writer and her public' in Manley's *New Atalantis* (108).

natural gift: 'we will make us Garments of the ambient Air, and be invisible, or otherways, as we shall see convenient' (i. 282).

Astrea goes on to insist that the satirist remains untainted by the crimes she observes: 'to fit the *Person* for a *Judge*, he must be inform'd of the most minute particular, neither can we be polluted but by our *own*, not the Crimes of *others*. They stain nor reflect back upon us, but in our approbation of them' (i. 301). Here, through her mythological judge, Manley provides an apologia for the eroticism of her text. The author of the satiric text acts as a pair of witnessing eyes on behalf of her absent audience. To report sexual crime in not necessarily to sanction it.

Early in her literary career, Manley found it necessary to answer charges of excessive 'warmth' in her writing. Her portrayal of unbridled sexual lust in the figure of a Persian queen, Homais, in *The Royal Mischief* (performed at Lincolns Inn Fields in April 1696) seems to have aroused criticism, judging by her comments in the preface to the printed edition of the play. Here, Manley employs a familiar disarming but witty sleight of hand:

> *The Principal Objection made against this Tragedy is the warmth of it, as they are pleas'd to call it; in all Writings of this kind, some particular Passion is describ'd, as a Woman I thought it Policy to begin with the softest, and which is easiest to our Sex; Ambition &c. were too bold for the first flight, all wou'd have condemned me if venturing on another, I had fail'd, when gentle love stood ready to afford an easy Victory, I did not believe it possible to pursue him too far, or that my Lawrel [sic] shou'd seem less graceful for having made an entire Conquest.*[3]

Like Aphra Behn, then, Manley concealed the 'transgression' of representing and embodying female political ambition beneath the 'lesser' transgression of representing and embodying active female sexual desire. Homais is an early prototype of the female politicians and rakes that populate Manley's scandal novels in the first decade of the eighteenth century. She is not only sexually but politically predatory, driven by political ambition as well as personal lust for her husband's nephew. Yet Manley insists that the play rejects the theme of ambition to remain within the feminine sphere of love, natural to its author's sex.

Similarly, in her (auto)biography, *The Adventures of Rivella* (1715), Manley/Rivella claims to be wholly preoccupied with the sphere of love in order to defend herself when she is questioned in court about

---

[3] Delarivier Manley, *The Royal Mischief: A Tragedy* (London, 1696), A3r.

the political content of her scandal fiction.[4] Manley/Rivella mocks her interrogators, asking: 'Whether the Persons in Power were ashamed to bring a Woman to her Trial for writing a few amorous Trifles purely for her own Amusement, or that our Laws are defective, as most Persons conceiv'd, because she had serv'd her self with Romantick Names, and a feign'd Scene of Action?' (*Novels*, ii. 850). The argument is to a certain extent, contradictory. Manley/ Rivella claims to be writing 'a few amorous Trifles' and then demands protection under the law because she gave her characters and location a set of feigned names.[5] If there is no political allegory embedded in this text then there is surely no need to claim that the characters have been given false names.

Manley's claims to be trafficking solely in love, the 'proper' sphere of the female novelist, are considerably more transparent than Aphra Behn's. The disguise is meant to be seen through. Rather than engaging with and reworking contemporary ideological debates with politically charged meanings (such as Behn's attention to the issue of vow-breaking), Manley focuses on specific and personal satire in her 'key' novels. Nearly every character in her novels has his or her correlative in the 'real' world of political intrigue. The disclaimer of producing a 'few amorous Trifles' is nothing more than a trope; answering charges of excessive 'warmth' is, it appears, a less difficult and perilous enterprise than answering those of libel.

Moreover, unlike Behn, Manley seems to have positively sought political patronage, in the shape of financial reward from those Tory politicians she had idealized in her novels. The only evidence of any material assistance for Manley from the Tory party is a letter in her own hand that records the receipt of a bill (for fifty pounds) from Robert Harley, Earl of Oxford in 1714.[6] Jonathan Swift's sympathetic

---

[4] Manley was in fact imprisoned briefly from 29 October to 5 November 1709 for the libellous content of the first two volumes of the *New Atalantis*. Her publishers (John Morphew and John Woodward) and printer (John Barber) were taken into custody with her and the second volume, published 20 October 1709, was suppressed. She was tried and discharged on 11 February 1710 at the Queen's Bench Court and went on to publish her *Memoirs of Europe*, in the same vein as the *New Atalantis* in the same year. See Narcissus Luttrell, *A Brief Relation of State Affairs from September 1678 to April 1714* (Oxford, 1857), vi. 505, 506 and 508.

[5] See Kropf on the loophole of 'innuendo' in British law which protected authors from prosecution if the victim was not specifically named. This resulted in the practice of substituting fictitious names and employing initials in scandal writing ('Libel and Satire in the Eighteenth Century', 159).

[6] See Gwendolyn Needham, 'Mary de la Rivière Manley, Tory Defender', *Huntington Library Quarterly*, 12 (1948–9), 283.

account in a letter to Stella of an encounter with Manley at Lord Peterborough's, suggests the neglect Manley experienced at the hands of the Tory ministry she had so ably defended: 'I met Mrs. Manley there, who was soliciting him to get some pension or reward for her service in the cause, by writing her *Atalantis*, and prosecution, &c. upon it. I seconded her, and hope they will do something for the poor woman.'[7]

As a woman, Manley could not receive the traditional recompense of public office for service to a political party, but she clearly felt bitter about their lack of acknowledgement of her services in terms of financial or legal protection. Her comments in *Rivella* on this neglect register the ambiguity that marks all her work between moral purism and self-serving interest, as models for political agency. Rivella's friend, Lovemore, points out that she has attached herself to the wrong party if she expected some reward. Criticism of the Tory ministers who had refused to acknowledge her publicly is transformed into a back-handed compliment. The moral superiority and impartiality of the Tory party means that they cannot recompense her: 'The most severe Criticks upon *Tory* Writings, were *Tories* themselves, who never considering the Design or honest Intention of the Author, would examin [sic] the Performance only, and that too with as much Severity as they would an Enemy's, and at the same Time value themselves upon their being impartial, tho' against their Friends' (ii. 846–7). Like her own Astrea, then, the Tory party, embodying moral justice, refuses to be tainted with the 'crimes' of others, choosing to remain an invisible and impartial observer.

There are other obvious differences between the careers of Behn and Manley. The facts of Manley's biography are well-documented, and indeed provide source material in her own writing.[8] She had a

---

[7] Jonathan Swift, a letter to Stella dated Saturday, 30 June 1711, in *Journal to Stella*, ed. Harold Williams, vol. i (Oxford, 1948), 306. Manley had painted Lord Peterborough in glowing colours as Horatio in her *Memoirs of Europe* (1710).

[8] Manley wrote her biography twice, first in the short story of Delia in the *New Atalantis* in 1709 (*Novels*, ii. 180–94) and then in *Rivella* in 1714 (*Novels*, ii. 729–856). For biographical studies of Manley, see, in particular, Dolores Diane Clarke Duff, 'Materials toward a Biography of Mary Delariviere Manley' (University of Indiana Ph.D. diss., 1965) and Fidelis Morgan, *A Woman of No Character: An Autobiography of Mrs. Manley* (London, 1986). See also Migdalia Sanchez, 'Mary Manley', in Janet Todd's *Dictionary*, 209–12; Paul Bunyan Anderson, 'Mistress Delariviere Manley's Biography', *Modern Philology*, 33 (1936), 261–78; Gwendolyn Needham, 'Mrs. Manley: An Eighteenth-Century Wife of Bath', *Huntington Library Quarterly*, 14 (1950–1), 259–85.

privileged childhood in a family with influential political connections as the daughter of a Royalist army officer and historian, Sir Roger Manley.[9] Following a bigamous marriage with her cousin, the Whig lawyer and politician, John Manley, Delarivier came under the protection of Charles II's notorious mistress, Barbara Villiers, Duchess of Cleveland. She left this patronage under a cloud and from 1694 onwards supported herself by writing. From December 1696 to December 1702, she was involved in an affair with John Tilly, a lawyer and Governor of the Prison at the Fleet, and from 1709 onwards she lived with John Barber, the printer, under the reputation of his mistress. Even on her death, Manley was determined to make it clear that she had not received her financial due for her literary and ideological services to the crown and state. She died on 11 July 1724 leaving a will that included a claim for overdue payment of a patent.[10]

Whereas Aphra Behn's search for government patronage seems to have ended with the disastrous Dutch expedition in 1666 that left her out of pocket and threatened with imprisonment, Manley remained throughout her life determined to gain some recognition from her sovereign and her party. Where Behn's amorous involvements are obscure, Manley made no secret of her love affairs, indeed, biographizing her own sexual intrigues is a frequent ploy in her prose fiction. However, in one important respect, Manley's literary career did continue in the tradition of Aphra Behn's. It was

[9] Sir Roger Manley was best known for his royalist history, *Commentariorum de Rebellione Anglicana* (1686). Manley was evidently raised as an ardent Royalist, but her uncle on her father's side, Major John Manley, was influential during the Commonwealth and his sons, Isaac (Post Master General of Ireland) and John, were active in the Whig cause in the late seventeenth and early eighteenth century (see Duff, 'Materials toward a Biography', 12–24). I am convinced by Dolores Duff's argument that Manley's Christian name was Delariviere, shortened to Delia, after the wife of her father's superior, Sir Thomas Morgan, governor of Jersey from February 1666 (12). There is no evidence to support the Christian name of Mary commonly used for her in nineteenth- and twentieth-century criticism, and Manley's use of the names Delia and Rivella in her autobiographical narratives suggests these are playful conversions of her given name. Her name was probably anglicized to Delarivier. See Patricia Köster, 'Delariviere Manley and the *DNB*: A Cautionary Tale about Following Black Sheep with a Challenge to Cataloguers', *Eighteenth-Century Life*, 3 (1977), 106–11.

[10] See the copy of Manley's will in *Notes and Queries*, 7th ser. 8 (1889), 156–7. Dated 6 October 1723 and proved 26 September 1724, the will claims she was owed £50 per annum in back payments for a salary promised from a patent of the King's printer obtained for Benjamin Tooke and John Barber and witnessed by Swift. Manley had received only one £20 advance from Tooke.

in the sphere of prose fiction, or the early novel, that Manley sought to extrapolate a specific place for the female writing subject as political agent. Like Behn, Manley experimented in other forms of literary production, but it was mainly in her novelistic prose that she explored and developed the place of the female writer, through the narcissistic presentation of a narrating female subject.

Manley's scandal novels were not her only sally into political commentary, but it is only in the genre of prose fiction that she experiments with gendered narrative voice. From late 1710 to early 1714, Manley produced no prose fiction and gave herself over to political journalism. In the winter of 1710–11 she became friendly with Jonathan Swift and a long alliance between the two authors began.[11] This friendship may have been one reason for her turn to political journalism, but she may also have been wary of further legal action following the publication of the *Memoirs of Europe* in October 1710, or disheartened by the lack of recognition her prose fiction had won from the Tory ministers she sought to impress. In April 1711 Manley published a pamphlet, to which Swift contributed the first page, which provided an account of the stabbing of Robert Harley, the Lord Treasurer, by the Marquis of Guiscard during examination of the latter on charges of plotting to invade England.[12] The pamphlet provides a scandalous biography of the French spy, as well as dividing the glory between two principal ministers, Harley, and the Secretary of State, Henry St John for preventing the assassin from achieving what Manley claimed to be his real object, the murder of the Queen. From his *Journal to Stella*, it is clear that Swift had employed Manley as a cloak for his theories about the Guiscard attempt, being himself 'afraid of disobliging Mr. Harley or Mr. St. John in one critical point about it' (i. 245).

He was to take a similar course when, from 14 June to 26 July 1711, he handed over the editorship of his Tory paper, the *Examiner*, to her. Her contributions (numbers 46 to 52) are taken up mainly by an exchange of abuse with the Whig paper, the *Medley*, along with some allegorizing of recent political history similar in structure to her scandal fiction. Swift took some delight in the confusion

[11] See Swift, *Journal to Stella*. In Letter 12 (26 December 1710) Swift mentions dining with 'a city printer', evidently John Barber (140) and in Letter 12 (4 January 1710) he says he dined again with 'people [Stella] never heard of, nor is it worth [her] while to know; an authoress, and a printer' (154).

[12] Delarivier Manley, *A True Narrative of What Pass'd at the Examination of the Marquis de Guiscard at the Cock-Pit, the 8th of March 1710/11* (London, 1711).

Manley's editorship produced, commenting that it will 'confound guessers' as to the true author of the paper.[13]

In October 1711, Manley further experimented with Swiftian irony in two mock 'Whig' pamphlets, ostensibly lauding the Duke of Marlborough's military prowess[14] and the perspicacity of Francis Hare, Chaplain-General to the King's Forces, who was encouraging the army to continue the war of the Spanish Succession against Tory designs to see it concluded by treaty.[15] Another pamphlet, published 29 November 1711, implicated Richard Steele in a Whig plot to encourage revolt by burning effigies during a parade to celebrate Queen Elizabeth's day.[16] Steele was also her major target in a pamphlet of August 1713 defending the Queen's decision to protect British shipping by exercising leniency toward the Magistrates of Dunkirk with respect to the Treaty of Utrecht's provision for the destruction of Dunkirk.[17] Finally, in February 1714, Manley published a 'dialogue' which accused the Whigs of planning to take advantage of the political unrest engendered by Queen Anne's severe illness.[18]

Manley's political journalism is evidence of her importance and instrumentality in Tory politics in the early eighteenth century, but it was all published anonymously and is, in the main, indistinguishable from the pamphlet style of her contemporaries. It makes no attempt to turn amatory conventions into political allegory in the vein of her prose fiction, nor does it make any reference to the gender of its author or projected readers. The only other journalistic writing attributed to Manley is the *Female Tatler*, which appeared in a variety of forms from 8 July 1709 to March 31, 1710.[19] The *Female*

[13] Letter 33 (23 October 1711), *Journal to Stella*, ii. 402.

[14] Delarivier Manley, *The Duke of M———h's Vindication in Answer to a Pamphlet Lately Publish'd Call'd* Bouchain, or a Dialogue between the *Medley* and the *Examiner* (London, 1711).

[15] Delarivier Manley, *A Learned Comment upon Dr. Hare's Excellent Sermon Preach'd before the Duke of Marlborough, on the Surrender of Bouchain* (London, 1711).

[16] Delarivier Manley, *A True Relation of the Several Facts and Circumstances of the Intended Riot and Tumult on Queen Elizabeth's Birth-day* (London, 1711).

[17] Delarivier Manley, *The Honour and Prerogative of the Queen's Majesty Vindicated and Defended against the Unexampled Insolence of the Author of the* Guardian, *in a Letter from a Country Whig to Mr. Steele* (London, 1713).

[18] Delarivier Manley, *A Modest Enquiry into the Reasons of the Joy Expressed by a Certain Sett of People upon the Spreading of a Report of Her Majesty's Death* (London, 1714).

[19] The *Female Tatler* has a complex publishing history. Nos. 1–18 were published by B. Bragge, nos. 19–44 by A. Baldwin simultaneously with a rival paper of the same name published by Bragge again, and nos. 45–51 by Baldwin alone.

Tatler is a mildly pro-Tory paper, ostensibly written by one Mrs Crackenthorpe, 'a lady who knows everything', which takes the form of a series of satirical portraits and collected gossip generated from her drawing room. Manley's authorship of this paper is disputed, however, and I am inclined to agree with the claims for Thomas Baker as author, not least because of the moderate tone of the paper's party politics.[20]

In conclusion, then, if we assume that the *Female Tatler* is not Manley's work, it appears that it was only in the realm of prose fiction that she attempted to adumbrate her political propaganda from within an amatory, and explicitly feminized, framework. In line with her predecessor, Behn, Manley found in amatory prose an opportunity for an exploration of the power of female representation—political and sexual—an opportunity that no other genre appears to have offered.

Manley's success in her ventures into fiction, if not manifested in financial reward from the Tory party, belies the ostensible message of that fiction, that the only possible career for women lies in romantic love and marriage. Manley's career in love takes a very different trajectory from the one she habitually assigns her innocent heroines. Each successive narration drives home another nail in another Whig politician's or propagandist's coffin. Contemporary representations of Manley's fiction as a form of murder reinforces this view. Joseph Addison satirized her in a letter from one 'Tobiah Greenhat' to the *Tatler* as an eighteenth-century Catherine de Medici, whose poisonous potions decimate the ranks of the mighty. Manley appears as Epicene, a tutor for young ladies in the art of Amazonian warfare at Madonella's (Mary Astell's) seminary:

Of these Military Performances, the Direction is undertaken by *Epicene*, the writer of *Memoirs from the Mediterranean*, who, by the help of some artificial Poisons conveyed by Smells, has within these few Weeks brought many Persons of both Sexes to an untimely Fate; and, what is more surprising, has, contrary to her Profession, with the same Odors, reviv'd others who had long since been drown'd in the whirlpools of *Lethe*. (*Tatler*, no. 63, 3 September 1709)

As late as 1944 we find this same kind of abjected imagery employed

---

[20] For Manley's claim, see Anderson, 'The History and Authorship of Mrs. Crackenthorpe's *Female Tatler*'; for Baker's, see Walter Graham, 'Thomas Baker, Mrs. Manley and the *Female Tatler*', *Modern Philology*, 34 (1936–7), 267–72; and John Harrington Smith, 'Thomas Baker and *The Female Tatler*', *Modern Philology*, 49 (1951–52), 182–8.

by Bridget MacCarthy in order to characterize Manley, who, we are told, 'collected filth with the relentless energy of a dredger, and aimed it with the deadly precision of a machine-gun'.[21]

The unabashed specificity, if not malice, of Manley's attacks on individual men and women associated with the Whig cause seems to unsettle her critics and commentators. This satire has more in common, it appears, with the 'slovenly butchering of a man' that Dryden despised, than the 'fineness of a stroke that separates the head from the body, and leaves it standing in its place'.[22] As I will go on to argue, however, the flagrant instrumentalism of Manley's scandal fiction, that is, her desire to see her texts have direct effects in the party political conflicts of her day, has blinded her critics to the complexity of her negotiation between and subversion of dichotomies of gender and genre. One of the instrumental effects she sought in her scandal fiction, beyond the political 'deaths' of various eminent Whigs, was the establishment of a moral, and hence social, purchase for the woman writer in a world traditionally debarred to her, that of politics and political agency.

Watching Women: Marie d'Aulnoy

The example of Aphra Behn was not the sole precedent available to Manley of a woman writer's use of romance and epistolary conventions to present contemporary scandal. In particular, Manley's scandal fictions consistently address and rework the fiction of the French travel and scandal writer, Marie d'Aulnoy. If Behn was her nearest predecessor in English prose fiction and thus an inevitable model to be invoked by critics and readers, Aulnoy appears to have been a 'heroine' consciously chosen by the author herself. Like that of d'Aulnoy, Manley's reputation rested upon the travel or scandal novel written in epistolary or narrative form. Her first published work was an epistolary travelogue entitled *Letters Written by Mrs. Manley* (1696) addressed to one 'J. H.' In his preface, J. H. admits that the letters '*were not proper for the Publick*', and that he has produced them without her permission.[23] The publication of the

---

[21] MacCarthy, *Women Writers*, 216.

[22] John Dryden, 'A Discourse concerning the Original and Progress of Satire' (1693), *Essays of John Dryden*, ed. W. P. Ker, vol. ii (New York, 1961), 94.

[23] J. H., 'Preface', *Letters Written by Mrs. Manley, to Which is Added A Letter from a Supposed Nun in Portugal to a Gentleman in France, in Imitation of the Nun's Five Letters in Print, by Colonel Pack* (London, 1696), A2ʳ.

letters appears to have been a piece of market exploitation, co-inciding with the appearance on the London stage of Manley's first two plays, *The Lost Lover* (1696) and *The Royal Mischief* (1696). J. H. presents himself as one among several male literary entrepreneurs eager to 'display' their new-found treasure to the public:

whilst the Town is big to see what a Genius so proportionate can produce, whilst Sir Thomas Skipwith and Mr. Betterton are eagerly contending, who shall bring you first upon the Stage, and which shall be the most applauded, your Tragick or Comick Strain, I cou'd not refuse the Vanity (my Soul whisper'd to me) of stealing you from the expecting Rivals, and dexterously throw you first into the World, as one that honour'd me with your Friendship before you thought of them. (Letters, A2ʳ⁻ᵛ)

Manley was clearly unimpressed by this act of presumptuous and unsolicited exposure, in that she promptly had the book withdrawn. The letters were not reprinted until 1725 when Edmund Curll produced them with a preface declaring that Manley had given him a copy in 1705 with the 'positive injunction that it should never more see the light of day till the thread of her life was cut'.[24] Whether Manley was indeed party to the publication of the letters or not, throughout her literary career she represented herself as the victim of male abuse and, in particular, the attempt by male literati to 'pimp' for her. Her history as a writer begins and ends, as my discussion of *Rivella* later in this chapter will demonstrate, with a drama of resistance to masculinist appropriations of her writings, metaphorized as her body.

The *Letters Written by Mrs. Manley* make explicit reference to Marie d'Aulnoy's most famous work in Britain, her *Travels into Spain*. Manley is travelling in the west country, too penurious to live in London and supposedly disillusioned by its hypocrisy and corruption (Morgan suggests that she was seeking to persuade her estranged husband to take their boy child into his care.[25]) She mentions a visit to Salisbury Cathedral and adds, 'If in a Foreign Country, as the Lady in her Letters of *Spain*, I cou'd entertain you with a noble Description; but you have either seen, or may see it; and so, I'll spare my Architecture' (*Letters*, 29). Here, Manley both invokes and mocks the contrived intimacy of Aulnoy's epistolary travelogues.

Another epistolary work by Manley, written for publication and entitled *The Lady's Pacquet of Letters* (1707), first appeared in the

²⁴ Delarivier Manley, *A Stagecoach Journey to Exeter* (London, 1725), n.p.
²⁵ Morgan, *A Woman of No Character*, 70–1.

same volume as a translation from d'Aulnoy entitled *Memoirs of the Court of England*.[26] Publishing her work with that of d'Aulnoy not only increased Manley's association in the public mind with a woman writer famed for her epistolary gifts, but it was also a shrewd marketing venture. D'Aulnoy's *Travels into Spain* went into sixteen editions from 1691 to 1740,[27] so Manley would have been assured of a large readership under the protection of d'Aulnoy's name.

The importance of d'Aulnoy's fiction to the development of Manley's distinctive form of scandal writing cannot be underestimated. First, they elaborated a special position for the woman in relation to the ambiguities of fact and fiction so central to the formation of early prose narrative, and second, they established politico-sexual intrigue as a narrative realm in which the woman writer had a privileged authority and interest. Both projects were to preoccupy Manley throughout her career in scandal. The influence of d'Aulnoy's work upon Manley's is nowhere better illustrated than in a close reading of their respective seduction scenes. Manley both adopts and subverts d'Aulnoy's amatory conventions, increasingly destabilizing the fact/fiction, nature/art dichotomies that d'Aulnoy habitually employs to structure her narratives.

The second letter of d'Aulnoy's *Travels into Spain* is largely taken up with the tragic love story of a hermit she meets at Mass. The hermit, Don Lewis, has retired from the world as penance for his responsibility in the death of his best friend's wife at the hands of her husband, the Marques de Barbaran. The Marques interrupts Don Lewis in his seduction of his wife, who is under the mistaken apprehension she is making love with her husband, and promptly murders her. The details of this seduction scene are replayed again and again in Manley's fiction:

She was in a Ground-Room which lookt into the Garden; all was fast and shut close, save a little Window, whereby he saw on her Bed this charming Creature: She was

[26] The translator's dedication explains that the second half of *The Lady's Pacquet* has had to be deferred because of the length of the *Memoirs* (n.p.). It appeared the following year in the same volume as another work by d'Aulnoy, *Memoirs of the Earl of Warwick* (London, 1708). *The Lady's Pacquet* was finally published in one volume as *Court Intrigues*. Letters 1 to 11, mainly consisting of Manley's correspondence with Richard Steele, in the days of their friendship, on alchemy and her assistance in procuring his mistress a midwife, were republished in Thomas Brown, *The Second Volume of Familiar Letters of Love, Gallantry and Several Occasions, by the Wits of the Last and Present Age* (London, 1718), 73–103. On the vicissitudes of Manley's relationship with Steele, see Morgan, *A Woman of No Character*, 106–20.

[27] Day, *Epistolary Fiction before Richardson*, 33.

in a profound Sleep, half undrest; he had the time to discover such Beauties as still
augmented the force of his Passion. He approacht so softly to her, that she did not
awake: It was already some moments that he had lookt on her with all the Transports
of a Man amazed, when seeing her naked Breasts, he could not forbear kissing them.
She arose on a sudden; she had not her Eyes open; the Chamber was dark, and she
could not have believ'd Don Lewis *could have been so bold. . . . [C]alling him*
several times, her dear Marquess and Husband, *she tenderly embrac'd him.*
(*Travels into Spain,* pt. 1, pp. 55–6)

Manley takes these ingredients—the garden, the sleeping woman,
the woman's body exposed to the lover's amorous gaze—and subtly
reorganizes them into configurations that disturb the dichotomy
established here between innocent woman and duplicitous male. Her
description of the seduction of Diana de Bedamore at the close of
the second volume of the *New Atalantis* is one such example.[28] Don
Thomasio Rodrigues [Thomas, Earl of Coningsby] draws Diana into
an illicit liaison when she and her husband go to stay at his country
seat. This time it is the wife who catches the couple *in flagrante
delicto.* Once again the woman is sleeping in a garden when the man
comes upon her, although there is no case of mistaken identity here:

It was the Evening of an excessive hot Day, she got into a shade of *Orange*
Flowers and *Jessamine,* the Blossoms that were fallen cover'd all beneath with
a profusion of Sweets. . . . *Diana,* full of the uneasiness of Mind that Love
occasion'd threw her self under the pleasing Canopy, apprehensive of no
Acteon to invade with forbidden Curiosity, her as *numerous perfect Beauties,* as
had the *Goddess.* Supinely laid on that repose of Sweets, the dazling Lustre of
her Bosom stood reveal'd, her polish'd Limbs all careless and extended,
show'd the *Artful* Work of *Nature. Rodriguez* (who only pretended to depart,
and had watch'd her every Motion) with softly treading Steps, stole close to
the *unthinking* Fair, and throwing him at his length beside her, fix'd his Lips
to hers, with so happy a *Celerity,* that his Arm was round her to prevent her
rising, and himself in possession of her lovely Mouth, before she either saw
or heard his Approach. (*Novels,* i. 759–60)

Diana succumbs to her lover's passion, inflamed by 'the *Rhetorick* of
one belov'd, his *strange bewitching Force*' (760). Innocence and sexual
knowledge become radically confused in this scene. Diana is the
victim not only of her lover's importunities but also of her own
desires, 'lull'd by the enchanting Poison Love had diffus'd
throughout her form' (760–1). Her lack of resistance is excused by

---

[28] Diana is identified by Patricia Köster as Frances Scudamore in her excellent
index developed from the various keys (*Novels,* ii. 859–927). All names from this index
are included in the main body of the text and enclosed in square brackets.

the author on the grounds of that 'beauteous Frailty' in women, the combined effects of '*Love* and *Nature*' (761). The rhetoric of this passage situates Diana as passive victim, indeed presents her to the reader's and her lover's gaze by analogy with the garden that frames her as a thing of nature to be exploited and shaped by man.

J. J. Richetti has argued that the scandal novel dramatized two basic conflicts, social and sexual, embodied in two key figures, 'the innocent persecuted maiden and the aristocratic *libertin*-seducer'. Manley's mythology of persecuted innocence, he suggests, provides its 'predominantly female audience' with 'an opportunity for extended erotic fantasy, even while it guarantees the moral innocence of the heroine and the readers who are invited to identify with her'.[29] Here, Richetti assumes that the female reader will identify with the female character. However, as April London points out with reference to the depiction of Diana's seduction above, Manley leaves the reader of either sex no other position to occupy in this scene than that of Acteon, 'the secret observer of a hidden scene'.[30] Indeed, this is precisely the position that the female audience within Manley's *New Atalantis*, the invisible Astrea, her mother Virtue, and their companion and sometime guide Intelligence, occupy in the text. The satirical observing eye thus comes perilously close to the voyeuristic gaze. Manley repeatedly calls our attention to this troubled scenario. What 'interest' does the woman spectator and, by extension, the female audience have in watching this spectacle of the man amorously contemplating the inviting female body?

Manley departs from d'Aulnoy, not only in her destabilisation of the gender dichotomies of the seduction scene, but also in the means she employs to establish the 'truth' of her texts. Whereas d'Aulnoy insists on the authenticity and contemporaneity of her stories, Manley locates hers in the ancient past or imagined worlds. In her preface to the reader that accompanies the *Travels into Spain*, d'Aulnoy insists that '*I write nothing but what I have seen, or heard from Persons of Unquestionable Credit; And therefore shall conclude with assuring you, That you have here no Novel, or Story, devised at pleasure; but an Exact and most True Account of what I met with in my Travels*'

---

[29] Richetti, *Popular Fiction before Richardson*, 124, 142, 146.
[30] April London, 'Placing the Female: The Metonymic Garden in Amatory and Pious Narrative 1700–1740', in Macheski and Schofield, *British Women Novelists 1670–1815*, 104.

(pt 1, sig. A3^{r-v}). Thus, as noted in Chapter 2, d'Aulnoy presents herself to her readers as an amatory 'spy', amassing information, details, and facts for the consumption of leisured genteel ladies in her home country. Here, facts serve as fiction, because the lady reader in her boudoir in France is interested, not in the political history of the countries d'Aulnoy visits, but the sexual mores and scandal.

Manley's texts, while she claims in *Rivella* that they are mere 'Tattle of Frailties . . . old Stories that all the World had long since reported' (*Novels*, ii. 846), have a much more directly instrumental purpose than d'Aulnoy's. D'Aulnoy transforms the information she gleaned as a spy for the French government into tales of sexual intrigue for the consumption of the French gentility after the fact. Manley transforms contemporary sexual scandal into political allegory with the purpose of making and breaking political careers, at moments of intense party political crisis.[31] *Queen Zarah* appeared in the same year that the Godolphin ministry and the Whig party won the election, their popularity enhanced by Marlborough's victory at Blenheim. The *New Atalantis* was instrumental in the propaganda war that resulted in the Tories overthrowing the Whig ministry in August 1710. Godolphin was dismissed and Robert Harley given the prime ministry. G. M. Trevelyan concludes that the *New Atalantis* was the single most harmful publication to the Whig ministry in the year of 1709.[32] Sarah, Duchess of Marlborough, favourite to the Queen and an important figure in Whig politics, was concerned enough about the *New Atalantis* to have her secretary, Maynwaring, read it and report back to her on its likely effects. Maynwaring in two letters in October 1709, the same month in which Manley was taken into custody, tried to assuage her fears, but an undercurrent of concern is evident: 'such weak slanderers as these, do not so much defame their enemies as they hurt their friends. . . . Yet I am afraid it will be very difficult quite to cure the mischief; for so long as the people will buy such books, there will always be vile printers ready to publish them; and low indigent

---

[31] On the timeliness of Manley's interventions in party politics, see Paul Bunyan Anderson, 'Delariviere Manley's Prose Fiction', *Philological Quarterly*, 13 (1934), 168–88.

[32] G. M. Trevelyan, *England under Queen Anne*, iii: *The Peace and the Protestant Succession* (London, 1934), 38.

writers will never be wanting for such a work.[33] Once the Tory party had gained the ministry, Manley produced her *Memoirs of Europe* (1710), a panegyric to the two major Tory leaders, Robert Harley and Lord Peterborough, at a point when her party was seeking to consolidate its supremacy at court.

Thus, Manley's scandal fiction serves a somewhat different purpose than that of her model, d'Aulnoy. Its author trod a delicate path in seeking to protect herself from legal retribution while ensuring that her allegorical structure was not so obscure that her readers could not recognize her fiction as the party political propaganda it was. As a result, she produced elaborate 'frames' to her texts, providing them with such far-fetched geneses that her reader could not fail to look nearer to home for their actual source.

If d'Aulnoy presents herself as a sexual spy, an itinerant voyeur, Manley most commonly adopts the persona of the sedentary translator and bibliophile. *Queen Zarah* (1705), the *New Atalantis* (1709), and *Memoirs of Europe* (1710) are all accompanied by prefaces that frame the texts as translations from long obsolete books that the author has stumbled upon by circuitous routes. *Queen Zarah*, we are told in a subtitle, is 'Faithfully Translated From the Italian Copy Now Lodged in the Vatican at Rome, and Never Before Printed in Any Language'. The dedication to the first volume of the *New Atalantis* supplements the motif of translation with a complex history of the manuscript's passage to the translator's desk:

> The following Adventures First spoke their own mixt Italian, a Speech Corrupted, and now much in Use thro' all the Islands of the Mediterranean; from whence some Industrious Frenchman soon Transported it into his own Country; and by giving it an Air and Habit, wherein the Foreigner was almost lost, seem'd to Naturalize it: A Friend of mine, that made the Campaign, met with it last Year at Bruxels; and thus, a la Francois, put it into my Hands, with a desire it might visit the Court, and Great Britain. (Novels, i. 268–9)

Here, Manley, through her play with the trope of translation (the turning of something foreign into something familiar), conveys to her readers the necessity of reading the text in relation to their own culture, while at the same time claiming its origin to be elsewhere.

<hr/>

[33] Sarah Churchill, *Private Correspondence of Sarah, Duchess of Marlborough*, i (London, 1838), 239. See also Maynwaring's comments in his previous letter (236) and the Duchess's to the Queen on the book, in which she upbraids Anne for her evident favouritism of Abigail Masham, new companion to the Queen and a close friend of Harley (244–5).

The *Memoirs of Europe* see the height of Manley's complex feigning of the foreign source. In this two volume novel, she sets about evolving a representation of early eighteenth-century political history by analogy with historical events in eighth-century Europe, ostensibly anthologized from a sixteenth-century French translation of a Latin manuscript by one Eginardus which the author came across in her father's library. Manley's extraordinary achievement with historical analogy in this text has largely been ignored by her twentieth-century critics. Richetti, for instance, dismisses her scandal fictions as 'formally nothing more than a series of anecdotes, some swollen to novella length and complexity', which only deserve attention because of their 'embarrassing popularity'.[34] In the *Memoirs of Europe*, Manley once again uses the trope of linguistic translation to signify her act of historical translation, claiming that '*The French is so obsolete, that [she has] bestow'd much Pains and Application in the Work*' (*Novels*, ii. n.p.). The 'translation' of content, from eighth-century political history to early eighteenth-century scandal, is encoded in the claim to translate language, from obsolete French to contemporary English.

In conclusion, then, if d'Aulnoy presents herself as the peripatetic source of a series of stable and indisputable texts/testimonies, Manley inverts the order to present herself as the sedentary translator toiling in libraries in the attempt to fix a series of peripatetic texts into some kind of stable meaning or utterance. Manley offers her readers 'facts' (an account of eighth-century European politics, the history of an imagined island called Atalantis) which are in reality fictions created by the author feigning the role of translator. In turn, these fictions point to a different set of 'facts', contemporary political and sexual scandal, disclosing the supposed 'truth' of Whig degeneracy and corruption. Finally, of course, these 'facts' are themselves 'fictions', in that the stories she tells of Whig politicians are largely invented or hearsay, deployed in the service of Tory ideology.

Both Lennard Davis and Michael McKeon have pointed out the importance of a certain fact/fiction ambiguity in the history of the early modern novel.[35] The development of an elaborate machinery

[34] Richetti, *Popular Fiction before Richardson*, 120, 121.
[35] Lennard Davis, *Factual Fictions*, 102–23; McKeon, *Origins of the English Novel*, 25–65.

for ascribing sources accompanied by repeated claims for its verity was, of course, by no means exclusive to Manley's writing. Jonathan Swift in his *Tale of a Tub* (1704) neatly satirizes both practices. His bookseller, in an address to the reader, declares: '*If I should go about to tell the Reader, by what Accident, I became Master of these Papers, it would, in this unbelieving Age, pass for little more than the Cant, or Jargon of the Trade. I, therefore, gladly spare both him and my self so unnecessary a Trouble.*'[36] While the bookseller provides a means of satirizing the convoluted histories of the passage of material from distant land to publishing house, the modern author of the *Tale of a Tub* is employed to poke fun at the meaningless function of the truth claim in fictional texts. In 'The Epistle Dedicatory to Prince Posterity', the modern author insists: 'I profess to *Your Highness*, in the Integrity of my Heart, that what I am going to say is literally true this Minute I am writing: What Revolutions may happen before it shall be ready for your Perusal, I can by no means warrant' (36). As Swift's satire proves, Manley was, in many ways, simply following narrative convention in constructing elaborate frames simultaneously to conceal and signify political intent. However Manley's use of narrative 'frames' is but one aspect of a wider project in her scandal novels: the attempt to figure the possibility of female political agency through the allegorical use of the seduction plot as substitute for the political plot. Manley's repetitious tales of seduction can be seen as a series of attempts to destabilize the structuring oppositions of contemporary ideology (fact versus fiction, love versus politics, feminine versus masculine) in order to privilege the woman as commentator upon and actor in the political realm. These stories offer us a number of allegories of female reading and writing. The attempts on the part of Manley's heroines either to 'read' the amatory language of their male seducers aright, or to 'write' their own version of their own love plots, can be seen as allegories of her own attempt to gain access to the scene of party political representation in early eighteenth-century England. The heroines of Manley's seduction plots must gain control of the scene of amatory representation if they are not to disappear from it altogether. The innocent reader, the heroine who believes the lies of her male seducer, is doomed to silence and death.

[36] Jonathan Swift, 'The Bookseller to the Reader', *A Tale of a Tub, to Which is Added The Battle of the Books and the Mechanical Operation of the Spirit* (1704), eds. A. C. Guthkelch and D. Nichol Smith, 2nd edn. (Oxford, 1958), 28.

The 'True Landmark': Allegories of Female Reading

At the end of the story of the love affair between Charlot [Stuarta Werberge Howard] and her guardian, the Duke [William Bentinck, First Earl of Portland], in the first part of Manley's *New Atalantis*, we are told that Charlot 'dy'd a true Landmark: to warn all believing Virgins from shipwracking their Honour upon (that dangerous Coast of Rocks) the Vows and pretended Passion of Mankind' (*Novels*, i. 355). Charlot's story is both the story of a landmark and a landmark story in Manley's text, in that it is an exemplary tale of seduction and betrayal to or from which all subsequent stories in the novel correspond or diverge. The allegorical web of this story is wide-ranging, encompassing as it does a specific attack upon the Earl of Portland, Whig favourite of William III, the more general myth of an innocent corrupted by power (or the Tory moralist struggling to hold out against the Machiavellian subtlety of the Whig politician), and finally the textual allegory of the innocent female reader seduced into debauchery by the power of erotic fiction. Charlot's story is one of a woman's total subjection to the control of a male patriarch, and her inability to resist or seize control of the text he writes for her life. Brought up in the Duke's household as one of his children in expectation that she will marry his son, Charlot is given an 'exemplary' education. The Duke, we are told:

banish'd from her Conversation whatever would not edify, Airy *Romances*, *Plays*, dangerous *Novels*, *loose* and *insinuating Poetry*, artificial Introductions of *Love*, well-painted Landskips of that dangerous Poison; her Diversions were always among the sort that were most Innocent and Simple, such as Walking, but not in publick Assemblies; Musick in Airs all Divine; reading and improving Books of Education and Piety. (*Novels*, i. 325)

The one distinguishing mark of Charlot's education is that she is taught to believe and trust in her books of 'Education and Piety' and in the authority of her guardian. The Duke orders her to 'shun all occasions of speaking upon Subjects not necessary to a Ladies Knowledge' (326), and thus effectively debars her from both the realm of sexual pleasure and that of political and intellectual power.

When he sees her performing Diana to his son's Acteon at a family entertainment in his country villa, however, the Duke's plans for his ward change, 'so admirably she varied the Passions that she gave Birth in his Breast, to what he had never felt before' (329). The

Duke now cynically redesigns his plans for Charlot's education, deciding to introduce her to 'every thing that might enervate the Mind, and fit it for the soft play and impression of Love' (333). Just as the Duke's passion for Charlot was created by art (her ability in play-acting), not nature, Charlot's passion for him is produced by the influence of art, in the shape of the erotic collection housed in his library. Providing Charlot with a key to the gallery, the Duke introduces her to its delights:

he took down an *Ovid*, and opening it just at the love of *Myrra* for her Father, conscious red overspread his Face; he gave it her to read, she obey'd him with a visible delight; nothing is more pleasing to young Girls, than in first being consider'd as Women.... She took down the Book, and plac'd herself by the Duke, his Eyes Feasted themselves upon her Face, thence wander'd over her snowy Bosom, and saw the young swelling Breasts just beginning to distinguish themselves, and which were gently heav'd at the impression *Myrra's* sufferings made upon her Heart. (335)

The erotic function of the book is highlighted here. It is art that seduces Charlot, rather than the Duke himself. Her sexual pleasure lies in the fiction in which she is immersed, while he takes the place of Acteon observing its effects. After this first taste of amatory fiction, Charlot's appetite for it becomes insatiable, and the Duke directs her to Ovid, Petrarch, Tibullus, tragic drama, and even instructional pornography. Charlot's 'education', it appears, has only been into the business of being educable. She as easily and eagerly learns the tricks of the courtesan as she did the virtues of the wife: 'She was become so great a Proficient, that nothing of the Theory was a stranger to her' (340).

After briefly providing Charlot with a taste of the court, nothing now remains for the Duke but to seize his opportunity, which he does on a sudden visit to the country villa to which he has sent her. Charlot, newly risen from her bath, is summarily raped: 'neither her prayers, tears, nor struglings, cou'd prevent him, but in her Arms he made himself a full amends for all those pains he had suffer'd for her' (344). Charlot, now the Duke's mistress, returns to court and makes a young widowed Countess [Martha Jane Bentinck née Temple, Countess of Portland] her confidante. The Countess, to whom the lover's amatory discourse is 'all Greek and Hebrew' (345), tries to introduce her protégé to a counter-culture, lending her the history of Roxelana, a courtesan in a seraglio who managed to manipulate the sultan into dividing his throne with her. Charlot, however, seems impervious to the reading direction of any but her mentor lover, 'sure that the Countess knew the World, but . . . knew not the Duke, who had not a Soul like other Men' (346). When the Duke sets Charlot up in a lonely country estate, she asks to have the Countess as company, and the affair comes to an end when the Duke's attentions turn to the latter. Charlot departs to die in solitary grief and the Countess, following her own amatory model, manages to elicit a proposal of marriage from the Duke by refusing his sexual advances.

The dangerous coast of rocks on which Charlot floundered, then, is amatory fiction itself. Like Behn's Oroonoko, Charlot's innocence, her inability to see through fiction, makes her both an ideal and a doomed 'reader' of the amatory/political plot. While this story ostensibly argues, through its allegorical structure, that politics and morality should be one and the same, its trajectory and outcome suggest that they are, in practice, incompatible. Moral purity can only be the dupe, not the undoer, of political intrigue. Charlot's belief in the moral perfectibility of mankind and, in particular, in the integrity of her lover, lead her to misread the text of her own love affair. The honest lover can only be a victim in this amatory system because he or she cannot see the code as a code.

Manley's persecuted virgins quite clearly symbolize the virtue of sincerity and political conviction in contrast with the corrupt fiction-mongering of their male counterparts. However, the woman's very innocence is her undoing, since it makes her vulnerable to deception. Thus, in two subsequent stories the brothers Hernando [William Cowper] and Mosco [Spencer Cowper] win and destroy their mistresses by exploiting their susceptibility to amatory impressions. The married Hernando is another rake who seduces his ward, Louisa [Elizabeth Culling], in this case by convincing her of the moral rectitude of polygamy and then secretly marrying her. Manley may have had a particular reason for attacking the lawyer William Cowper (1665–1723), and Lord Chancellor from October 1705 to 1710 and a moderate Whig, in that he was a friend of John Manley and Richard Steele, and a particularly zealous Whig agent against the Tory press. It is not inappropriate, considering his connection with her own husband, that Manley should have made his story one of bigamy.[37]

[37] On Cowper, see J. A. Downie, *Robert Harley and the Press: Propaganda and Public Opinion in the Age of Swift and Defoe* (Cambridge, 1979), 86–7.

Hernando takes his ward and his wife to an opera, in which a bigamous heroine stabs herself on discovering that her first husband is still alive: 'Louisa, who did not often see such Representations, became extremely mov'd at this; Her young Breasts heav'd with Sorrow; the Tears fill'd her Eyes; . . . he was infinitely pleas'd, and employ'd a world of pains to applaud, instead of ridiculing, as his Lady did, that sensibility of Soul' (Novels, i. 490). Louisa's doom is assured when she allows herself to get into a late-night discussion with Hernando on the moral justice of polygamy. Intelligence warns: 'When once a young Maid pretends to put her self upon the same Foot with a Lover at Argument, she is sure to be cast' (498). Louisa is punished, it seems, more for her gullibility than her lapse in virtue. Both she and Hernando's wife die of the venereal disease with which he infects them both, Louisa with 'Polygamy . . . an unshaken Article of her Faith' (i. 516). Hernando, in contrast, qualifies as a judge and marries again. The parallel story of Mosco's affair is equally a question of the woman's commitment to truth, in contrast with the male seducer's hypocrisy. Zara [Sarah Stout], a wealthy independent heiress who belongs to a strict religious sect that interprets the vow to marry as equivalent to the ceremony itself, pursues and wins Mosco who is, however, only interested in her money. Zara declares herself 'bred in the plain road of Sincerity', explaining that within her religion 'their very Word to them is a Law' (506). When Mosco fails to keep his promise to leave his current wife, Zara is thrown into despair and drowns herself. Rumour has it that Mosco first strangled, then drowned her.[38]

Sincerity, then, is always a losing card in the business of love and, thus, by analogy, in that of politics. Within the fictional economy of Manley's text, masculine and feminine appear to be radically divided. Female sincerity and male duplicity, fact and fiction, fight an unequal battle in which virtue can only lose. Intelligence comments with gloom, that 'Enjoyment (the death of Love in all Mankind) gives Birth to new Fondness, and doating Extasies in the

[38] Manley was reproducing a contemporary scandal. Spencer Cowper defended himself in a famous trial in which he, Ellis Stephens and William Rogers (both attorneys), and John Marston (a scrivener), were indicted at the Hertford summer Assizes of 1699 for the murder of the Quaker, Sarah Stout, on 13 March 1698. They were acquitted since it could not be established whether Stout, evidently Cowper's mistress, had been killed before drowning or drowned herself. For a transcript of the trial, see State Trials: Political and Social, ed. H. L. Stephen, vol. ii (London, 1899), 139–231.

what about Zarah? — Anne = the virtuous one.

Women' (501). Thus beleaguered and victimized, Manley's sincere heroines face an inescapable future of misery and/or death.

Manley appears to have entangled her heroines and, with them, her political allegory in an unresolvable paradox. Virtue can never be rewarded, nor can it offer any viable resistance to the multifarious and duplicitous strategies of vice. The virtuous are offered only one role in a fictional economy too secular to receive any comfort from the idea of a heavenly recompense for worldly pain, that of embodying iconic suffering. Manley's stories of suffering virtue thus leave us with an ambiguous moral, that women must seek a new relationship to the amatory text/political order if they are not to remain its victims and if they are to become agents of change within it. A suitable regard to 'interest' is necessary to survival.

The party allegory, then, to some extent transforms the sexual myth of the text, restoring this notion of a necessary cynicism and distrust of masculine power. Accordingly, the repetitious motif of seduction and betrayal is repeatedly reworked in her novels, introducing and exploring the possibilities of a number of strategies of resistance on the part of her female characters in order to alleviate an otherwise embracing political pessimism. These strategies fall into two main categories: first, the use of gender inversion and second, the manipulation of narrative voice or satirical 'masks'. Both, I suggest, offer a way into the amatory text for the woman reader, enabling her to become a writer of her own plot and, thus, in terms of the dominating allegory of the work, an agent in the socio-political order.

Cross-dressing and Cabals: Allegories of Female Writing

The pages of Manley's scandal fiction are filled with examples of cross-dressing and gender inversion, in the shape of both individual plots and the overall 'key' structure of her scandal narration. Contemporary female figures often appear as men in these narratives. Queen Anne is represented as Emperor Constantine VI in the *Memoirs of Europe*, a weak monarch dominated by his mother, the Empress Irene [Sarah Churchill]. Manley provides Anne/Constantine with two 'wives', Mary the Armenian [Prince George of Denmark, her husband] and Theodecta [Abigail Masham, her favourite from 1705 onwards]. Abigail Masham also appears in this same novel as the Duchess of Savoy, in the dedication to the second part, and as

Leonidas, the Emperor's young male favourite whom the Empress plots to have removed from court.[39] A more complex instance of gender inversion lies in Manley's frequent creation of female characters who have chosen to adopt a masculine subject position in the amatory world they inhabit.

Manley unequivocally condemns those women who 'cross-dress' by attempting to operate within the social and political order of her imagined world in the same manner as their male counterparts, that is, those women who imitate the 'masculine' practice of exploiting and victimizing the innocent. An adoption of patriarchal power and its methods of control proves to be no resistance at all. Desire is an inescapable given for all human subjects in her fiction, but its exploitation in order to gain power and gratify personal greed is a specifically masculine practice. Indeed, opprobrium and even death are preferable to a cynical rehearsal of masculine power moves on the part of women. Thus, the Whig female 'politicians' of her age, Sarah Churchill and Barbara Villiers in particular, are virulently attacked as, at best, poor mimics and, at worst, vicious perpetuators of masculine corruption.

The Machiavellian practice of Zarah in Manley's earliest work of scandal fiction is denounced, less because it inverts male supremacy than because it undermines the symbolic power of femininity.[40] Zarah is described as 'the Mirror of her Sex, and the Phoenix of a Qu—n' (*Novels*, i. 154). The mirror reflects everything in reverse, while the phoenix famously gives birth to itself in defiance of 'natural' law (Zarah takes on the political power of the Queen, but feels none of the regal obligations attendant on inheritance).

Sarah, Duchess of Marlborough appears in all Manley's texts as an abuser and invertor of those sacred powers invested in the woman. Thus, in the *Memoirs of Europe* she appears as an 'unnatural' mother, abusing her authority in relation to her son, Constantine [Anne] in order to accrue political power for herself. She is con-

---

[39] Anne's passionate attachments to her female friends are well documented. She herself adopted a male persona in her letters to Frances Apsley during the year 1679 when she was living in exile in Brussels with her father and stepmother. Anne wrote to Frances as the romance hero, Ziphares, pining for his 'faire Semandra' (see Edward Gregg, *Queen Anne* (London, 1980), 21).

[40] It is not absolutely certain that Manley was the author of Queen Zarah. See *Novels*, vol. i, pp. x–xi. Despite Köster's arguments that the novel does not conform to Manley's usual habits of punctuation and is for her unusually severe on Robert Harley, I am inclined to accept the attribution, if only because its exploration and use of gender inversion is so similar to that of her other known works.

trasted with Abigail Masham, the woman who superseded her in Anne's affections, in the shape of Constantine's second wife, Theodecta, who shows all the wifely virtues of duty and selflessness in relation to her 'husband'.

The Empress Irene [Sarah Churchill] is associated with the most notorious of unnatural mothers in classical history, the Empress Livia. Like Livia, she turns the supposedly 'natural' maternal habit of indulgence toward a child to her advantage:

She got an insensible ascendant over him, never speaking to his Reason, but his Pleasures, never giving him to consider he was one Day to reign for the Benefit of Mankind, but to indulge himself: 'Tis well he was not Cruel, Voluptuous, or positively Evil . . . ; the Encouragement all his Desires met with by this artful Mother, wou'd have made him another *Nero*, and caus'd *Constantinople* to blaze with Fires, as obscene, as those that destroy'd *Rome*. (*Novels*, ii. 182)

Anne is represented as an emasculated man tied to his mother's apron strings, and unable to assert his autonomy without the influence of a 'good' woman, Theodecta.

Theodecta is, however, not without her own brand of cunning. She had, we are told, 'a latent Ambition, Greatness of Soul, Humanity, Ingenuity, Religion and other conceal'd Vertues, that she had made no noise of, for fear of allarming *Irene*' (ii. 211). She sets up secret meetings between the Emperor and Herminius [Robert Harley], the leader of the orthodox [Tory] opposition to Irene's Roman [Whig] party. Irene/Sarah's 'masculinity' is, then, a more complex instance of gender inversion than it might at first appear. Masculinity, it seems, is marked by a compulsion to exploit traditional feminine virtues (sincerity, tenderness, fidelity, gullibility) for the purposes of self-interest. Proper femininity, in contrast, though it can be equally manipulative as Theodecta's protective caution implies, is directed toward enhancing and developing virtue for its own sake.

Female cross-dressing is less unambiguously criticized in Manley's fiction than an identification with the masculine quality of 'interest' on the part of women. Like Madeleine de Scudéry, Manley frequently idealizes female friendship as an alternative model of sentimental affection to the abusive power struggles of heterosexual romance. Cross-dressing and role reversal are not infrequent entertainments in Manley's depictions of female friendship, most memorably in her presentation of the 'Cabal' in her *New Atalantis*.

The Cabal consists of a number of women artists and aristocrats who reject heterosexual love and familial structures. It is significant that a number of the Cabal members are artists and writers, and it is these women who are most given to cross-dressing. If, as Manley's sexual oppositions suggest, the power of fiction lies with men, then it is perhaps appropriate that the woman artist should be addicted to male disguise, thus figuring her own interest in the power of representation. Manley makes it perfectly clear that it is precisely this power of representation, rather than the men themselves, that the women of the Cabal desire, when Intelligence comments that: 'They do not in reality love *Men*; but doat of the Representation of *Men* in *Women*. Hence it is that those Ladies are so fond of the Dress *En Cavaliere*' (*Novels*, i. 738). The adoption of male disguise is thus excused and the fact that the women of the Cabal love women *as women* is reinforced, on the grounds that the wearing of male disguise is not an endeavour to pass as men, but an indulgence of the pleasure of artifice and fictionality traditionally denied to women in heterosexual economies.

In many ways the Cabal embodies the exact reverse of the strategies employed by Manley's female politicians and rakes. The women of the Cabal reject those notions of value they identify with masculinity in favour of a set of values traditionally associated with femininity. In particular, they reject the masculine pursuit of 'interest'. The loving friendships established within the Cabal are a denial of the principle of property, and thus female commodification at the hands of men: 'In this little *Commonwealth* is no *Property*; whatever a *Lady* possesses, is, *sans ceremone*, at the service, and for the use of her *Fair Friend*, without the vain nice scruple of being oblig'd. 'Tis her *Right*; the other disputes it not; no, not so much as in *Thought*, they have no reserve; mutual *Love* bestows all things in *common*' (i. 589).

The Cabal is, however, relentless in its expulsion of all taint of the masculine. There is no mercy toward those who slip from the community's strictures in relation to men: 'they momently exclude the *Men*, fortify themselves in the Precepts of *Virtue* and *Chastity* against all their detestable undermining Arts, arraign without Pity or Compassion those who have been so unfortunate as to fall into their Snare' (i. 578–9). Janet Todd has argued that Manley's representation of this separatist Cabal is 'less satiric than utopian'.[41] Manley, in

---

[41] Janet Todd, *Women's Friendship in Literature* (New York, 1980), 342.

fact, as the quotation above suggests, seems to be caught between these two poles, an ambiguity which is registered peculiarly strongly in Intelligence's confusion over the Cabal's sexual practices. Manley has some specific satirical targets among her Cabal women, in particular Lucy Wharton, wife of the Whig minister Thomas Wharton, and Catherine Trotter Cockburn, a fellow writer. At certain points in her description of the Càbal she appears simply to be employing the popular satiric convention of the Amazonian all-female community in order to attack individual contemporary women for sexual crimes or political ambition.

The figure of the learned lady is, as Felicity Nussbaum has argued in her *The Brink of All We Hate*, a central focus for male fear of women's independence in such satiric representations.[42] Manley is clearly drawing, to some extent, on a long tradition of anti-feminist satire concentrating on the women's community as a threat to male dominance, in which the Amazon separatist is viewed as an embittered and vengeful woman rejected or slighted by the men she secretly desires. Within this tradition the female community invariably collapses because of its members' secret desires for men. A number of Manley's Cabalists indulge secret liaisons with male lovers. However, Manley presents these women's illicit desires as momentary lapses within a utopian framework that is, generally, endorsed.

The slur of lesbianism that haunts Intelligence's attempts to describe the Cabal is also dismissed as an aberrant perversion of the community's 'higher' objective of platonic, yet passionate, friendship between women. Intelligence is overtaken with an uncharacteristic prudishness when she exclaims:

Two beautiful Ladies join'd in an Excess of *Amity* (no word is tender enough to express their new Delight) innocently embrace! for how can they be guilty? They vow eternal *Tenderness*, they exclude the Men, and condition that they will always do. What irregularity can there be in this? 'Tis true, some things may be strain'd a little too far, and that causes Reflections to be cast upon the Rest. (i. 576)

If Manley stopped short of representing her women of the Cabal as endorsing lesbian sexual pleasures, she had no hesitation in valorizing their separatist ideology, that is, their resistance to a masculine social and sexual order of exchange and appropriation.

[42] Felicity Nussbaum, *The Brink of All We Hate: English Satires on Women 1660–1740* (Lexington, Ky., 1984), 43.

It was clearly not prudery or incomprehension of lesbian sexual encounters that made Manley shy away from representing them as part of the Cabal's social economy. One of the male narrators in the *Memoirs of Europe*, the Count de St Gironne, takes up the now familiar position of voyeur in describing a series of erotic scenes he observes in the private apartments of Julius Sergius.[43] They include an encounter between that aberrant Cabal member, Ariadne [Lucy Wharton], her male lover Bacchus [Sir Richard Temple, Viscount Cobham], the singer Philomela [the opera singer, Catherine Tofts], and Ariadne's maid, who tactfully dims the light at the apposite moment. Ariadne uses the female singer as an erotic object of exchange between herself and her lover: 'she drew her to her, and kiss'd her Lips, with Eyes swimming in Delight and a peculiar Satisfaction: Let me Die, my lovely Girl, said she, if thou hast not all the Deliciousness and Flavour in thy Breath that one can imagine. My dear *Bacchus*, try the Pleasure of her moist Kisses' (*Novels*, ii. 300). Here, then, the lesbian beloved is property to be exchanged between the heterosexual couple as evidence of their mutual desire. The specific challenge the Cabal offers to the masculine order lies in their rejection of this form of appropriation. Ariadne here adopts a masculine subject position, not so much because of her desire for a woman, but because of her willingness to employ the 'other' as a commodity for appropriation and exchange, in which the woman functions solely as the signifier of male homosocial desire.[44]

In her essay, 'The Laugh of the Medusa', the twentieth-century theorist Hélène Cixous outlines just such a utopian model of a feminine economy as Manley's Cabal glimpses:

Elsewhere, she gives. She doesn't 'know' what she's giving, she doesn't measure it; she gives, though, neither a counterfeit impression nor something she hasn't got. She gives more, with no assurance that she'll get back even some unexpected profit from what she puts out. She gives that there may be life, thought, transformation. This is an 'economy' that can no longer be put

---

[43] Gironne appears to be an entirely fictional creation. Julius Sergius is Charles Montagu, Earl of Halifax (1661–1715), a prominent Whig and Chancellor of the Exchequer from 1692–9. He was accused in 1702–3 of malpractice in his Exchequer years by the Commissioners of Public Accounts but finally voted guilty only of a breach of trust. See Geoffrey Holmes and W. A. Speck (eds.), *The Divided Society: Party Conflict in England 1696–1716*, (London, 1967), 139, 237.

[44] For an analysis of this form of homosocial exchange of the figure of the woman in English literature, see Eve Kosofsky Sedgwick, *Between Men: English Literature and Male Homosocial Desire* (New York, 1985).

in economic terms. Wherever she loves, all the old concepts of management are left behind. At the end of a more or less conscious computation, she finds not her sum but her differences.[45]

Manley's Cabal does provide one of the most remarkable early attempts at figuring an alternative female community, an attempt that was to take on renewed life later in the century with the publication of Sarah Scott's *Millenium Hall* (1762).[46]

However, the satirical structure of Manley's text to some extent undermines the utopian aspects of her representation of the Cabal. Finally, Astrea, always the arbiter and provider of the moral 'frame' within which to read the action of the *New Atalantis*, condemns and silences the community. As I have already noted, Astrea herself ambiguously partakes in the masculine economy, voyeuristically observing female suffering and turning all the amatory plots conveyed to her to her own 'interest', the education of her young male charge. Her judgement upon the Cabal is one of censure that validates the authority of male property relations by arguing that the women are abandoning their proper 'wifely' duties:

> If only *tender Friendship*, inviolable and sincere, be the regard, what can be more meritorious, or a truer Emblem of their Happiness above? ... But if they carry it a length beyond what *Nature* design'd and *fortifie* themselves by these new-form'd *Amities* against the *Hymenial Union*, or give their Husbands but a second place in their *Affections* and *Cares*; 'tis wrong and to be *blam'd*. (i. 589–90)

Astrea recuperates the radical otherness of the Cabal by restoring hierarchy. Friendship between women is only praiseworthy if it reinforces, rather than undermines, the property relation of marriage.

'Framing' the Woman

The importance of Astrea's framing judgements to the sexual and political ideology of the *New Atalantis* leads us to the role of the narrative frame in Manley's fiction in general. As I have noted, Manley sets femininity and masculinity at odds, privileging the

---

[45] Hélène Cixous, 'The Laugh of the Medusa', in *New French Feminisms: An Anthology*, trans. and ed. Elaine Marks and Isabelle de Courtivron (Brighton, 1981), 261.

[46] See Sarah Scott, *A Description of Millenium Hall and the Country Adjacent* (1762; London, 1986).

former over the latter in a move that has become conventional in twentieth-century romantic fiction. Manley's gendering of subject positions on the level of plot extends to her presentation of story-tellers and audience. In imitation of the French romance, Manley presents her stories as a series of narratives, rendered and tailored to the reading interests of a group of auditors. The differentiation of texts by sex is perhaps most sharply illustrated in contrasting the two volumes of the *Memoirs of Europe.*

The dedication to Volume 1 is addressed by Manley to her erstwhile friend and now political opponent, Richard Steele, whom she attacks through his well-known *Tatler* persona, Isaac Bicker-staff.[47] Referring to the satirical representation of herself as Epicene in the *Tatler*, Manley upbraids Bickerstaff for bothering to expend his energy on a 'weak unlearned Woman's Writings!' (*Novels*, ii. n.p.) Bickerstaff is emasculated, she suggests, by considering a woman a worthy opponent in the heroic conflicts of contemporary satirical prose: 'Heavens! how valuable am I? How fond of that *Immortality*, even of *Infamy*, that you have promised! I am ravish'd at the thoughts of *living a thousand Years hence* in your indelible Lines, tho' to *give Offence*. He that burnt the Temple of *Diana* was Ambitious after much such a sort of Fame, as what your Worship seems to have in store for me' (*Novels*, ii. n.p.)

In contrast, the second volume of the *Memoirs of Europe* is dedicated to Louisa, Duchess of Savoy [Abigail Masham], rejecting irony for panegyric in an address which identifies the Duchess with Manley's own heroines: 'Your *undeserv'd Sufferings! Innocence persecuted!* makes you dearer to our Hearts!' (ii. 381). Manley apologizes to the Duchess 'If some part of it be thought too *light*' and asks her to 'be pleas'd to consider it as *Shades* and *Colours* in Painting, the *Deformity* of *Vice* expos'd, to heighten the *Beauty* and *Shine* of *Vertue!*' (ii. 382). The 'lightness' referred to here is presumably the bawdy content which might be considered improper for a lady to hear, but it is conventionally excused as necessary in order to expose vice in its true horrors.

The gender differences that are clear in the dedications to the two

---

[47] On Manley's troubled relations, personal and political, with Steele, see Fidelis Morgan, *A Woman of No Character*, 106–20 and Duff, 'Materials toward a Biography', 111–59. He is satirized in her novels as Monsieur L'Ingrat in the *New Atalantis* (*Novels*, i. 459–65) and as Stelico, chief propagandist for Irene and her Junto, in *Memoirs of Europe* (*Novels*, ii. 236–8).

volumes are replayed in the texts themselves. Both take the form of a series of scandalous narratives delivered by a number of different narrators to an assembled company. Within each company a single auditor is privileged as the addressee of the tales. In the first volume, Horatio [Lord Peterborough] is the main addressee in an exclusively male company and the stories are tailored toward his interest in learning the state of contemporary politics in Constantinople [Britain] since his self-imposed exile to mourn the death of his wife. In the second volume, Horatio and his companions visit the beautiful Ethelinda [Maria Köngismark] and the stories are addressed to her as a means of entertainment designed to divert her thoughts from her onetime lover, Prince Theoderick [Charles XII of Sweden]. In the preface to this second volume, the translator (Manley) comments that, 'The Entertainment being to a Lady, there's not so much of the Politick, as in the first Part, more of the Gay' (ii. 383–4). Volume 2, in contrast with Volume 1, does indeed privilege the short seduction story over the long-winded political history but both retain Manley's habitual explanation of all historical events by amatory causes.

Even in Volume 1, the 'author', Eginardus, finds it necessary to point out that, although it was first delivered to an entirely male audience, he has 'edited' the narrative so that it will appeal to those women who will read the written version. Commenting that the main focus of the story is war, he adds: 'But to take in and compleat our Circle with the lovely Sex, to attempt their Heart, Eyes and Attention by something *less* dreadful, tho' not less fatal than the native Horrors of the Warriour God [Mars]; we shall not forbear to introduce the *Queen* of *Love*, her *bitter Sweets*, her *Hours* of *Pain* and *Joy*' (ii. 2–3). In order to 'take in' his women readers, the author is obliged to present amorous intrigues along with martial conflicts. The second volume, with its almost exclusive address to women, makes no such effort to incorporate the male reader. As in the French romance, then, women readers are necessary to 'compleat' the world of culture. Manley's fiction employs a diverse range of narrative frames, all, however, directed toward the affective goal of stimulating a posited reader's erotic interest under the guise of moral outrage. Her narrators and auditors are always 'interested' in the fullest sense of the term, that is, stimulated by a moral, sexual, or political investment in the scandalous text they seek to re-present or interpret.

The *New Atalantis* appears to be the most thoroughly femino-centric of her novels, almost exclusively narrated to women by women and about women. Astrea herself never tells stories, remaining an auditor throughout. She thus remains a muse to the fictions that are mediated and controlled by the more mundane figure of the 'gossip', in the shape of the allegorical Intelligence or the midwife Mrs Nightwatch. Intelligence, we are told, 'bustles up and down, and has a World of Business upon her hands; she is first lady of the *Bedchamber* to the *Princess Fame*, her Garments are all *Hieroglyphicks*' (i. 290). Intelligence's stories are indeed hieroglyphics, from which the reader, to some extent represented by Astrea, must distill the 'real' meaning or moral import. Intelligence is by no means a discriminating story-teller, admitting, 'I take *Truth* with me when I can get her. Sometimes indeed she's so hard to recover, that Fame grows impatient, and will not suffer me to wait for her slow *Approach*' (i. 593).

Interpretation, or judgement, then, is the reader's, not the narrator's, business. Manley neatly gives her ideologically over-determined and politically partisan text an appearance of democracy. As she argues in the preface to *Queen Zarah*, the role of the writer of 'histories' is to satisfy the reader's 'impatient Desire to see the End of the Accidents, the reading of which causes an Exquisite Pleasure when they are Nicely handled', since 'Moral Reflexions, Maxims and Sentences, are more proper in Discourses for Instructions than in Historical Novels, whose chief End is to please' (Ioaon Williams (ed.), *Novel and Romance* 36, 38).

Zara's comments to Mosco in the *New Atalantis* echo this sentiment of the necessity of 'satisfying' the impatient reader in an explicitly sexual context. Mosco's refusal to fulfil his promise to co-habit with her (to complete their own amatory plot) has, she tells him, driven her to distraction: 'you have screwd me by your delays, up to the very height; you must now stop, or I break and fall to pieces' (*Novels*, i. 506–7). Zara brings her own end to the story by committing suicide. The narrator's intention in delivering a fiction is to prevent any such wilful disengagement from the seduction narrative on the part of the 'reader'. Thus, Intelligence frequently interrupts Astrea's and Virtue's moral musings to turn her reader's attention elsewhere. At the beginning of the second part of the *New Atalantis*, she brusquely interrupts a meditation on the malign effects of love, with the words, 'Whilst your *Eminences* are declaiming a Length beyond my Understanding, give me leave to get what Information I can of that new Adventure before us' (i. 539).

It is at this point that Manley introduces a second narrator in the shape of the talkative midwife Mrs Nightwatch, a true 'gossip' in contrast with Intelligence in that she is a confidante as well as a spreader of idle tittle-tattle.[48] Intelligence criticises Mrs Nightwatch for repeating stories told in confidence but the midwife insists that the dissemination of scandal is part of her job: 'without this indirect *Liberty*, we should be but ill Company to most of our Ladies, who love to be amused with the failings of others, and would not always give us so favourable and warm a Reception, if we had nothing of Scandal to entertain them with' (i. 545). Scandal is now firmly associated with an exclusively female sphere. It is part of the world of reproduction; scandal breeds scandal.

The *Memoirs of Europe* to some extent departs from the femino-centric exclusivity of the *New Atalantis*. Its opening, in which Horatio [Lord Peterborough] encounters two allegorical female figures, Solitude and Sincerity, seems to imply a similar narrative frame to that of its predecessor, but Manley swiftly abandons the use of an embodied moral perspective in the shape of an allegorical or mythic commentator. The stories within the *Memoirs of Europe* are all narrated by human characters, often ironically presented, without the presence of an over-arching moral perspective (such as Astrea) to enable the reader to judge the truth or interpret the meaning of the tale.

The main bulk of the scandal narration in the first volume of the *Memoirs of Europe* is delivered by the French adventurer and raconteur the Count de St Gironne, one of Manley's few entirely fictional characters. Gironne is a confessed specularizer, voyeur, and gatherer of unconsidered trifles of contemporary gossip. He is also a traveller, like Marie d'Aulnoy, whose lack of investment in the factions in Constantinople [England] validates the 'objectivity' of his tale-telling. 'I have no personal Quarrel to those I have been speaking of', he asserts, 'they have done me no particular Injury, it is only because they are great and glaring Enemies to Vertue that I am an Enemy to them' (ii. 253). However, although he is cleared of party political prejudice, Gironne's sexual politics are swiftly

---

[48] See 'Gossip', *Shorter Oxford English Dictionary on Historical Principles*, 3rd edn. (Oxford, 1973). The word derives from an old Norse term for a godfather or godmother, and can mean a familiar acquaintance as well as a tattler.

revealed to be virulently misogynistic. In telling the story of the innocent Isabella's [Elizabeth Somers] seduction by Alarick [Phillip Königsmark], Gironne suddenly embarks on a lengthy misogynistic rant, rehearsing traditional anti-feminist arguments about woman's role in introducing man to sin: 'they have set us the Pattern, but Man has prov'd so excellent an Imitator as to refine upon the Invention, and now we may pretend even to out-do 'em at their own Weapon: They may thank themselves for giving us a Sample of their Artifice' (ii. 143). Gironne's attack on Isabella is, it is clear, quite unjustified, and from this point onwards he remains an unstable and ironized commentator on the narratives he renders.

In the figure of Gironne, Manley explores a new variation on her presentation of woman as victim. Gironne is an old-fashioned rake, who is enraged by the fact that in Constantinople, 'Gallantry is no longer the Theme, the greatest Beauties seem to forget that they have Charms . . . ; all are buried in Politicks and Strugglings which Opinions shall prevail' (ii. 133). The masculine attempt to impose amatory conventions on women whose interest lies in politics was to become the central theme of Manley's subsequent work, *The Adventures of Rivella* (1714). *Rivella*, too, has a male narrator, one Sir Charles Lovemore.[49] The story of Rivella, as the names of its narrator and auditor (the Chevalier d'Aumont) suggest, is indeed the story of the attempt on the part of male arbiters to stamp the mark of 'more love' on the too manl(e)y writing of a woman.

Lovemore struggles throughout the novel to contain Rivella within the private sphere he considers proper to the woman. Listing her charms to d'Aumont, he comments that they are better revealed in private conversation than in public audience: 'Few who have only beheld her in Publick, could be brought to like her; whereas none that became acquainted with her, could refrain from loving her' (ii. 744). He describes her as particularly gifted at letter writing: 'there was something surprizing in her Letters, so natural, so spiritous, so sprightly, so well turned, that from the first to the last, I must and ever will maintain, that all her other Productions however successful they have been, came short of her Talent in writing Letters' (ii. 753). As I argued in Chapter 2, the letter form was seen as peculiarly

---

[49] Edmund Curll's key to *Rivella* identifies Lovemore as General John Tidcomb (1642–1713), but this attribution makes Lovemore far too old to be the supposed callow youth who first flirts with the 12-year-old Rivella in 1685. See Köster's introduction to *Novels*, vol. i, p. xxi.

appropriate to the woman writer, and here Lovemore reveals his desire to see Rivella remain within the bounds of proper feminine behaviour, eschewing political satire for the love letter.

Elsewhere in her fiction Manley satirizes the truism that women are natural letter writers by virtue of their artlessness as an example of masculine prejudice. Letter twenty-four in the collection *Court Intrigues* (1711) details a young man's infatuation with a mysterious lady he meets on a country ramble, one Mrs S—. She successfully engineers the encounter so that her visitor cannot find the house in which she lives in retirement with her lover, Mr King, until after they have moved. The lovelorn narrator's only consolation is the discovery of a hidden collection of love-letters between the couple in the garden. Mr King's letters, he comments disparagingly, show 'a poorness of Stile, a meanness of Expression, a studied Passion . . . ; whilst hers were full of luxuriant Nature, rich in Love and Beauty' (109). Her facility with deceit in preventing his further pursuit of her is forgotten in the narrator's eulogies about the unstudied artlessness of her letter-writing technique. The male lover only 'reads' in the woman what he wants to see, the woman's vulnerability to sexual desire and the concomitant possibility of amatory pleasure with her.

Lovemore and d'Aumont couch all their praise of Rivella in similar terms. Her womanly knowledge of the power of love mitigates her unhealthy political interests. Rivella, however, stubbornly resists all attempts on the part of Lovemore to direct her to a life of virtue and a career in the literature of love alone. Following the success of her first tragedy, she embarks on a life of hedonism and political prose, while Lovemore comments self-righteously that 'she still went on in her own Way, without any Regard to [his] Doctrine, till Experience gave her enough of her Indiscretion' (ii. 781). His doctrine finally prevails when Rivella is imprisoned for the publication of a 'party' novel. He triumphantly declares that he 'brought her to be asham'd of her Writings' (852) and persuaded her to 'entertain her Readers with more gentle pleasing Theams' (853). There is, of course, a significant inaccuracy here in that after her imprisonment, Manley, unlike her auto-biographical persona, went on to publish an equally partisan political novel, her *Memoirs of Europe*, and showed no sign at this stage of submitting to the 'more gentle and pleasing Theams' Lovemore considers more fitting to the woman writer. This 'autobiography' thus finishes with the ostensible triumph of the man in his attempt to impose a particular form, amatory fiction, upon the female writer, but its historical inaccuracy suggests an alternative reading of the amatory plot in *Rivella*.

Appropriately, Lovemore finishes his narrative by offering his young listener a vision of the prospect of a physical as opposed to textual encounter with the author herself. Lovemore imagines, on behalf of d'Aumont, a fictional rendezvous at Rivella's house:

I should have brought you to her Table well furnish'd and well serv'd; . . . From thence carried you (in the Heat of Summer after Dinner) within the Nymphs Alcove, to a Bed nicely sheeted and strow'd with *Roses*, *Jessamins* or *Orange-Flowers*, suited to the variety of the Season; her Pillows neatly trim'd with Lace or Muslin, stuck round with *Jonquils*, or other natural Garden Sweets, for she uses no Perfumes, and there have given you leave to fancy your self the happy Man, with whom she chose to repose her self, during the Heat of the Day, in a State of Sweetness and Tranquility: From thence conducted you towards the cool of the Evening, either upon the *Water*, or to the *Park* for Air, with a Conversation always new, and which never cloys. . . . (ii. 855–6)

The descriptive prose of this passage echoes that employed to represent the young Germanicus awaiting his Duchess in the first story rendered in Manley's *New Atalantis*:

the Weather violently hot, the *Umbrelloes* were let down from behind the Windows, the Sashes open, and the Jessamines that covered 'em blew in with a gentle Fragrancy; *Tuberoses* set in pretty *Gilt* and *China Posts*, were placed advantageously upon Stands, the Curtains of the Bed drawn back to the *Canopy*, made of yellow Velvet embroider'd with white *Bugles*, the Panels of the Chamber Looking-Glass, upon the Bed were strow'd with a lavish Profuseness, plenty of *Orange* and *Lemon Flowers*, and to compleat the Scene, the young *Germanicus* in a dress and posture not very decent to describe. (*Novels*, i. 305)

As with this 'framing' depiction of Germanicus (a young man mimicking the posture of the distressed virgin female for the gaze of a lustful woman who mistakes him for her male lover, Fortunatus), what is being described is precisely a trick or *trompe-l'œil*. The woman is, in fact, nowhere to be seen in this scene—only her table, pillows, flowers, and bed. Lennard Davis describes the closing passage of *Rivella* as a 'colossal autoerotic reverie the likes of which had probably never occurred so directly between author and reader in the history of narrative up to this point';[50] yet surely the auto-eroticism must be attributed to the fictional 'author', Lovemore, rather than Manley herself. What is striking about this scene is precisely its indirectness.

In this passage, then, 'proper' femininity is disclosed to be nothing more than a patriarchal fiction within which the woman herself is absent. What Lovemore pimps to his male reader is his own fantasy of the absent author. However, the absent author is in reality *his* author. It is, after all, Lovemore who is the fictional creation. Manley's consummate irony is evident here. While the man appears to have 'authored' the perfect female object she is, in reality, elsewhere 'authoring' him.

The history of *Rivella*'s commissioning bears out my suggested reading of the novel.[51] Early in 1714, Manley received word that Charles Gildon had started work on a scandalous biography of her life entitled *The Adventures of Rivella*, and that two sheets had already been printed. The publisher, Edmund Curll, set up a meeting between Gildon, himself, Manley, and her sister Cornelia, at which Manley agreed to produce her own manuscript.[52] In March of the same year Curll received the work with instructions to publish it anonymously. In the light of these facts it seems more than fortuitous that Manley should have framed her text as a dialogue between two men seeking the answer to one solitary question, 'Do Her Eyes love as well as Her Pen?' (ii. 744). *Rivella*, I would argue, is a brisk riposte to masculine appropriations of the female 'form', physical and textual. Its erotic withholding of authorial identity mimics the strategies of Aphra Behn, herself a victim of Gildon's biographizing ambitions.

The text of *Rivella* contrasts strongly with Manley's other sally into autobiography, the story of Delia rendered in the *New Atalantis* (*Novels*, i. 712–26) and narrated by Delia herself. Lovemore, absent for that part of Rivella's life which involved her bigamous marriage, reinforces the fictional status of his own narrative when he is obliged to refer d'Aumont 'to her own Story, under the name of *Delia*, in the

---

[50] Lennard Davis, *Factual Fictions*, 119.

[51] This history is given by Edmund Curll in his address 'To the Reader', accompanying the 4th edn. of *Rivella* under a different title. See *Mrs. Manley's History of her Own Life and Times*, 4th edn. (London, 1725), p. vi.

[52] Gildon and Curll were both notorious: Gildon was a hack writer of scandalous biographies and Curll a publisher of pornography. See Ralph Straus, *The Unspeakable Curll, being Some Account of Edmund Curll Bookseller* (London, 1927).

Atalantis' (ii. 765). The story of Delia is an unabashed attempt at whitewashing Manley's complicity in her bigamous marriage. Told by Delia to a priest and overheard by Astrea, Virtue, and Intelligence, it presents Manley as the exemplary suffering virgin *par excellence*. Delia excuses her sin of continuing to live with her husband for three years after he had disclosed the fact of an earlier marriage, on the grounds that she was 'young, unacquainted with the World, had never seen the Necessities of it, knew no Arts, had not been expos'd to any Hardships' (i. 721). This is a far cry from the persona of Rivella, whose very knowingness in the arts of love is what makes her so attractive to the young male auditor of her story, d'Aumont. Jane Spencer, in her analysis of the differences between these two autobiographical studies, concludes that: 'Manley's fiction can be seen as a meeting-ground for two conceptions of womanhood: one of the passionate, sexual being as often depicted in Restoration drama, the other of the innocent, passionless, easily deceived creature gaining ascendancy in the early eighteenth century' (58). I would argue, however, that if careful attention is paid to its sophisticated use of the narrative frame, Manley's fiction can be interpreted as a challenge to, rather than a reproduction of, this dichotomy. Manley was no doubt obliged to admit her sexual indiscretions if she was to provide a satisfactory alternative to Gildon's Rivella, but she succeeded in making a virtue out of a necessity. *Rivella* and the story of Delia read side by side constitute a resistance to the madonna/whore opposition imposed on women by masculinist ideologies, subverting them by exposing their status as 'fictions' and insisting on the prerogative of the woman to write her own fictions of the female self.

Manley's fiction stands perpetually on the borders of what are perceived as discrete discursive territories. The political and the personal, the erotic and the pathetic, the real and the fictive, scandal and satire, all undergo a series of inversions and re-articulations until their supposed exclusivity is undermined. These 'invented' tales point to their resistance to the imposition of generic norms through the insistent dramatization of the imposition of form upon the body of the woman. The virgin reader is seduced by the experienced rake's deployment of amatory fictions, the male libertine reader can only interpret the female satirist's text as biography or romance. Invariably, Manley's response is to argue for a resistance to such impositions through the practice of writing itself. Here, the satiric 'mask' gains a special significance for the woman writer. Like the women of her Cabal, Manley covets the masculine purchase on representation, rather than masculinity itself. She does not 'in reality love *Men*, but doat[s] of the Representation of *Men* in *Women*' (*Novels*, i. 738). 'Manleyness' proves to be the power of fiction itself.

5

'Preparatives to Love': Fiction as Seduction in Eliza Haywood's Amatory Prose

Love Triumphant: The Decline in Scandal Fiction

Eliza Haywood's rise to fame as an amatory novelist coincided almost exactly with Manley's final sally into the field of fiction. Manley's last work of fiction, *The Power of Love in Seven Novels*, appeared in 1720, the same year in which Haywood published the concluding part to her first novel, *Love in Excess* (1719–20).[1] *Love in Excess* was an immediate success, running into four editions before it was collected with her other novels to date in *The Works of Mrs. Eliza Haywood* in 1724 and the following year in her *Secret Histories, Novels and Poems*.[2] Only the now better-known novels, *Gulliver's Travels* (1726) and *Robinson Crusoe* (1719), rivalled it as the most popular work of fiction in Britain before the publication of Richardson's *Pamela* in 1740.[3]

As their titles suggest, both Manley's *The Power of Love* and Haywood's *Love in Excess* mark a shift in the nature of amatory fiction by women. *The Power of Love* abandoned the complexity of the rediscovered, translated, and reconstructed source commonly employed as a means of simultaneously concealing and signifying political intent in Manley's fiction. The 'fiction' of translation is maintained but Manley simply declares in her dedication to Lady Lansdowne: 'These Novels, Madam, have Truth for their Foundation; several of the Facts are to be found in Ancient History: To which,

---

[1] *Love in Excess, or, The Fatal Enquiry* (London, 1720). The *Daily Post* for 26 February 1720 carried an advertisement for the third part of *Love in Excess*. There is no record of an advertisement for the first, and the second part appeared with no date, but we may presume they were published in 1719.

[2] *The Works of Mrs. Eliza Haywood, Consisting of Novels, Letters, Poems, and Plays* (4 vols.; London, 1724), i; *Secret Histories, Novels and Poems. In Four Volumes*, i (London, 1725). All references to Haywood's works, unless otherwise noted, are to those novels collected in *Secret Histories, Novels and Poems*, 2nd edn. (vols. i and ii; London, 1725) and 3rd edn. (vols. iii and iv; London, 1732), cited as *SH*, with title, original date of publication, volume (4 numbered separately) and page numbers, and included in the main body of the text.

[3] See W. H. McBurney, 'Mrs. Penelope Aubin and the Early Eighteenth-Century Novel', *Huntington Library Quarterly*, 20 (1957), 250.

adding divers new Incidents, I have attempted in Modern *English*, to draw them out of Obscurity.'[4] The simple truth claim signals a less sophisticated interplay between fact and fiction in this work, and, indeed, the novel is not a work of scandal, but rather a reworking of a number of medieval and Renaissance Italian and French tales found in William Painter's *The Palace of Pleasure* (1566).[5]

This, then, is that work on 'more gentle pleasing Theams' promised by Lovemore in Manley's *Rivella*. The allegorical duplicity of scandal fiction, its complex double movement between the amatory and party political plot, is superseded by the more direct aim of representing the eternal power of the disruptive force of desire, specifically female desire. The opening pages of the first novel, entitled *The Fair Hypocrite*, set the stage:

> Of all those Passions which may be said to tyrannize over the Heart of Man, Love is not only the most violent, but the most persuasive.... When Love truly seizes the Heart, it is like a malignant Fever which thence disperses itself through all the sensible Parts; the Poyson preys upon the Vitals, and is only extinguished by Death; or, by as fatal a Cure, the accomplishment of its own Desires. (1)

All seven stories are solely concerned with the deleterious effects of love upon the human subject. As in the French *nouvelle* or *petite histoire*, love brings only destruction and disaster upon its victims. The 'secret history' is now one of sexual intrigue, divested of its specific allegorical correlatives in the world of party politics. From 1720 onwards women's amatory fiction turned away from employing sexual desire as a substituting metaphor for political interest. Sexual desire, in these 'new' novels of the 1720s is too protean and absolute a quality to be the vehicle for any other form of 'interest'. A characteristic authorial interjection in Haywood's *The Agreeable Caledonian* (1728) echoes Manley's sentiments, complaining that:

> 'tis Destiny alone rules Love; Reason, Religion, and even the Will is sub-servient to that all-powerful Passion which forces us sometimes to Actions our Natures most detest; Mother against Daughter, Father against Son,

---

[4] Delarivier Manley, *The Power of Love: In Seven Novels* (London, 1720), p. xv.

[5] Of the seven novels, only one, *The Physician's Strategy*, appears to be wholly of Manley's making and may have its source in a contemporary scandal that has yet to be identified. Another, *The Perjur'd Beauty*, is loosely based on the St Gregory legend and the remaining five are all close adaptations of novels to be found in Painter. See William Painter, *The Palace of Pleasure: Elizabethan Versions of Italian and French Novels from Boccaccio, Bandello, Cinthio, Straparoal, Queen Margaret of Navarre and Others* (1566), ed. Joseph Jacobs, 2nd edn. (London, 1890).

contrives; all Obligations of Blood and Interest are no more remembered; over every Bound we leap, to gratify the wild Desire, and Conscience but vainly interposes its Remonstrances.[6]

Even when Haywood denominated a text a 'secret history', she made it clear that the discovery of the real identity of a character would not illuminate interpretation of the text. Thus, the preface to *The Fair Hebrew, or, A True, but Secret History of Two Jewish Ladies, Who Lately Resided in London* (1729), in which an upright young Englishman is seduced into marriage and then abandoned by a beautiful Jewess, Kesiah, employs the trope of the truth-claim only to support its critique of the dangers of succumbing to sexual passion. Do not imagine, Haywood argues, that such things only happen in fiction:

There are so many Things, meerly the effect of Invention, which have been published, of late, under the Title of SECRET HISTORIES, that, to distinguish this, I am obliged to inform my Reader, that I have not inserted one Incident which was not related to me by a Person nearly concerned in the Family of that unfortunate Gentleman, who had no other Consideration in the Choice of a *Wife*, than to gratify a present Passion for the Enjoyment of her Beauty. (Ioaon Williams (ed.), *Novel and Romance*, 85)

Here, then, Haywood resorts to the substantiating claims typical of Aphra Behn, rather than Delarivier Manley. This story, she insists, has been provided to her on good authority, and it leaves 'so much Room for the most useful and moral Reflections to be drawn from it' that she would 'be guilty of an Injury to the Publick in concealing it' (*Novel and Romance*, 85).

There were pragmatic political and ideological reasons for a return to romance proper in the 1720s. Following the death of Anne in 1714, the Hanoverian succession, and the failure of the 1715 Jacobite rebellion, the Whig ministry (reconstructed from the Junto Manley had attacked in her *Memoirs of Europe*) went from strength to strength. As W. A. Speck has argued, after 1714 the Tories 'no longer had the strength to be effective rivals for power', and the traditional power struggle between Tories and Whigs was displaced into the more unstable conflict between Court and Country, the former made up of a strong Whig majority at the centre of power, and the latter of Country Whigs and the remnants of the old Tory

---

[6] Eliza Haywood, *The Agreeable Caledonian, or, Memoirs of Signora di Morella, a Roman Lady, Who Made her Escape from a Monastery at Viterbo, for the Love of a Scots Nobleman*, pt. 1 (London, 1728), 84–5. The second part was published in 1729.

party supporters.[7] It was not until 1726 that an effective parliamentary opposition emerged to the ministry of Robert Walpole, in the shape of an alliance between Bolingbroke and William Pulteney, one-time confederate of the prime minister. The literary-political opposition offered by such Scriblerians as Pope, Gay, Swift, and Arbuthnot was by no means an organized campaign.[8] Indeed, both Swift and Defoe, noted for their political journalism in the last four years of Anne's reign, turned to fiction as their major medium in the 1720s.

It is significant that, unlike Manley, Haywood did not indulge in any form of political journalism. She produced three novels that owe clear debts to the scandal fiction of Manley, even echoing the latter's famous title of the *New Atalantis*, but the seduction/betrayal motif was now exploited for the purposes of a more general moralism and Haywood betrays no interest in direct political intervention or allegiance to other opposition figures or forces.[9] Haywood's targets in the two scandal novels of the 1720s are not leading politicians but court figures and private individuals. These novels show none of the 'insider's' knowledge that made Manley's work so threatening to the Whig politicians who brought her to trial and the stories are presented as moral exempla. The over-arching structure of a Tory ideology remains in place, but the mercenary self-interest Manley had identified as the defining characteristic of the male Whig politician is now identified with court culture in general and contrasted with the pleasures of country retirement. Cupid, in the *Memoirs of a Certain Island*, has settled into rural retirement in disgust at the profligacy and sexual perversion that reigns in the city, and is only persuaded to emerge from his retreat in order to acquaint the traveller with the horrors of court life.

It was not until 1736 that Haywood produced the sort of specific politically motivated scandal fiction that Manley had excelled in, with the publication of her *The Adventures of Eovaai*. This novel was a

[7] W. A. Speck, *Stability and Strife: England 1714–1760* (Cambridge, Mass., 1977), 7. See also V. H. H. Green, *The Hanoverians 1714–1815* (London, 1948), 128–9.

[8] See Bertrand A. Goldgar, *Walpole and the Wits. The Relation of Politics to Literature, 1722–42* (London and Lincoln, Nebr., 1976), 42.

[9] The novels were *Memoirs of a Certain Island Adjacent to the Kingdom of Utopia* (London, 1725); *The Secret History of the Present Intrigues of the Court of Caramania* (London, 1727), and *The Adventures of Eovaai* (London, 1736). *Bath Intrigues, in Four Letters to a Friend in London* (London, 1725), modelled on Manley's *Court Intrigues*, and *Letters from the Palace of Fame* (London, 1727), a pseudo-Oriental series of epistolary tales, have both been ascribed to Haywood also.

concerted and damning attack on Robert Walpole represented as the evil and lascivious Prime Minister of Hypotosa, Ochihatou, who, by his magic arts, blinds his king (George II) to the well-being of the nation, deprives the young prince (the Pretender, James Edward Stuart) of his birthright, and attempts to seduce the princess Eovaai in order to win a crown for himself. *The Adventures of Eovaai*, with its complex narrative frame (the text is supposedly a translation into English from a Chinese translation of a pre-adamitical language now defunct) and extreme particularity of satiric representation, demonstrates that Haywood was as expert as Manley in the strategies of the scandal chronicle. This novel, however, appeared after the Walpole administration had fallen into decline, and at a point where the opposition had succeeded in amassing considerable popular and literary support, particularly around the figure of Prince Frederick.[10]

The Adventures of Eovaai stands virtually alone in Eliza Haywood's extraordinarily numerous writings as an attempt to reproduce the political instrumentality of Manley's scandal fiction during the reign of Anne. However, it also demonstrates the extent to which the party political dichotomies so central to Manley's texts had been undermined. Haywood's only clear object of attack is the prime minister, and her scandal text endorses at different points both republican and divine-right monarchist sentiments as a means of unseating the overweening Walpole. Her Eovaai, exiled from her throne, engages in a long debate with an old man in Oozoff (the country of Impartiality) who acts as the advocate for republicanism. By the end of this discussion, we are told, that 'if she were not a Convert to all the Republican Principles, she at least thought some of them so highly reasonable, that she resolved, if she was ever happy enough to regain her Crown, she wou'd make them Part of the Constitution' (127). Like the opposition itself, conservative ideology in this period seems to have consisted of an uneasy piecemeal alliance of otherwise contradictory positions. Literary-political writing, then, had to seek other ways of representing ideological conflict than the simplified moral dichotomies of Whig and Tory that had proved so successful for scandal fiction in the age of Anne.

Haywood's greatest innovation in the field of amatory fiction was to revitalize the representation of a desiring conflict into social, rather than party political, myth. In contrast to both Behn and

[10] Goldgar, *Walpole and the Wits*, 134–7.

Manley, Haywood was unequivocal in her address to a female audience and her commitment to the discourse of love. Female desire is no longer a ruling metaphor in her fiction, but rather the subject and generating ground of its plot. The Walpole government's lack of interest in supporting and controlling party-motivated literature meant that all the 'Tory wits' of the 1720s were obliged to seek new means of encoding their political critique and maintaining their literary reputations. Haywood's response was virtually to corner the market in amatory representation, to establish herself as the 'Great Arbitress of Passion'.[11] This chapter will concentrate on Haywood's amatory novels of the 1720s, which, I would argue, mark the beginnings of an autonomous tradition in romantic fiction, primarily addressed to and authored by women.

The 'Great Arbitress of Passion': Romance Transfigurations

Haywood's name, from the 1720s onwards, was synonymous with the most extreme excesses of romance. Even when she turned to writing more respectable domestic fiction in the 1750s she published anonymously, since evidently the associations of her name would have been enough to discredit the enterprise.[12] Of all the amatory novelists I have so far considered, it is Haywood whose textual production was most consistently identified with sexual promiscuity. Her immense corpus of texts both fascinates and repels contemporary commentators, and the equation of text and body so repeatedly made with respect to women writers takes on a new and grotesque configuration in these representations.

The only twentieth-century biography of Haywood, George Frisbie Whicher's *The Life and Romances of Mrs. Eliza Haywood* (1915), echoes this equation in its very title.[13] It is not clear whether this 'biography' will lead us through Haywood's sexual adventures (romances) or her books (romances). Indeed, in the absence of much

---

[11] See James Sterling, 'To Mrs. Eliza Haywood on her Writings', prefixed to *SH* vol. i, sig. a'.

[12] *The History of Miss Betsy Thoughtless* (London, 1751) is probably the best known of all Haywood's work and the first publishing success of her later career. The first fiction of this later period, *The Fortunate Foundlings* (London, 1741) was also published anonymously. Other subsequent novels were *Life's Progress through the Passions, or, The Adventures of Natura* (London, 1748); *The History of Jemmy and Jenny Jessamy* (London, 1753); and *The History of Leonora Meadowson* (London, 1788).

[13] George Frisbie Whicher, *The Life and Romances of Mrs. Eliza Haywood* (New York, 1915).

information about the woman, and in the presence of some sixty-seven works directly attributable to her authorship (see Whicher's excellent bibliography, 176–204), it appears that the books stand in for the life. Very little is known about Eliza Haywood, beyond the fact that she left her husband, the Norfolk clergyman Valentine Haywood, toward the end of 1720, that is, around the time that *Love in Excess* saw enormous popular success. Whicher suggests she was the daughter of a London hosier named Robert Fowler and finds evidence of the birth of one son to the Haywoods who was christened in 1711 (2).

Haywood, according to her earliest biographer, David Erskine Baker, positively shunned any attempt to reveal the facts of her life. In his *Companion to the English Stage* (1764), he asserts that he has 'been credibly informed that, from a Supposition of some improper Liberties being taken with her Character after Death, by the Inter-mixture of Truth and Falshood [sic] with her History, she laid a solemn Injunction on a particular Person, who was well acquainted with all the Particulars of it, not to communicate to any one the least Circumstance relating to her.'[14] In her later career, when she had turned to domestic moral fiction and denounced romance fiction, Haywood herself commented on an early life of promiscuity and pleasure:

I have run through as many Scenes of Vanity and Folly as the greatest Coquet of them all.—Dress, Equipage, and Flattery, were the Idols of my Heart.—I should have thought that Day lost which did not present me with some new Opportunity of shewing myself.—My Life, for some Years, was a continued Round of what I then called Pleasure, and my whole Time engrossed by a Hurry of promiscuous Diversions.[15]

However, these comments are made in the persona of the mature lady editor of her anonymously published journal, the *Female Spectator* (1744–6), and, as such, might more fruitfully be read as a fictional device than biographical insight. Indeed, in the knowledge that during the 1720s Haywood produced a novel on average every

[14] David Erskine Baker, 'Eliza Haywood', *The Companion to the Play-House, or, An Historical Account of all the Dramatic Writers (and their Works) That Have appeared in Great Britain and Ireland, from the Commencement of our Theatrical Exhibitions, down to the Present Year 1764. Composed in the Form of a Dictionary* (London, 1764), vol. ii, sig. Q^v.

[15] Eliza Haywood, *The Female Spectator*, 1 (London, 1745), 2. All subsequent references are to this edition, cited as *Female Spectator* and included in the main body of the text.

three months, it is hard to imagine she had much time for the 'promiscuous diversions' to which she refers above.

It was her textual promiscuity, however, that became the brunt of satirical attacks in the late 1720s. Haywood is perhaps best known in the twentieth century for her appearance in Alexander Pope's *Dunciad*, where she has the dubious honour of being one of the few named women authors. Haywood is the prize for which two publishers compete by seeing who can urinate to the greatest distance in the goddess Dulness's 'Olympic' games.[16] Excepting the excision of two lines in the *Dunciad Variorum* of 1729 and all subsequent editions, the description of Haywood remained unchanged throughout all the versions of the *Dunciad* from 1728 to 1743. Pope caricatures a portrait of Haywood by Elisha Kirkall that was prefixed to a four-volume edition of her works in 1724. Here, the *Dunciad*'s technique of eliding book and author acquires a particularly sexualized overtone as Eliza's 'works' represent both her writings and the result of illicit sexual liaisons:

> See in the circle next, Eliza plac'd
> Two babes of love close clinging to her waste;
> Fair as before her works she stands confess'd.
> In flowr's and pearls by bounteous Kirkall dress'd.
> The Goddess then: 'Who best can send on high
> 'The salient spout, far-streaming to the sky;
>   'His be yon Juno of majestic size,
> 'With cow-like udders, and with ox-like eyes.
> 'This China-Jordan, let the chief o'ercome
> 'Replenish, not ingloriously, at home.'
>
>   (ii. 149–58)

Eliza's works, then, are her body which she shamelessly exposes to public view and sells to the highest bidder (the most powerful bookseller).

The 'two babes of love' are not, as commentators on Haywood have generally assumed, her two children, but rather her two scandal novels, figured as the offspring of this unsavoury mercenary alliance

---

[16] Among his many revisions and substitutions in *The Dunciad* from 1729 through to 1743, Pope retained the citation to Haywood. Chetwood, one of the publishers who competes for her in the 1728 edition (and one of her most regular publishers in fact), was first replaced by Chapman in 1735, then Osborne in *The Dunciad in Four Books* (1743). All references to *The Dunciad* are to *The Dunciad*, ed. James Sutherland, vol. v of *The Twickenham Edition of the Poems of Alexander Pope*, ed. John Butt, 3rd edn. rev. (6 vols.; London, 1963), cited as *Dunciad* with book and line numbers.

between female writer and male bookseller, as Pope's own footnote makes clear.[17] The footnote informs us that Eliza is 'the authoress of those most scandalous books call'd *The Court of Carimania* [*sic*] and *The New Utopia*' and adds that:

In this game is expos'd in the most contemptuous manner, the profligate licentiousness of those shameless Scriblers (for the most part of That sex, which ought least to be capable of such malice or impudence) who in libellous Memoirs and Novels, reveal the faults and misfortunes of both sexes, to the ruin or disturbance, of publick fame or private happiness. (*Dunciad*, ii. 149n)

It is not so much the use of a personalized satire itself to which Scriblerus objects, since, after all, this is the dominant mode of his own poem, but rather the 'unnatural' use of it by women. Women, the gentle sex, 'ought least to be capable of such malice or impudence'. Pope's particular grievance with Haywood lay in her attack upon his neighbour and friend, Lady Henrietta Howard (later Countess of Suffolk), who is represented as Ismonda, mistress to the married Prince Theodore (George, Prince of Wales) in her *Court of Caramania*. It was this attack, also, that led to Swift's dismissal of Haywood as 'a stupid, infamous, scribbling woman', although he had 'not seen any of her productions', in a letter to the Countess of Suffolk herself of 26 October 1731.[18] Both Pope and Swift, one publicly and the other privately, figure themselves as the champions of women against the abuse of other women.

Haywood, then, inverts natural order by 'displaying' her shameful works (and the shameful works of other women) in public. Women's writing is here metaphorized as a form of unrepentant prostitution, in which the woman's body is turned to profit. Even worse, Pope implies, Haywood displays no shame in 'confessing' these illegit- imate productions (her books/babies) to be her own. Not only did Haywood have the boldness to write licentious fiction, but she put

---

[17] Edmund Curll's *A Compleat Key to the Dunciad* (London, 1728) claimed that the two 'babes of love' were 'the Offspring of a *Poet and a Bookseller*' (12). All of Haywood's modern biographers take this slight evidence as proof that she was the mother of two illegitimate children. See Mary Anne Schofield, *Eliza Haywood* (Boston, 1985), 2; Dale Spender, *Mothers of the Novel* (London, 1986), 101; Jane Spencer, 'Eliza Haywood', in Todd's *Dictionary*, 158. Only Helene Koon in her article, 'Eliza Haywood and the *Female Spectator*', *Huntington Library Quarterly*, 42 (1978–9), 43–57 notes that 'the more likely explanation for Pope's charge is that the "two babes of love" were the two works cited in his footnote' (44).

[18] Jonathan Swift, *The Correspondence of Jonathan Swift*, ed. Harold Williams, vol. iii (Oxford, 1963), 501.

her name to it and her picture on the frontispiece.[19] The synonymity that the *Dunciad* had so deftly exploited between the romance author's body and the romance text, was further elaborated by Richard Savage, one-time admirer of Haywood.[20] In 1729, Savage, who, it has been suggested, was Pope's Grub Street informant for the *Dunciad*, published a prose satire in the vein of Pope's poem, entitled *An Author to be Lett*.[21] The very title of Savage's satire puts Haywood at the centre of the dunces' controversy, since it echoes that of her comedy, *A Wife to be Lett*, first performed at the Theatre Royal, Drury Lane, in August 1723.[22]

Savage's satirical portrait of Haywood in his 'Publisher's Preface' takes Pope's presentation of her as a prostitute a step further. She now appears as a procuress '*writing Novels of Intrigue, to teach young Heiresses the Art of running away with Fortune-hunters, and scandalizing Persons of the highest Worth and Distinction*' (A3ʳ). In an allusive reference to Haywood's critique of the mercenary greed engendered by the British Government's involvement with the South Sea Company (the famous South Sea Bubble) in her *Memoirs of a Certain Island*,[23] Savage suggests a more properly feminine form of employ-

[19] Whicher notes that of forty publications authored by Haywood before the first appearance of *The Dunciad* in 1728 only fifteen were not published or advertised under her name, and five of these were too libellous to risk naming the author (*Life and Romances of Mrs. Eliza Haywood*, 130).

[20] His panegyric to her *Love in Excess*, 'To Mrs. *Eliza Haywood, on her Novel, call'd Love in Excess, &c.*', was prefixed to the novel (*SH* i. n.p.).

[21] Richard Savage, *An Author to be Lett. Being a Proposal Humbly Address'd to the Consideration of the Knights, Esquires, Gentlemen, and Other Worshipful and Weighty Members of the Solid and Ancient Society of the Bathos. By their Associate and Well-Wisher, Iscariot Hackney* (London, 1732). See Sutherland's Introduction to *The Dunciad*, pp. xxv–xxvi.

[22] Eliza Haywood, *A Wife to be Lett* (London, 1723). Haywood was obliged to play the lead part of the virtuous married woman, Mrs Graspall, when the actress fell sick. In 1715 she appeared in Shadwell's revival of *Timon of Athens, or The Man-Hater* at Smock Alley, Dublin. Haywood only made four ventures into dramatic writing, the tragedies *The Fair Captive* (London, 1721), *Frederick Duke of Brunswick-Lunenburgh* (London, 1729), and an adaptation of Fielding's *Tragedy of Tragedies* entitled *The Opera of Operas, or, Tom Thumb the Great* (London, 1733) in which she collaborated with William Hatchett. See *The Plays of Eliza Haywood*, ed. Valerie C. Rudolph (Garland Eighteenth Century English Drama Series; New York and London, 1983).

[23] The first narrative provided by Cupid is that of the magician Lucitario's [J. Craggs the elder] claim to turn water into liquid gold. The people of Utopia bring their belongings to Lucitario's priests in hopes of receiving a dividend from his 'enchanted well' [the South Sea company] but the wealth is only redistributed to a few of the magician's favourites (*Memoirs of a Certain Island*, 5–10). On the South Sea Bubble, see John Carswell, *The South Sea Bubble* (London, 1960) and John G. Sperling, *The South Sea Company* (Kress Library Series of Publications; Boston, 1962).

ment for a notorious handler of other people's dirty linen would be that of washerwoman:

When Mrs. H–yw—d grew too homely for a Strolling Actress, *why might not the Lady (tho' once a* Theatrical Queen*) have substituted by turning* Washer-Woman? *Has not the Fall of Greatness been a frequent Distress in all Ages? She might have caught a beautiful Bubble as it arose from the Suds of her Tub, blown it in the Air, seen it glitter, and then break! Even in this low Condition, she had play'd with a Bubble, and what more is the Vanity of human Greatness? She might have also consider'd the sullied Linen growing white in her pretty red Hands, as an Emblem of her Soul, were it well scour'd by Repentance for the Sins of her Youth . . .* (A2ᵛ–A3ʳ)

Savage's attack, like Pope's, highlights the impropriety of Haywood's literary ambitions. Women's unacknowledged domestic and private heroism is to restore order and beauty to the world; in other words, they are to clean the linen, rather than display it in public. It is the desire of public display, the role of the theatrical queen, that Savage finds so unorthodox in Haywood. Instead of staying by the side of her washing tub, Haywood takes up the peripatetic life of a strolling actress; even worse, she encourages other women to wander from the kitchen sink into the arms of unscrupulous men.

Savage had satirized Haywood earlier in her literary career in a poem entitled *The Authors of the Town* (1725), which foreshadows Pope's equation of the female body with the female text by representing her turn to the writing and acting of drama with her heroic tragedy *The Fair Captive* (1723) as a desire for self-display:

> A cast-off Dame, who of Intrigue can judge,
> Writes Scandal in Romance—A Printer's Drudge!
> Flush'd with Success, for Stage-Renown she pants,
> And melts, and swells, and pens luxurious Rants.[24]

Again, Haywood's crime is to invert the natural business of women, seeking to display, rather than conceal, the erotic blush, the heaving breast of the amorous woman. Although comic, both Savage's and Pope's representations of the female body as borderless (melting)

---

[24] Richard Savage, *The Authors of the Town: A Satire. Inscribed to the Author of the Universal Passion* (London, 1725), n.p. Savage's particular grievance with Haywood was her depiction of his mother, Anne Mason, formerly Lady Macclesfield, as Masonia in her *Memoirs of a Certain Island* (167–86). The married Masonia elopes with Riverius (the Earl of Rivers) but, repenting of her adultery, abandons him and rejects their illegitimate son. In this same novel, Haywood had presented Savage's mistress, Martha Fouke, as a libidinous whore with literary pretensions named Gloatitia (47–8).

and engulfing (swelling) reveal a certain paranoid anxiety about the power of the woman to disrupt masculine authority and autonomy.

The figure of Haywood in Pope's *Dunciad* bears certain resemblances to that of the goddess Dulness herself. If Eliza is a 'Juno of majestic size, | With Cow-like udders' (ii. 155–6), Dulness, 'Daughter of Chaos and eternal Night', is 'Gross as her sire, and as her mother grave' (i. 12). The entire 'plot' of the *Dunciad* hinges, after all, on the female's seductive power to diminish and destroy the world of masculine epic heroism. In these misogynist satiric representations, Dulness and Haywood appear as manifestations of the 'literary fat lady', a figure Patricia Parker has identified as essential to the concept of romance from the classical period to the nineteenth century. Parker notes that male writers of the romance (Virgil, Homer, Sidney, Spenser in particular) consistently deploy the trope of the fat female body to figure the copious verbosity of the romance text and its resistance to closure and mastery. Within this trope, the 'figure or body of a female enchantress' (Circe, Excesse, Penelope) enacts a wayward dilation of plot trajectory, coaxing the prodigal son away from his predestined return 'home', and impeding the progress of narrative toward its end.[25] Such verbal prolixity, identified with the fat female body, inhibits interpretation and mastery of the text's meaning, indulging in its place word-play and linguistic inversion.

Dulness, it is clear, is firmly within this tradition, an enchantress who seduces the 'prodigal son' (Theobald/Cibber) from the march of masculine epic into the wayward paths of feminine romance. Dulness is the queen of rhetorical inversion; 'the Chaos dark and deep, | Where nameless somethings in their causes sleep' (*Dunciad*, i. 53–4) is revealed to be her own 'wild creation' which she narcissistically views with 'self-applause' (i. 80). Dulness's 'womb', her 'wild creation', is thus outside her body and from this already inverted body/chaos where the distinction between outside and inside has been dissolved, appear a mass of inverted literary and natural phenomena:

> There motley Images her fancy strike,
> Figures ill-pair'd, and Similes unlike,
> She sees a Mob of Metaphors advance,
> Pleas'd with the Madness of the mazy dance:

[25] Patricia Parker, 'Literary Fat Ladies and the Generation of the Text', in *Literary Fat Ladies: Rhetoric, Gender, Property* (London and New York, 1987), 8–35.

How Tragedy and Comedy embrace;
How Farce and Epic get a jumbled race;
How Time itself stands still at her command,
Realms shift their place, and Ocean turns to land.
Here gay Description Ægypt glads with showers;
Or gives to Zembla fruits, to Barca flowers;
Glitt'ring with ice here hoary hills are seen,
There painted vallies of eternal green,
On cold December fragrant chaplets blow,
And heavy harvests nod beneath the snow.

(i. 63–76)

The female body, then, is the source of a variety of irregularities and improprieties. Like Haywood, Dulness stands 'confess'd' with pride before her 'works', the shameful and fatherless products of her imagination. The complaint that romance inverts 'proper' hierarchies of fact, history, temporality, and place under its enchanting wand of the absolute and transformative power of love, was, as noted in Chapter 2, a well-established trope of masculinist criticism. Both Dulness and Haywood are associated with this dangerous power of transfiguration through the female body.

Even James Sterling's panegyric to Haywood, prefixed to her *Secret Histories*, comes perilously close to this kind of satiric representation. Here, Haywood, like Dulness, observes from a position of distanced pleasure the chaos of feeling she has generated from her romance text:

> You sit like Heav'n's bright Minister on High,
> Command the throbbing Breast, and watry Eye,
> And, as our captive Spirits ebb and flow,
> Smile at the Tempests you have rais'd below:
> The Face of Guilt a Flush of Vertue wears,
> And sudden burst th'involuntary Tears:
> Honour's sworn Foe, the Libertine with Shame,
> Descends to curse the sordid lawless Flame.

(*SH* i. a2)

Haywood's powers of inversion are here employed to transform wickedness into virtue. In an effort to naturalize this unnatural exercise of female power, Sterling presents Haywood as the moon ('Heaven's bright Minister on High'), a traditional symbol of feminine influence with its capacity to control the 'female' element of water through the tides, and associations with female sexuality.

However, the moral conversion that Haywood's text generates in her reader (the libertine) or character (Sterling may be referring to the hero of *Love in Excess*, Count D'Elmont, who is converted to true love by his beautiful ward, Melliora) is brought about by an act of seduction. The female romance writer seduces her readers into shame. The ambivalent nature of this victory is indicated by the use of the blush to signify conversion. John Mullan, in his comments on eighteenth-century representations of hysteria, points out that 'the distinction between the flush of an improper excitement and the virtuous blush of an entranced sensibility is a difficult and shifting one'.[26] Here, then, the distinction between moral conversion and illicit sexual excitement is collapsed.

Haywood's refusal to reveal anything of her personal history, or to pass comment upon her own texts, only adds to this confusion. Her only response to her detractors was to produce another romance text. When Edmund Curll pieced together a female response to the *Dunciad* in the form of a collection entitled *The Female Dunciad* (1728), he included a novella by Haywood entitled *Irish Artifice, or, The History of Clarina*.[27] However, the novella had been sent to Curll for an entirely different purpose in connection with the project of a weekly paper entitled *The Rover* and bears no relation to the *Dunciad*; instead it consists simply of an amatory tale about an Irish housekeeper who engineers a marriage between her son and the young heiress, Clarina. Although the publication of this novel was probably merely fortuitous, it proves the most appropriate response of all. If, as I have argued, Pope's poem seeks to check the proliferation of corrupted and improper writings from the woman writer—to stem the flow of romance—the publication of another romance by Haywood, once again signed with her name, and registering no response to the enclosing strategies of her male detractor, becomes the most effective symbol of his impotence.[28]

[26] John Mullan, 'Hypochondria and Hysteria: Sensibility and the Physicians', *The Eighteenth Century: Theory and Interpretation*, 25 (1984), 169.

[27] Eliza Haywood, *Irish Artifice, or, The History of Clarina* in *The Female Dunciad*, ed. E. Curll (London, 1728), 17–41.

[28] Whicher, *Life and Romances of Mrs. Eliza Haywood*, 123–4. Whicher argues that Pope's attack did, in fact, have very serious effects for Haywood, obliging her to lapse into anonymity for the rest of her literary career (127–30). This seems to overestimate the power of a single text which included, after all, attacks on nearly every other popular writer of the day. Pope's *Dunciad* cannot be considered the single cause of either Haywood's change to anonymous publication or of her supposed moral conversion which led to her domestic moral fiction of the 1740s.

Similarly, when Daniel Defoe in 1720 published his narrative of the life of a deaf and dumb fortune-teller, *The History and Adventures of Mr. Duncan Campbell*, a novel which explicitly declared itself an anti-romance, Haywood simply 'cashed in' on its success by transforming the text into an amatory fiction.[29] The dedicatory epistle to Defoe's novel, addressed 'to the Ladies and Gentleman of Great Britain', ostensibly by Campbell himself, forthrightly informs those readers who had thought the text designed '*to make one half of the fair Species very merry, over the Blushes and Mortifications of the other half*' that they will be '*very agreeably disappointed*' (p. iv). In the midst of a narrative that explores questions of the veracity of the super-natural and the nature of the perception of spirits, as well as outlining sign language for the deaf, the narrator intervenes to comment that he has no intention of providing his readers with an account of the amatory adventures of the ladies who come to consult with the prophet. He has chosen, he says, to 'leave that Method of swelling distorted and commented Trifles into Volumes, to the writers of Fable and Romance' (242). Haywood could not fail to take up the challenge in her *A Spy on the Conjurer* of 1724, 'swelling' and 'distorting' the Duncan Campbell myth into a series of amatory tales around the same ladies the original novel had chivalrously protected.[30]

As my analysis of satirical representations of Haywood and the 'romance authoress' has suggested, romance writing in this period came to be increasingly associated with female transgression and, in particular, with the female body as a grotesque 'dilation' and inversion of narrative teleology and linguistic order. Eliza Haywood both capitalized on and critiqued this trope of the female form in her romances of the 1720s. However, unlike Aphra Behn and Delarivier Manley, she demonstrates little or no interest in employing the strategy of ironic self-representation, or (auto)biographizing, through which her predecessors had concentr-

---

[29] Daniel Defoe, *The History of the Life and Adventures of Mr. Duncan Campbell, a Gentleman, Who, tho' Deaf and Dumb Writes Down Any Stranger's Name at First Sight, with their Future Contingencies of Fortune* (London, 1720).

[30] Eliza Haywood, *A Spy on the Conjurer, or, A Collection of Surprising and Diverting Stories, with Merry and Ingenious Letters. By Way of the Memoirs of the Famous Mr. Duncan Campbell. Revised by Mrs. Eliza Haywood* (London, 1724). Haywood may have been encouraged in this venture by William Bond, a mutual friend of both Haywood and Defoe who, Whicher suggests, may have been responsible for the few sentimental passages in Defoe's novel (78–9).

ated their resistance to masculinist interpretation. The few comments on her role as female writer that Haywood inserts in her narratives are largely conventional. If Behn and Manley had asserted the will to power of the female writer by marking her difference from the women victims she re-presented to her readers, Haywood presents herself as a sufferer on a par with her heroines. Where Behn and Manley figure themselves as heroes transcending all obstacles to acquire literary fame, Haywood describes herself as an abused victim.

Like the seduced and abandoned virgins of her fiction, Haywood argues, she cannot be blamed for indulging her 'natural' female propensity for love:

as I am a woman, and consequently depriv'd of those advantages of education which the other sex enjoy, I cannot so flatter my desires, as to imagine it is in my power to soar to any subject higher than that which nature is not negligent to teach us. Love is a Topick which I believe few are ignorant of; there requires no Aids of Learning, no general Conversation, no Application; a shady Grove and purling Stream are all Things that's necessary to give us an Idea of the tender Passion. This is a Theme, therefore, which while I make choice to write of, frees me from the Imputation of vain or self-sufficient:—None can tax me with having too great an Opinion of my own Genius, when I aim at nothing but what the meanest may perform.[31]

However, despite her self-deprecation, she does find herself 'taxed' with self-aggrandisement. Another dedication, in this case to her tragedy *The Fair Captive* (1721), again presents her as inadequate to the task of resistance, a weak woman who 'wanted many more Arguments than the little Philosophy [she is] Mistress of could furnish [her] with, to enable [her] to stem that Tide of Raillery, which all of [her] Sex, unless they are very excellent indeed, must expect, when once they exchange the Needle for the Quill' (*Plays*, n.p.)

The woman writer, like the female lover, is beset by dangers. Her inevitable fate is abuse, neglect, contempt, rejection. Thus, in the preface to her *The Memoirs of the Baron de Brosse* (1725), Haywood presents herself as one of her solitary and embattled heroines, the victim of public scorn and envy:

It would be impossible to recount the numerous Difficulties a Woman has to

[31] Eliza Haywood, Dedication, *The Fatal Secret* (1724), in *The Masquerade Novels of Eliza Haywood*, ed. Mary Anne Schofield (New York, 1986), n.p.

struggle through in her Approach to Fame: If her Writings are considerable enough to make any Figure in the World, Envy pursues her with unweary'd Diligence; and if, on the contrary, she only writes what is forgot as soon as read, Contempt is all the Reward, her Wish to please, excites; and the cold Breath of Scorn chills the little Genius she has, and which, perhaps, cherished by Encouragement, might in Time, grow to a Praiseworthy Height.[32]

Writing a work of fiction in search of public fame entails the same risks for a woman as entering into a criminal 'conversation' with a man. As Haywood comments in a disquisition on the love letter appended to her *Letters from a Lady of Quality to a Chevalier* (1721), the woman who refuses to follow the prescribed forms (by taking a lover or taking up the pen) 'walks as in a narrow Path, hedged on each side with Thorns, which there is scarce a possibility of passing through unhurt, either by domestick Jealousy, or foreign Malice'.[33] Despite all attempts at secrecy, the woman behind the love intrigue will be discovered and destroyed.

The profound melancholia and pessimism of Haywood's depiction of female possibilities make her, for the feminist critic, the least attractive of the 'fair Triumvirate of Wit'.[34] The ebullient resilience of Behn's and Manley's narcissistic self-representations is nowhere in evidence in the fiction of Haywood. However, as this chapter hopes to demonstrate, Haywood's romances of the 1720s do locate a form of feminine resistance precisely in the compulsive re-inscription and display of the hysterical female body. The remainder of this chapter explores the means by which Haywood's narrative strategies subvert the seemingly rigid gender oppositions through which her romance plots are constructed. Here the victory of the masculine 'plot' over the female 'form' (the traditional tale of seduction and betrayal) is repeatedly subverted from within by a recurrent female 'counter plot', which seeks to empower the heroine by allowing her rhetorical

[32] Eliza Haywood, *Memoirs of the Baron de Brosse, Who Was Broke on the Wheel in the Reign of Louis XIV* (London, 1725), n.p.

[33] Eliza Haywood, 'A Discourse Concerning Writings of this Nature, by way of Essay', *Letters from a Lady of Quality to a Chevalier*, 2nd edn. (London, 1724), 19 (separately numbered).

[34] See James Sterling, 'To Mrs. *Eliza Haywood* on her *Writings*':

> *Read, proud Usurper, read with conscious Shame,*
> *Pathetick Behn, or Manley's greater Name,*
> *Forget their Sex, and own when Haywood writ,*
> *She clos'd the fair Triumvirate of Wit. . . .*
>
> (*SH* i. a2.)

control of the 'forms' of love, her own proper body. The figure of the female 'plotter' is offered to an audience specifically identified as female as a means of challenging gender determinations. If Behn and Manley ascribed women's victory in amatory struggle to the woman writer by virtue of her difference from her own suffering heroines, Haywood locates it in the woman writer by virtue of her identification with them.

Unfortunate Mistresses

The business of Haywood's amatory plots is to engage the female reader's sympathy and erotic pleaure, rather than stimulate intellectual judgement. These texts explicitly call upon the female reader to identify with the troubled heroine, yet paradoxically enjoin her to interpret the tale as moral admonition. To this purpose, Haywood frequently employs the novelistic convention of the interjected narrative of seduction delivered by one woman to another. Thus, in *The Agreeable Caledonian*, Ismena narrates her own story of seduction and betrayal to the heroine, Clementina, requiring her first to 'recollect the first dear Moments of discovered Passion; Think what you felt, and by yourself, pity me, in so amazing, and at the same time, so transporting a Juncture' (pt. 2, p. 13). As in the case of Katteriena's narrative to Isabella in Behn's *The Fair Vow-Breaker*, however, this story-telling serves to further inflame and ratify rather than curb the heroine's illicit passion.

Haywood's heroines are both indulged and punished for succumbing to sexual desire. Through this paradoxical movement Haywood's fiction sets about constructing the modern female reader of romance fiction. Erotic fantasy on the part of the woman reader, a heterosexual fantasy of subjugation and self-abandonment, is encouraged in the secure knowledge that ultimately female sexual pleasure will be punished or tamed. This seeming contradiction is maintained through the specific metaphysics of love that structure the ideology of the text and through Haywood's representation of a 'hystericized' female body.

Haywood's heroines, though ruined, are 'innocent' because of their inability to resist sexual passion. The narrator of *Love in Excess* informs us that 'Passion is not to be circumscrib'd; and being not only, not *Subservient*, but absolute *Comptroller* of the *Will*, it would

be mere Madness, as well as ill Nature, to say a Person was blame-
worthy for what was unavoidable' (*SH* i. 176). Although these
comments refer equally to the effects of passion on men and women,
it is upon the body of the woman that such effects are most
frequently and forcefully inscribed. Thus Belinda of *The British
Recluse* describes her submission to the advances of Sir Thomas
Courtal (who, unbeknownst to her is also the seducer of Cleomira,
the friend to whom she is narrating her story) in terms of a
hysterical inability to control her unconscious desires from being
manifested through her body: 'my trembling Limbs refus'd to oppose
the lovely Tyrant's Will! and, if my faultering Tongue entreated him
to desist, or my weak Hands attempted to repulse the approaching
Liberty of his, it serv'd but, as he said, the more to inflame his
Wishes, and raise his Passion to a higher Pitch of Fury!' (*SH* ii. 93).
Similarly, in the story that opens *Love in Excess*, in which the as yet
unreformed Count D'Elmont takes advantage of a young virgin's
hopeless passion for him, the heroine, Amena, is incapable of
preventing her body from signifying desire despite her virtuous
misgivings:

she had only a thin Silk nightgown on, which flying open as he caught her in
his Arms, he found her panting Heart beat Measures of Consent, her
heaving Breast swell to be press'd by his, and every Pulse confess a Wish to
yield; her Spirits all dissolv'd, sunk in a Lethargy of Love; her snowy Arms,
unknowing, grasp'd his Neck, her Lips met his half way, and trembled at the
Touch. (*SH* i. 26)

Later in the novel, D'Elmont falls in love with his ward, Melliora.
Despite her strenuous advocacy in her waking hours 'against the
giving way to Love, and the Danger of all softening Amusements'
(82), Melliora is unable to control her dream life. When D'Elmont
covertly enters her bedroom at night he finds her in the midst of a
dream which 'made her throw her Arm (still slumbering) about his
Neck, and in a soft and languishing Voice, cry out, O! D'ELMONT,
cease, cease to Charm, to such a Height—Life cannot bear these
Raptures!—And then again embracing him yet closer,—O! too, too
lovely Count—Extatick Ruiner!' (94). Under cover of the dream
state, Haywood can even bring her heroines to orgasm without
undermining the conviction of their virtuous principles.

The 'symptoms' of Haywood's desiring virgins correspond closely
to those Sigmund Freud and Joseph Breuer identified in hysterical

female patients in their 1893 essay, 'On the Psychical Mechanism of Hysterical Phenomena'.[35] Freud and Breuer describe hysteria as manifested most commonly in 'dispositional hypnoid states' (13) and 'failures of function' in particular parts of the body such as paralyses of certain limbs, coughing, anaesthesia (7). The hysteric converts psychological trauma into physical symptoms. The hypnoid states and failures of function which descend upon Haywood's heroines might then be interpreted as hysterical responses to the 'trauma' of seduction. In his *Madness and Civilization*, Michel Foucault lights upon this link between 'amatory' and 'hysterical' ardour in eighteenth-century theories of hysterical disorder:

> Often hysteria was perceived as the effect of an internal heat that spread throughout the entire body, an effervescence, an ebullition ceaselessly manifested in convulsions and spasms. Was this heat not related to the amorous ardor with which hysteria was so often linked, in girls looking for husbands and in young widows who had lost theirs? Hysteria was ardent, by nature; its symptoms referred more easily to an image than an illness.[36]

Hysteria, then, had come to be perceived as an 'image' rather than an 'illness', a set of amatory signs over which the woman has no interpretative control. It is, after all, the men in these seduction scenes who interpret the woman's body as desirous and submissive. In his comments on the rush of popular scientific publications on nervous disorders from 1720 to 1770 in Britain,[37] John Mullan comments that 'For the eighteenth-century practitioner of 'Physick', the female body is construed . . . as an ever visible corpus of signs given over to their practice of interpretation, but also as that which might bespeak a dangerous opacity of passion and imagination' (157). Haywood's texts put popular contemporary theories of madness to use in her attempt to represent and justify female desire.

Hysteria is, however, as both Mullan and Foucault suggest, a form of mimicry which produces a certain interpretative ambiguity into the scene of representation (the woman's body). Haywood's

---

[35] Joseph Breuer and Sigmund Freud, 'On the Psychical Mechanism of Hysterical Pheonomena: Preliminary Communication' (1893), *SE* ii. 3–17.

[36] Michel Foucault, *Madness and Civilization: A History of Insanity in the Age of Reason*, trans. Richard Howard (New York, 1988), 139.

[37] Mullan and Foucault cite, in particular, Richard Blackmore's *A Treatise of Spleen and Vapours, or, Hypochondria and Hysterical Affections* (London, 1725) and George Cheyne's *The English Malady, or, A Treatise of Nervous Disorders of All Kinds* (London, 1733).

hapless heroines mimic the desirous environment of the wood and garden in which they are commonly found at the scene of seduction. Belinda, again, in describing her fatal seduction by Courtal, describes the setting of the wood:

Never was a Night more delectable, more aiding to a Lover's Wishes! the arching Trees form'd a Canopy over our Heads, while through the gently shaking Boughs soft Breezes play'd in lulling Murmurings, and fann'd us with delicious Gales! a thousand Nightingales sung amorous Ditties, and the billing Doves coo'd out their tender Transports!—Every Thing was soothing—every Thing inspiring! The very Soul of Love seem'd to inform the Place, and reign throughout the Whole. (*SH* ii. 93)

Belinda's trembling limbs, inarticulate cries, and fluttering hands appear to mimic the shaking boughs, murmuring breezes, and billing doves that surround her. However, this is one interpretation of the amatory signs emanating from Belinda. Another reading, more threatening perhaps, lies in the presence of the nightingales, classically associated with the tragic victim of rape, Philomela, and the inability to articulate female rage and resistance.

I do not wish to suggest that we are not expected to interpret Haywood's heroines as desiring, but that the hysterical symptom is in and of itself ambivalent. The opacity of the hysterical symptom/ amatory sign troubles a reading of Haywood's text as simply 'direct effusions of fantasy . . . that imply the delight of full commitment to the unconscious'.[38] This is indeed the stuff of rape-fantasy, but it carries with it an anxiety about the risks of irresponsibility and the necessary abnegation of all control that it implies. Catherine Clément in a timely feminist intervention on contemporary theories of hysteria notes the powerlessness of the hysteric. Displaced from the scene of language and writing, entirely the victim of the arbitrary signifying capacities of her own body, 'the hysteric does *not* write, does *not* produce, does nothing—nothing other than make things circulate without inscribing them'.[39] The uninterpretability of the hysterical body may endow it with a certain effective power, but the hysteric herself has no control over the representational scene her body creates.

[38] Spacks, 'Ev'ry Woman Is at Heart a Rake', 39.
[39] Catherine Clément, 'The Guilty One', in Hélène Cixous and Catherine Clément, *The Newly Born Woman*, trans. Betsy Wing, (Theory and History of Literature Ser. 24; Manchester, 1986), 147.

The disempowering aspects of the hysteric's capacity to 'make things circulate without inscribing them' is perhaps best demonstrated in the story of Idalia, whom Mary Anne Schofield has described as 'Haywood's incarnate figure of female exploitation'.[40] Like Behn's dumb virgin, Maria, Idalia is simply a mirror onto which male desire is projected. 'Her Beauty', Haywood tells us, 'like a fatal Comet, was destructive to all on whom it had any influence' (*SH* iii. 39). Idalia is abducted and raped by Ferdinand with the connivance of her pretended lover, Florez. The man entrusted by Ferdinand to convey Idalia to his country seat, Henriquez, also falls in love with her, and both Ferdinand and Henriquez die in their ensuing duel. Myrtano, Henriquez's brother, is the next man to fall for Idalia's fatal beauty, but before their love can be consummated, his prospective bride, Antonia, commissions her brother, Honorius, to abduct Idalia. Inevitably Honorius too falls in love with Idalia and when she flees from him in fear, he retires to a monastery having lost his hair and eyebrows out of grief.

After another attempted rape by the captain of the ship on which she embarks, followed by a storm and a shipwreck, Idalia arrives in Italy, having disguised herself as a man. She is promptly attacked by banditti, only to be saved by a mysterious lady who, smitten by the young man's charms, takes her home to recuperate. The lady, it transpires, is Myrtano's wife, Antonia, who, on discovery of the real identity of her supposed lover and the recommenced affair between Idalia and Myrtano, attempts to poison both of them. Idalia, separated from her lover by edict of the Pope, Antonia's uncle, sights Florez, the original cause of her ruin, on the street. She arranges to meet him and stabs the man who attends the rendezvous only to discover it is her beloved Myrtano who has substituted for Florez as a result of his suspicions about her fidelity. Idalia takes her own life and Florez is executed for a murder he committed in Venice.

As my brief synopsis of the main plot of *Idalia* demonstrates, every point at which the heroine attempts to become an agent in her own history (fleeing from the in fact worthy Honorius, disguising herself as a man, planning to murder her betrayer) results in further disaster. Idalia trails death, disease, and psychic torment everywhere in her wake.

[40] Mary Anne Schofield, ' "Descending Angels": Salubrious Sluts and Petty Prostitutes in Haywood's Fiction', Marcheski and Schofield (eds.), *British Women Novelists 1670–1815*, 197.

Haywood's novels then, in the main, present their female readers with a thoroughly melancholy view of the world of heterosexual romance. Male desire is, with rare exceptions, short-lived and end-directed, constituting a series of metonymical displacements of woman for woman in search of an impossible and unattainable satisfaction. Female desire is masochistic, self-destructive and hysterical. However, like Behn and Manley before her, if less obviously, Haywood does explore alternatives to this model, specifically in the notion of hysterical 'mimicry' which I have noted is so fundamental to her seduction scenarios. In these short romances of the 1720s, even more explicitly perhaps than in Behn's novellas of the 1680s and Manley's scandal fiction in the first decade of the eighteenth century, the seduction scene is presented as a struggle for power and, more particularly, a gendered conflict over the interpretation of the woman's body as amatory sign.

Mistresses of Artifice

As Delarivier Manley had done in her fictionalized representations of Sarah Churchill, Duchess of Marlborough, Haywood rejected, as a model of female empowerment, the possibilities of a female adoption of the self-interested and end-directed desire her novels consistently associate with masculinity. Her novels abound with representations of vicious, libidinous, usually older women who threaten the virtuous heroine's hold over the hero. Ciamara in *Love in Excess* and the Baroness de Tortillée in *The Injur'd Husband, or, The Mistaken Resentment* (1723; *SH* ii. 115–260) are representatives of this malign type and both are contrasted with their virtuous opposite, Melliora and Montamour. These women transform themselves into art objects in order to seduce the young lovers they pursue in their attempt to control and direct the amatory scene. When D'Elmont first encounters Ciamara, a wealthy Italian widow captivated by his charms when she sees him at chapel, it is already under conditions of deception. He has arrived in Ciamara's house intent on obtaining an interview with her niece, the mistress of Frankville (his friend and Melliora's brother), in order to arrange an elopement on the latter's behalf. Ciamara entertains D'Elmont in a room 'contriv'd in such a manner, as might fitly be a Pattern, to paint the Palace of the Queen of Love by' (*SH* i. 202). Ciamara frames herself in amatory representations; the walls are covered with tapestries 'in which, most artificially were woven, in various colour'd Silk, intermix'd with Gold and Silver, a great number of amorous Stories' (202), in particular Venus and Adonis, Jupiter and Leda, Diana and Endimion, Cupid and Psyche. The visual effect of satiating amorous pleasure is enhanced by the wall-length looking-glasses between each tapestry 'out of which sprung several chrystal Branches, containing great Wax Tapers so that the Number of Lights vy'd with the Sun ... which lately was withdrawn' (202). Ciamara's attire is of a piece with this hall of mirrors:

she was drest in a Gold and Silver stuff Petticoat, and a Wastecoat of plain blue Sattin, set round the Neck and Sleeves, and down the Seams with Diamonds, and fasten'd on the Breast with Jewels of a prodigious Largeness and Lustre; a Girdle of the same encompass'd her Waste; her Hair, of which she had great Quantity, was black as Jet, and with a studied Negligence, fell part of it on her Neck in careless Ringlets, and the other was turn'd up, and fasten'd here and there with Bodkins, which had pendant Diamonds hanging to 'em, and as she mov'd, glitter'd with a quivering Blaze, like Stars darting their Fires from out a sable Sky. (203)

The sable sky is Ciamara's face, which is concealed by a heavy black veil, further enhancing her mimetic representation of the woman as mirror. Ciamara appears as a grotesque parody of Haywood's faceless heroines, whose morphology reproduces in the eyes of the lover the amatory frame (the garden, the wood, the room) in which she is set. Unfortunately, however, it only convinces D'Elmont, under the assumption that the veiled woman is Camilla, of the latter's hypocrisy, and he departs to persuade Frankville to abandon his mistress.

Camilla's furious letter in response to this rejection oddly aligns her with her promiscuous aunt. Like Ciamara, she has come to recognize that men only see in their mistresses the image of their own desire: '*the few Charms I am Mistress of*', she writes '*look'd lovely at a Distance, but lose their Lustre when approach'd too near; your Fancy threw a glittering Burnish o're me, which free Possession has worn off, and now the* Woman *only stands expos'd to View*' (222). A passionate love-letter from Ciamara to D'Elmont exposes the mistake and D'Elmont is obliged to agree to a second encounter in order to provide Frankville with an opportunity to be reconciled with Camilla. Ciamara, her true identity now disclosed, adopts a different form of parody, this time of the 'hysterical' virgin. Dressed 'loose as wanton Fancy cou'd invent' (224), she throws herself upon the bemused

D'Elmont: 'Lost to all Sense of Honour, Pride or Shame, and wild to gratify her furious Wishes, she spoke, without reserve, all they suggested to her; and lying on his Breast, beheld, without Concern, her Robes fly open, and all the Beauties of her own expos'd, and naked to his View' (227). As with Amena, in an earlier seduction scene, Ciamara's clothes 'fly open' of their own accord, but there is a fundamental narcissism in this scene which is lacking in the former. Here, Ciamara controls and observes the display and turns the openness and accessibility of the female body into an opportunity to gratify her own interest, rather than suffering as victim because of it.

Ciamara's facility with amatory (self) representation, though in many ways presented as a peculiarly feminine mode of appropriation, is, Haywood makes clear, at root a masculine identification. It is purely end-directed and, as Haywood warns, 'that Passion which ends chiefly at Enjoyment, in Enjoyment ends; the fleeting Pleasure is no more remembred, but all the Stings of Guilt and Shame remain' (226). The fulfilment of that passion is, in this case, frustrated, though not through D'Elmont's agency. Frankville's presence in the house is discovered and the lovers and D'Elmont are obliged to flee the city to escape the wrath of Ciamara and Camilla's father. Ciamara, destroyed by her own lusts, takes poison and dies.

The Baroness de Tortillée also takes her own life with poison when the pursuit of her sexual lusts is curtailed. Haywood's representation of the Baroness owes much to Bussy-Rabutin's depiction of hypocritical court ladies in his *Amorous History of the Gauls*: 'No Woman that ever liv'd was Mistress of more Artifice, nor had less the Appearance of being so: Nature had given her a Countenance extremely favourable for her Purpose; and whenever she was pleas'd to join to those Looks of Sincerity and Innocence any Asseverations that she was so, it was hardly possible to believe her otherwise' (*SH* ii. 125). Like Bussy-Rabutin's Madame de Châtillon, the Baroness takes lovers for the sake of power and wealth, despite her advantageous marriage to the doting Baron. The essentially masculine quality of her desire is revealed by the fact that it wanes with enjoyment. Her attention turns to the virtuous Beauclair, contracted to his longtime love, Montamour, precisely because 'he was *unenjoy'd*, and *therefore* most *desirable*' (133). She succeeds in winning him by discrediting Montamour's integrity and presenting herself as a modest and reserved woman of honour in the grip of an uncontrollable passion, in other words by mimicking the hysterical female role. In the midst of all this complex role-playing, Montamour stubbornly resists any activity, insisting, 'shou'd *he* be ever *blind, she* ever *cunning*, I am resolv'd, in Justice to myself, to continue entirely passive' (173). Montamour retires to a convent and does not reappear again until the Baroness's villainies have been exposed by her numerous lovers. The Baron, cured by a country surgeon of the lethargy brought on by the narcoleptic drugs administered by his wife, returns determined to be revenged on wife and her lovers alike, and is treacherously stabbed in the back by the latter's co-conspirator, Du Lache, while he is duelling with Beauclair. Beauclair is only saved from execution for this murder by the testimony of the mysterious Vrayment. Vrayment, it is revealed, is Montamour in male disguise and the lovers are finally reunited.

The significant aspect of this novella is that its resolution is engineered through the strenuous activity of a heroine previously characterized by total passivity. The Baroness's 'masculine' artifice (prompted by the desire for ever new objects of conquest) cloaked in the appearance of femininity is counteracted by Montamour's 'feminine' artifice (prompted by the desire to retain a single lover) from within the disguise of a man. It is only in male disguise that Montamour can deliver certain truths to her lover about the female condition, as the pseudonym of Vrayment (truth) implies. Vrayment befriends Beauclair when he is in despair because Montamour has rejected his attempts at reconciliation following the discovery of the Baroness's duplicity. In male disguise, Montamour delivers a passionate piece of proto-feminist argument to her lover:

Reputation is so nice a Thing, so finely wrought, so liable to break, the least false Step disjoints the beauteous Frame, and down we sink in endless Infamy.—Consider ... the Reasons why Women are, by our *Salique* Law, debarr'd from reigning? Why, in all Nations of the Earth, excluded from publick Management? Us'd but as Toys? Little immaterial Amusements, to trifle away an Hour of idle Time with? Is it not because their Levity of Nature, their weak Irresolution, pleas'd and displeas'd oft at they know not what, and always in Extreams, makes them unfit for Counsel, for Secrecy, or Action?—If one among them can tow'r above the Follies of her Sex, and awe her encroaching Passions with superior Reason, we should admire a Virtue so uncommon. (242–3)

Vrayment asks Beauclair to admit his mistress's superiority in proving capable of allowing reason and self-respect to conquer passion. However, within this story it is Beauclair who has demon-strated 'levity of nature' and 'weak irresolution' with respect to his mistress. The vices traditionally ascribed to women are, it transpires, those of men. Yet Vrayment's statement is in itself a lie. Montamour has not conquered her passion, but has rather set about finding a way to preserve her 'reputation' and secure her lover again on her own terms. It is, then, loss of reputation, the sacrifice of the appearance of respectability, that ruins women, rather than their sexual desire itself. The female reader of romance fiction must be offered some resolution whereby the 'beauteous Frame' of feminine virtue can be retained, sexual desire gratified, and the moral superiority of female constancy confirmed. Women must be made fit for action by learning 'counsel' and 'secrecy' rather than honesty.

Masqueraders

Hitherto I have considered Haywood's representations of the female subject position within the amatory plot as largely negative and disempowering. She offers her female readers either the model of the 'hysterical' virgin who can only 'make things circulate without inscribing them' or that of the vicious 'masculine' woman who, like the men she mimics, ceaselessly circulates in the world of sexual exchange without the possibility of securing absolute satisfaction in a single love object.

The dilemma of the heroine in Haywood's novellas of the 1720s might be metaphorized as precisely that of the desire to dilate the amatory plot (the desire of romance) despite the conflicting masculine desire of the libertine hero for closure (the desire of the novel). Proper femininity, in Haywood's romances, is always associ-ated with absolute fidelity to a single male lover. It is not, however, always commensurate with a total lack of artifice. Rather I would suggest that in this early fiction, Haywood glimpses a means of empowering the female within amatory conflict, of making her a weaver and dilator of her own amatory plot, through the elaboration of a familiar concept-metaphor of the early eighteenth century, that of the masquerade. Here, the masquerade functions as a site in which gender inversion and amatory activity is licensed under the sanction of organized 'secrecy'.[41]

[41] I have adopted Gayatri Spivak's coinage of the term 'concept-metaphor' as elaborated in her essay, 'Explanation and Culture: Marginalia', in *In Other Worlds:*

Terry Castle, in her ground-breaking study of the motif of the masquerade in eighteenth-century British fiction, has commented that:

Though typically represented as a moral emblem, the image of a corrupt and pleasure-seeking populace, the masquerade was also an indispensable plot catalyst, the mysterious scene out of which the essential drama of the fiction emerged. All the ambivalence that the masquerade aroused in English public life—where it was at once the sign of depravity and freedom, corruption and delight—was thus replicated in its fictional representation.[42]

The links between the masquerade and amatory fiction are obvious: both are forms in which sexual pursuit and conflict are acted out and both, as Castle argues, are invested with a certain interpretative ambivalence, confusing the distinction between sexual pleasure and sexual abuse. Moreover, both are licensed transgressions of gender and class boundaries. In the masquerade, whores appeared as fine ladies, fine ladies as whores. Allon White and Peter Stallybrass have argued that the eighteenth-century theatre was the focus of the construction of a new bourgeois public sphere which regulated and demarcated class distinction by spatial separations of the audience, thus negating seventeenth-century traditions of the 'carnivalesque'.[43] The masquerade, in contrast, combined elements of both seventeenth-century carnival and masque, low and high culture. Unlike the carnival it was located indoors and it was only open to those who could afford admission by ticket, thus offering a form of controlled anarchy, a licensed and bounded lifting of repression. Unlike the masque, however, the masquerade did not recognize any division betweeen audience and theatrical company.

The attractions of the metaphor of the masquerade for the female writer of amatory fiction are equally obvious. Castle notes that, through satirical representations of the masquerade, 'the metonymic

Essays in Cultural Politics (London, 1987), 103–17. Specifically, Spivak argues: 'If we would deconstruct ... [the] marginalization between metaphor and concept, we would realize not only that no pure theory of metaphor is possible, because any metaphoric base of discussion must already assume the distinction between theory and metaphor, but also that no priority, by the same token, can be given to metaphor, since every metaphor is contaminated and constituted by the conceptual justification' (115).

[42] Terry Castle, Masquerade and Civilization: The Carnivalesque in Eighteenth-Century English Culture and Fiction (Stanford, Calif., 1986), p. ix. See also her article, 'The Carnivalization of Eighteenth-Century English narrative', PMLA 9 (1984), 903–16.

[43] Allon White and Peter Stallybrass, 'The Grotesque Body and the Smithfield Muse: Authorship in the Eighteenth Century', The Politics and Poetics of Transgression (London, 1986), 80–124.

relation between masquerades and sex becomes a metaphorical one'.[44] The anonymity of the masquerade provides women with the opportunity of maintaining public reputation and indulging private sexual desire. Whether women in the early eighteenth century actually availed themselves of this opportunity is, to some extent, immaterial to my discussion of the role of the masquerade in Haywood's texts of the 1720s, since it is the metaphorical possibilities that its representation in eighteenth-century culture may have suggested to her that I intend to explore.

The dangerous duplicity of the disguise was celebrated in the masquerade. 'The masquerade', Castle writes, 'was a revelling in duplicity, a collective experiment ... in semantic betrayal and violation of the sartorial experiment'.[45] Castle concentrates, in the main, on the appearance of the masquerade in fictional texts that were produced after the practice's heyday of the 1720s (the second part of Richardson's *Pamela* (1742), Fielding's *Amelia* (1751), Burney's *Cecilia* (1782), Inchbald's *A Simple Story* (1791)), paying only cursory attention to Haywood's *The Masqueraders, or, Fatal Curiosity* (1724), which she dismisses as one of many 'salacious tales of masquerade disaster' of the earlier period (214). Moreover, because of her emphasis on this later period in the history of the English novel, she emphasizes the role of the masquerade as simply that of 'plot-catalyst', a moment of transgressive disruption introduced into the otherwise moral and domestic framework of the mid- to late eighteenth-century novel. A closer reading of Haywood's novel, however, within the context of the possibilities of romance fiction in the 1720s, opens out other readings of the place of the masquerade topos in the feminocentric world of amatory fiction.

The Masqueraders (1724; *SH* iv. separately numbered) employs the masquerade as a controlled space of mimicry of amatory conventions, revealing in its course the extent to which representation, far from being the adjunct to desire, is its source. This novel, I will argue, along with her *Fantomina* (*SH* iii. 257–92), published a year after it, marks Haywood's attempt to 'plot' a way out of the negative opposition of the unfortunate mistress and the mistress of artifice, proferring in its place the model of a female experimentation with amatory codes in order to defer closure of heterosexual romance without falling into hysteria. The novel opens by establishing the

[44] Castle, *Masquerade and Civilization*, 43.
[45] Ibid. 57.

masquerade as, like sexual passion, a universal and levelling experience: 'Great-Britain has no Assembly which affords such variety of Characters as the Masquerade; there are scarce any Degrees of People, of what Religion or Principle soever, that some time or other are not willing to embrace an opportunity of partaking this Diversion' (5). The libertine-seducer Dorimenus, is an afficionado of the masquerade, which he employs as a cover for his romantic liaisons with a variety of ladies who 'would give him a Description of their Habits, each in hope to be the Favourite She, which should that Night be singled out' (6). In other words, Dorimenus is a master of the amatory codes of the masquerade, with a privileged knowledge of the real identities of the women behind their disguises. It is the hermeneutical enterprise of 'cracking the code', discovering the woman, that affords him his pleasure, rather than the continued enjoyment of his mistresses' favour. Every new woman who enters the masquerade is, for Dorimenus, another potential amatory plot upon which to embark and to abandon once solved (possessed).

The rapidity with which he dis-covers the identity of a young widow Dalinda in costume as a shepherdess (by removing her mask when she faints) foreshadows the precipitancy of their affair. He conducts her home and has sex with her that very night. Dalinda's fate is sealed when she proves incapable of concealing the affair and confides in her friend, Philecta. It is clear that narrating the story of seduction is in itself a sexual experience for both the addresser and addressee. Dalinda 'long'd to impart the mighty Bliss; she panted to pour out the over-whelming Transport' (11) and she 'felt in the delicious Representation, a Pleasure, perhaps, not much inferiour to that which the Reality afforded' (12). The masquerade and the confession, the representations of amatory experience, are pleasurable substitutes for it.

Unfortunately, in this case, Dalinda, unsophisticated in the workings of amatory codes (as her first appearance in the pastoral garb of the shepherdess implies), does not recognize the effect of her erotic monologues upon Philecta. The latter, previously betrayed by a lover and cynical about men's capacity for constancy, determines to 'test' Dorimenus. She persuades Dalinda to prepare the costume of an Indian slave for the next masquerade, replicates the costume, and enjoys Dorimenus's advances in the place of her friend before the latter arrives. Terry Castle notes that whereas the shepherdess costume in the masquerade denoted 'a purely ornamental world of labour', the oriental or primitive costume suggested 'an erotic commingling with the alien' (62). Dorimenus has expected to find a familiar face behind the 'alien' costume, but Philecta lives up to the semantic logic of the costume, when she allows him a brief glimpse of her 'alien' (not known) face, thus challenging his mastery of the code. She departs without revealing her identity, heightening Dorimenus's sexual curiosity.

Philecta continues to inhabit Dalinda's identity, forging her handwriting in order to set up a tryst with Dorimenus and once again preparing the ground for a scene of alienation in which Dorimenus, expecting to find the familiar, will encounter the strange. She prepares for this encounter in the daylight world of sexual intrigue with as much care as she would for the night-time masquerade, but already her command of the 'masquerade' code is beginning to slip:

a thousand, and a thousand times were the Patches plac'd, alter'd and replac'd,—the position of the Curls as often chang'd,—now *this*, anon *that* Fashion she thought most becoming—sometimes one sort of Glance, then its contrary seem'd the likeliest to attract—and she remain'd unfix'd in Determination, how she shou'd Look, or Speak, or Act, when she was told he was enquiring for her. (22)

Without the safety of the masquerade code, Philecta finds herself at a loss. She cannot fix on a masquerade identity outside the delimited environment of the assembly hall that will ensure both her 'secrecy' (concealing her anonymity and her interest in Dorimenus) and bring her the pleasure of sexual conquest. On this occasion, however, Dorimenus is not to gain the lady's sexual favours on the first encounter outside the masquerade setting, or, as Haywood puts it, he 'was not always to triumph at first sight; he could not find a DALINDA in PHILECTA' (25). Philecta, here, continues to protect herself through her friend's identity. Every advance Dorimenus makes is answered solely with the invocation of Dalinda's name, as a reminder of her friend's prior claim.

After this troubled encounter, realizing her growing sexual passion for him, Philecta visits Dalinda, reveals her duplicity, and begs her to win him back, promising to avoid any further contact with him. She leaves filled with 'a kind of gloomy Transport, that she had pass'd the fiery Tryal, and secured her Honour from all the Attacks of Love and her own Wishes' (34). Philecta's confidence is of course misplaced. Ironically, in employing her friend's identity first as a means of gaining access to the male lover and then as a means of protecting herself from him, Philecta has come to substitute for her, not only as the object of Dorimenus's desire, but in the nature of her own, and her inability to occupy anything but the position of victim in the amatory plot. When Dorimenus breaks into Philecta's bedroom in the early morning he finds her in the dream-state typical of Haywood's hysterical suffering virgins. She is sunk in dreams and 'Imagination, always a Friend to Love, had given her, in *Sleep*, a full Idea of those Joys, which, when *Awake*, she durst not allow herself to think of' (40). Nothing remains but for Dorimenus to press home his advantage until 'at last, amidst Delight and Pain, a Rack of Extasy on both sides, she more faintly denying, he more vigorously pressing, half yielding, half reluctant, she was wholly lost' (41). The familiar rhetoric of this seduction scene reveals that Philecta has lost the upper hand in the masquerade drama of amatory 'plotting' and is now relegated to the role of hysterical victim.

The story concludes tragically. Dorimenus abandons both women to marry a wealthy heiress, Lysimena, leaving Philecta pregnant and the object of universal contempt.[46] Pregnancy, in this novel, marks the final defeat for the masquerading woman in her attempt to control the significatory capacities of the female body. All the heroine's artifice and facility with disguise cannot, in the end, conceal this final corporeal and evident sign of her secret sexual desires. Philecta's 'Pangs' of regret, and by association pangs in labour, are 'made more sharp by a Reflection that she owed them to herself' (26). For the 'witty' women, such as Philecta, in Haywood's novels, seduction signifies not only sexual but intellectual defeat. Or, as Haywood herself put it in her 'Discourse' appended to the *Love-Letters from a Lady of Quality to a Chevalier*: 'The happy *Idiot*, blest in Security, postpones not her Misfortune; and perhaps, for many Years enjoys a state of Tranquillity; while the *Woman of Wit*, with aking heart, perceives from far, the Ruin she is sure to meet, and fain would fly, but cannot' (5).

Joan Rivière's polemical article entitled 'Womanliness as a Masquerade', and first published in 1929, is illuminating in this

[46] *The Masqueraders* has a continuation, published as *The Masqueraders: or, Fatal Curiosity, Being the Secret History of a Late Amour. Part II* (London, 1725), but this story abandons Philecta, Dalinda, and the masquerade trope, providing an account of Dorimenus's infidelity to his wife with another woman, Briscilla.

context.[47] Rivière's essay on the intellectual woman's use of masquerade as a means of expressing a 'masculine' identification was in itself a piece of masquerading. When her own long analysis under Ernest Jones from 1916 to 1920 failed to satisfy her, she appears to have written her own case history under the cover of presenting that of another female analysand, a successful university lecturer, who, despite her academic brilliance found it necessary to seek reassurance from men following the performance of her lectures by soliciting their sexual admiration. Rivière argues that 'women who wish for masculinity may put on a mask of womanliness to avert anxiety and the retribution feared from men' (35). In other words, in order to challenge her male analyst's 'reading' of her story, Rivière presents the story of another fictional woman. She adopts the place of another woman in order to substitute for the man, or rather, the male position of mastery over interpretation and evaluation. Thus, like Philecta, the woman who is adopting the 'masculine' part of sexual aggression or seduction endeavours to conceal her activity by playing the role of 'another' woman, accentuating rather than suppressing her femininity in order to compensate for her self-perceived impropriety. The performance of submissive femininity, engaged upon with self-conscious irony, becomes a more effective means of disguising active female desire than the adoption of a visibly 'masculine' persona.

Rivière comments that the use of the masquerade of femininity stems from a sadistic need to triumph over both sexes and does not engender any solidarity with other women against male abuse, but rather rivalry. She comments that 'It is significant that this woman's mask, though transparent to other women, was successful with men, and served its purpose very well' (41). Men, in this fictional display, are cast in the role of dupes, while women recognize it for what it is. Within masquerade logic the power lies with women in their strategic deployment of the mask, but frequently at the expense of other women.

Here too, Rivière's interpretation illuminates Haywood's romance fictions. Haywood's novels are rarely resolved through the friendship of women. Dalinda is used by Philecta as an identity to assume and with which to protect herself, but there is no sympathy between the

---

[47] Joan Rivière, 'Womanliness as a Masquerade' (1929), repr. in Burgin, Donald, and Kaplan (eds.), *Formations of Fantasy*, 35–44.

two women. The only examples of plot resolution through female friendship among these romances of the 1720s occur when there is no possibility of rivalry between the women for the attention of a man. In *The Surprize, or, Constancy Rewarded* (1724; *SH* iii. 167–202), Alinda dismisses one of her suitors when she discovers her cousin, Euphenia, is in love with him, but we are assured that her affections were not deeply engaged. In *The British Recluse* (1722; *SH* ii. 1–114) the two women become friends through narrating their mutual stories of seduction and betrayal by the same man to each other and retire to the country together, 'where they still live in a perfect Tranquility, happy in the real Friendship of each other, despising the uncertain *Pleasures*, and free from all the *Hurries* and *Disquiets* which attend the Gaieties of the Town' (114). However, it is only in this retirement, away from the presence of men, and without the possibility of either retrieving the lost lover, that the friendship is allowed credence. Compassion from one woman to another, whether between fictional characters, or solicited by the narrator from the female reader on behalf of the heroine, is only licensed if the heroine is posited as 'victim' and her feminine submission/suffering revealed to be 'authentic'.

Yet it is precisely the authenticity of this femininity that the masquerade fiction undermines, as Rivière came to realize. At the conclusion of her essay, she asserts:

Womanliness therefore could be assumed and worn as a mask, both to hide the possession of masculinity and to avert the reprisals expected if she was found to possess it. . . . The reader may now ask how I define womanliness or where I draw the line between genuine womanliness and the 'masquerade'. My suggestion is not, however, that there is any such difference; whether radical or superficial, they are the same thing. (38)

Applied to my reading of *The Masqueraders*, Rivière's comments would suggest that Philecta's ruin is not brought about by the transformation of her masquerade performance into 'genuine womanliness', so much as her inability to perceive the latter as nothing more than another fictional identity that she can turn to serve her purpose. Rivière adds that the 'weak point' of her subject's masquerade activity was the 'megalomaniac character, under all the disguises, of the necessity for supremacy. When this supremacy was seriously disturbed during analysis, she fell into an abyss of anxiety, rage and abject depression . . .' (42). This returns us to Haywood's repeated commentary on the difficulties for the intellectual woman of admitting defeat in amatory conflict. Such conflict is, it is clear, a struggle for power. It is the inability to see beyond the dichotomy of victor and victim that entraps Philecta. When her creative resources dry up, she succumbs to the position of hysteric, the 'abyss of anxiety, rage and abject depression'. Stephen Heath points out in his analysis of Rivière's thesis: 'Hysteria is what? *Failed* masquerade. The hysteric will not play the game, misses her identity as a woman'.[48] Theories of hysteria in the eighteenth century associated hysteria with women of superior intellectual powers. Sir William Stukely, in a work exactly contemporary to Haywood's romances, remarked 'that the modish disease call'd the vapors, and from it's supposed seat, the SPLEEN, does most frequently attack scholars and persons of the soft sex most eminent for wit and good sense'.[49] Over a century and a half later, Freud and Breuer were to substantiate this argument, commenting that 'among hysterics may be found people of the clearest intellect, strongest will, greatest character and highest critical power' (*SE* ii. 13). Hysteria in women, and its eighteenth-century equivalent for men, hypochondria, is associated with art and the powers of the imagination.

An artistic nature paradoxically serves as both the greatest stimulus of hysteria, and the only possibility of escape from it. If the hysteric can transform her trauma into art (as Kamuf's reading of the Portuguese nun suggests), she can divest herself of her symptoms, not by suppressing the significatory capacities of her body but by 'renarrating' them in order to 'master' them. We could see the adoption of masquerade identities on the part of women in Haywood's texts as providing her heroines with an opportunity to engineer a 'renarration' of the seduction scene until they can effect a cure. The ambiguous place of art in curing or generating hysteria in psychological theory could be seen as analogous to the ambiguous power Haywood accords to her text to generate or cure sexual desire in the female reader.

Fiction, Fantasy, Fantomina

It is in her *Fantomina, or, Love in a Maze* (1725; *SH* iii. 257–92) that

⁴⁸ Stephen Heath, 'Joan Rivière and the Masquerade', in Burgin, Donald, and Kaplan (eds.), *Formations of Fantasy*, 51.
⁴⁹ William Stukely, *Of the Spleen: Its Description and History, Uses and Diseases, Particularly the Vapors, with their Remedy* (London, 1723), 25.

Haywood exploits to the full the possibilities of the concept-metaphor of the masquerade as a 're-enactment' of the seduction scene deployed by the woman for her own empowerment. This complex story of 'womanliness as a masquerade' even withholds from the reader the true identity of its heroine. The nameless heroine is an independent heiress, who is first introduced to us as typical material for the role of suffering hysterical virgin in that she is 'young, a Stranger to the World, and consequently to the Dangers of it' (260). On a solitary excursion to London from the country, she visits the theatre. Intrigued by the dalliance between the men of quality and the prostitutes in the pit below her, she determines to disguise herself as a prostitute in order to discover how such women are addressed by the men she encounters only in the formal assemblies and balls of her own bourgeois culture. She is courted by many, but is particularly charmed by the gallant Beauplaisir who 'was transported to find so much Beauty and Wit in a Woman, who he doubted not but on very easy Terms he might enjoy; and she found a vast deal of Pleasure in conversing with him in this free and unrestrain'd Manner' (261). The disguise of 'Fantomina', the name she gives herself, allows the heroine the freedom that Castle argues the masquerade licensed for women, 'a kind of psychological latitude normally reserved for men' (44). The new divisions of place and culture that bourgeois hegemony was carving out for itself may have offered new opportunities for bourgeois men but were peculiarly restrictive to bourgeois women. While their male counterparts could move from coffee-house to ale-house, gallery to pit, between élite and populist cultures, bourgeois women found themselves increasingly confined to the home and the 'polite' assembly. Only the masquerade provided a sanctioned space for a lifting of restrictions on women's social mobility.

Fantomina engages to meet Beauplaisir the following night at the theatre and takes lodgings near the playhouse. Here she entertains him but finds her play-acting has gone further than she imagined. Despite her revelation that she is a virgin, Beauplaisir rapes her. Haywood employs her characteristic rhetoric of victim and victor to describe the scene, and it appears that Fantomina will go the way of her sisters, seduced, abandoned, and falling into hysteria: '*He* was bold;—he was resolute: *She* fearful,—confus'd, altogether unprepar'd to resist in such Encounters' (264). Beauplaisir is already writing Fantomina's future plot for her, expecting her to become a hardened prostitute. He 'did not doubt by the Beginning of her Conduct, but that in the End she would be in Reality, the thing she so artfully had counterfeited' (262).

However, the heroine herself has other plans. She maintains both identities, entertaining her lover in her lodgings during the day, and appearing at the balls and assemblies in her 'real' persona:

The Business of her Love has engross'd her till Six in the Evening, and before seven she has been dress'd in a different Habit, and in another Place.—Slippers, and a Nightgown loosely flowing, has been the Garb in which he has left the languishing *Fantomina*;—Lac'd, and adorn'd with all the Blaze of Jewels, has he, in less than an Hour after, beheld at the Royal Chapel, the Palace-Gardens, Drawing-Room, Opera, or Play, the haughty Awe-inspiring Lady. (268–9)

Thus, 'Fantomina' turns class demarcations of place that habitually impede women's mobility to her advantage. Indeed, she keeps Beauplaisir's 'Inclination alive something longer than otherwise' (269), precisely because of her uncanny physical resemblance to the lady he views from a distance at society assemblies.

Ultimately, of course, Beauplaisir varies 'not so much from his Sex, as to be able to prolong Desire, to any great Length after Possession' (269). It is at this point that the story of *Fantomina* diverges from the usual trajectory of seduction, betrayal, and hysterical decline of amatory fiction. Unlike the Baroness de Tortillée, Fantomina, despite her 'masculine' desire to control the amatory plot, does not suffer from congenital infidelity. Like the hysterical virgins she has so far resembled, her passion has only increased with possession and her desire is now to 'dilate' her own romance, to see it continue: 'She lov'd *Beauplaisir*; it was only he whose Solicitations could give her Pleasure. . . . Her Design was once more to engage him, to hear him sigh, to see him languish, to feel the strenuous Pressures of his eager Arms, to be compelled, to be sweetly forced to what she wished with equal Ardour' (270). In other words, Fantomina wishes to 're-enact' the scene of seduction, to return to the momentary power that the woman experiences in courtship.

When Beauplaisir pretends to visit an aunt in the country, but instead heads for new pursuits in the city of Bath, the heroine follows him and plots to regain access to the heady delights of their early courtship. Blacking her eyebrows and hair and dressing in the clothing of a country rustic (adopting a new masquerade disguise), she is engaged as a chamber-maid under the name of Celia at Beauplaisir's lodgings. True to form, Beauplaisir 'seduces' the innocent country maid. She now mimics the 'half-yielding, half-reluctant' gestures of the embattled virgin she had involuntarily displayed in their first encounter (271). When a month later her lover loses interest in this new conquest and heads back to London, the heroine waylays his coach in disguise as the Widow Bloomer, her hair concealed in a widow's cap and dressed in sober black. The widow asks the young gallant to conduct her to an urgent meeting in London and, during an overnight coach stop, feigns a faint in shock at his sexual overtures. This time, she enjoys the pleasures of being ravished while semi-conscious, another familiar scenario in Haywood's amatory fiction (Philecta and Melliora are only two examples).

At this point, the narrator feels obliged to explain her heroine's continued success in disguise, commenting that she 'was so admirably skill'd in the Art of Feigning, that she had the Power of putting on almost what Face she pleas'd, and knew ... exactly how to form her Behaviour to the Character she represented' (276). Beauplaisir's own intentness on 'acting' the part of the sincere lover, of course, favours her own deceit. The libertine driven by lust only 'sees' in the woman the image of his own desire, casting her as victim in his own narcissistic drama. 'Fantomina' congratulates herself upon her inversion of traditional gender opposition with the thought that she has 'out-witted even the most subtle of the deceiving Kind, and while he thinks to fool [her], is himself the only beguiled Person' (279).

On her return to London she continues to entertain her lover both as Fantomina and the Widow Bloomer, until his interest wanes in the latter. Our heroine now shifts into a different tradition of masquerade disguise. Up until this point her masquerade identities have fallen under the genre of the 'class' of character as opposed to representing a specific historical, allegorical, or literary figure or adopting the 'neutral' guise of the domino. This genre of masquerade disguise could range from shepherdesses, orange girls, and flower-sellers through to nuns, priests, bawds, animals, and birds.[50] Now, in the role of the mysterious Incognita, the heroine dons the disguise of the domino. Where 'character' dress is

[50] Castle, *Masquerade and Civilization*, 58.

expressive, demanding the adoption of certain generic traits associated with the costume and eliciting responses from fellow
masqueraders in tune with the class of character portrayed
(Beauplaisir engages in horseplay with the chambermaid, but courts
the bourgeois widow), the domino is a concealing habit and mask
that completely obscures the wearer, transforming him or her into a
mere cipher. The domino, then, was 'the quintessential sign of erotic
and political cabal, the mask of intrigue itself'.[51] To play this final
role, the heroine rents a well-furnished house and hires two down-
and-outs to act the part of go-betweens and servants. She solicits
Beauplaisir by letter, makes a rendezvous at the house and offers
him the delights of her body only on the terms that their sexual
encounters take place in a shuttered room, and that he may only see
her in daylight when she is veiled.

The adoption of the disguise of the domino appears to mark the
end of the heroine's masquerading. No costume, it appears, can
succeed the utterly blank and hence infinite significatory possibilities
of the domino. As Incognita, Haywood's heroine presents the nadir
of feminine representation. She embodies the exchangeable female
body, the empty sign into which both male and female readers can
project their own fantasy and desire. In fact, her masquerading
ventures are curtailed by the fact that she is pregnant. Once again,
the indomitable materialism of the body defeats the woman's play
with the ambiguity of signification. Pregnancy is the irrefutable sign
of female difference that calls a halt to the woman's 'mimicry' of
femininity.

The heroine does attempt to resist even this 'imposition' upon the
body she has so far controlled and manipulated to serve her own
amatory ends: 'By eating little, lacing prodigious strait, and the
Advantage of a great Hoop-Petticoat, . . . her Bigness was not taken
notice of' (289). She finally goes into labour at a ball and her 'fall'
from virtue is now publicly displayed. Haywood's description of this
moment restores her heroine to the tradition of the hystericized
victim. Her body signifies, against her will, the secret of her active
sexual desire in a grotesque parody of the love-struck virgin's
paralyses and fevers at the scene of seduction: 'She could not
conceal the sudden Rack which all at once invaded her; or had her
Tongue been mute, her wildly rolling Eyes, the Distortion of her

---

[51] Ibid. 59.

Features, and the Convulsions which shook her whole Frame, in spite of her, would have reveal'd she labour'd under some terrible Shock of Nature' (289). The heroine names Beauplaisir as the father of her baby girl. He, of course, denies all responsibility, since she has never exposed her real identity to him and her mother turns on her daughter with the enquiry, 'have you deceived me by a fictitious Tale?' (291) Even, then, at this most material of events, a pregnancy which discloses a 'truth', the heroine can be 'read' only as a piece of artifice. Yet the conclusion of *Fantomina* is one of the least melancholy of Haywood's endings. The heroine is dispatched to a convent in France showing no signs of repentance, while her lover is cleared of blame and charged only not to 'divulge the distracted Folly she has been guilty of' (292). This heroine suffers none of the psychological torment that leads so many of her counterparts, such as Philecta, to the grave. The story of *Fantomina* offers a challenge to the conventional plot structure and gendered subject positions of the amatory tale. Here the heroine acts out a series of tales of seduction through the adoption of a variety of masquerade identities that transport the duped man from female form to female form. In the melancholy reiteration of female defeat at the hands of the fictionalizing male libertine, *Fantomina* provides a small oasis of possibility through the practice of feminine mimicry.

Mimicking Femininity: Romance and the Female Reader

In Haywood's later domestic fiction, the use of the masquerade topos highlights the ambiguities of its liberatory possibilities that her earlier work had, to some extent, masked. The 'masquerade' stories included in the first number (April 1744) of her monthly periodical, the *Female Spectator* (1744–6), stress the dangers attendant upon the masquerade's sanction of anonymity. 'The glitter with which it is adorned', writes the older and wiser editor of the journal, 'strikes the eye at a distance, and you perceive not the spirit within, till, by too near an approach, you are in danger of being infected with its venom' (i. 16). As Terry Castle points out, the darker side of the promise of liberation from bourgeois sexual repression that the masquerade encoded, was that 'inclusive as it was, the masquerade made no exception for the sadistic or psychopathic' (45). Haywood provides two stories in the *Female Spectator* which dramatize the sexual threat of the masquerade to women. The first involves a husband who sets about curing his wife of her addiction to the masquerade by persuading a friend to wear an exact replica of his own costume. Mistaking this man for her husband, the wife leaves the masquerade with him, is transported to a sordid lodging-house, and threatened with rape. Her husband miraculously appears to save her both from the supposed rape and her fascination with the masquerade itself (i. 34–7). A more tragic story is that of Erminia (i. 45–56), in which the heroine, an innocent country girl on her first excursion to the masquerade, leaves with a man dressed in a duplicate of her brother's blue domino. The libertine rapes her and Erminia, too ashamed to accept her country sweetheart's generous offer to marry her despite her disgrace, retires to live with a dull aunt and seclude herself from the world.

These stories develop the plot of *The Lucky Rape, or, Fate the Best Disposer* (1727), an early story which had already identified women's vulnerability to abuse as a result of masquerade anonymity and inversion.[52] Emilia, a strictly reared Spanish heiress visiting her liberal aunt in the Andalusian countryside, is encouraged to attend the carnival. Her worldly aunt instructs her to 'enjoy all the Freedoms that Season allow'd with only one Restriction, which was that whoever, taking the Liberty of the Time, should happen to address her, she should with the utmost Care conceal her real Name' (81). In this case the worldly advice that all pleasures can be indulged so long as public reputation is not besmirched proves misguided. Emilia, calling herself 'Florella' falls in love with a young gallant under the name of Berinthus and agrees to meet him at the masquerade on the following night on the basis that 'the Freedom, which the time of Carnival permits, is but a short Duration, and that then ensues Restrictions and Restraints' which might make their meetings difficult (86). At the masquerade, Berinthus's friend, Alonzo, abducts her, under the pretence of saving her from the unwanted attentions of an unknown cavalier. He takes her to an inn and rapes her, and when Berinthus enters in search of his friend she reveals her high-born background and name, calling upon the latter to revenge her honour. Upon the disclosure of her name it emerges that Berinthus is in fact her long-estranged brother who has been educated abroad. The plot is neatly resolved with Alonzo's offer to

---

[52] Eliza Haywood, *The Lucky Rape*, appended to *Cleomelia, or, The Generous Mistress*, 2nd edn. (London, 1727), 80–94.

repair the damage by marrying Emilia. Haywood concludes with delight that 'This Rape therefore which had the Appearance of the most terrible Misfortune that Female Virtue cou'd sustain, by the secret Decrees of Destiny, prov'd her greatest Good, since by it she was not only deliver'd from that manifest Danger of Incest she was falling into, but also gain'd a Husband' (94). Clearly, then, rape in Haywood's sexual economy is not so much a physical or emotional outrage, but a form of theft. Rape, if not 'repaired' by marriage, deprives the woman of her only commodity of any value in the sexual marketplace, her virginity. *The Lucky Rape* recalls Aphra Behn's *The Dumb Virgin*, another masquerade fiction (the two sisters and brother first meet at a masquerade), in which the tragic effects of incest are not averted.

The Lucky Rape and the masquerade stories of the *Female Spectator*, then, recuperate women into the model of oppression which dominates Haywood's representation of heterosexual romance in general. The female body finally defeats the fertile plots of the female imagination. However, I would suggest that the 'masquerade' novels do not only solicit the reader's identification with the struggles of the heroine in order to escape exploitation and repression. The masquerade is more than a plot device from which to explore the pleasures and perils of female sexuality. It stands as a metaphor for the practice of Haywood's female romance writing itself, the transformation of the mute and 'written upon' female body into the active profit-making of the female writing subject.

Where her heroines fail in turning the romance to profit, Haywood succeeds. Ultimately Haywood's romance plots are not offered to the female reader as simple models for female strategies of resistance in the 'real' world of heterosexual exchange, but as substitutes in themselves for that world. The act of making fiction, the seduction of female reader by female writer, is offered as a substitute in and of itself for the disappointments of heterosexual love. If Haywood's heroines only suffer at the hands of romance, Haywood herself makes a profit from it. The only 'guilty evidence' of her involvement in romance is the financial return that enables her to survive to write another fiction. In this sense, Haywood's novels are themselves examples of 'womanliness as masquerade', in which the witty woman (Haywood or her reader) employs the persona of another woman, a substitute (her heroine), to re-enact the story of seduction as a history of coming to power. Haywood turns the seduced and violated body of the romance heroine to her own profit.

Fictional 'generation' of romance, then, transforms physical oppression into formal subversion. Consumption of the romance text by the female reader is a means of avoiding 'that Fate which all Women must expect, when to gratify their Passion they make a Sacrifice of their Honour, that of being slighted and forsaken'.[53] The eroticism of these fictional texts extends to the reader a means of 'gratifying passion' without 'sacrificing honour', releasing guilt from the practice of rape-fantasy. Fiction both compensates for and challenges the limits of reality. Haywood thus offers her readers a method of escape from masculine closure through the re-enactment of fictional feminine identities, or the practice of subversive mimesis.

At one point in *Love in Excess* Melliora argues with her lover, D'Elmont, commenting that 'Books were, as it were, Preparatives to Love, and by their softening Influence, melted the Soul, and made it fit for amorous Impressions' (*SH* i. 84). My reading of Haywood's early fiction would suggest that far from encouraging her readers to move from the fictional to the real 'romance', her novels seek to substitute the fictional for the real. This act of mimicry, of masquerade discourse, is paradoxically both an unveiling and a re-veiling. Unrealistic though Haywood's fictional romance world is, it constantly reinscribes the 'truth' of women's oppression at the hands of men, and seeks to compensate them with the pleasures of fiction. In the words of Luce Irigaray:

To play with mimesis is thus, for a woman, to try to recover the place of her exploitation by discourse, without allowing herself to be simply reduced to it. It means to resubmit herself—inasmuch as she is on the side of the 'perceptible', of 'matter'—to 'ideas', in particular to ideas about herself, that are elaborated in/by a masculine logic, but so as to make 'visible', by an effect of playful repetition, what was supposed to remain invisible: the cover-up of a possible operation of the feminine in language. It also means 'to unveil' the fact that, if women are such good mimics, it is because they are not simply resorbed [*sic*] in this function. *They also remain elsewhere*: another case of the persistence of 'matter', but also of 'sexual pleasure'.[54]

[53] Eliza Haywood, *Reflections on the Various Effects of Love. According to the Contrary Dispositions of the Persons on Whom it Operates* (London, 1726), 17.

[54] Luce Irigaray, 'The Power of Discourse and the Subordination of the Feminine', in *This Sex Which is Not One*, trans. Catherine Porter (New York, 1985), 76.

6

The Decline of Amatory Fiction: Re(de)fining the Female Form

Love in itself, when under the Direction of Reason, harmonizes the soul, and gives it a gentle, generous Turn; but I can by no means approve of such Definitions of that Passion as we find in Romances, Novels and Plays: In most of those Writings, the Authors seem to lay out all their Art in rendering that Character most interesting, which most sets at Defiance all the Obligations, by the strict Observance of which, Love can alone become a Virtue.—They dress their *Cupid* up in Roses, call him the God of soft Desires, and ever-springing Joys, yet at the same Time give him the vindictive Fury, and the rage of *Mars*;—shew him impatient of Controul, and trampling over all the Ties of Duty, Friendship, or natural Affection, yet make the Motive sanctify the Crime.—How fatal, how pernicious to a young and inexperienced Mind must be such Maxims, especially when dress'd up in all the Pomp of Words! The Beauty of the Expression steals upon the Senses, and every Mischief, every Woe that Love occasions, appears a Charm. (*Female Spectator*, i. 8)

In this statement of April 1744 from the first number of her anonymously published periodical, *The Female Spectator*, Eliza Haywood appears to inveigh against her own short romances of passion of the 1720s and 1730s. The sober and industrious editor of the *Female Spectator* draws on her own youthful experience of the dangerous and seductive power of romance in order to warn her young female readers of its dangers. Haywood, it seems, had seen the error of her ways. This was, indeed, the attitude that commentators on Haywood's career toward the end of the century adopted toward her dismissal of the charms of romance in her domestic fiction, periodical and conduct writings of the 1740s and 1750s. Thus, Euphrasia, the spokeswoman for romance in Clara Reeve's *The Progress of Romance* (1785), cites the *Female Spectator* as one of the works that would remember Haywood to posterity, presenting her early career as itself an unfortunate 'seduction' narrative at the hands of her two 'fallen' predecessors, Behn and Manley: 'There is reason to believe that the examples of the two ladies we have spoken of, seduced Mrs. *Heywood* into the same track; she certainly wrote some amorous novels in her youth, and also two books of the same kind as Mrs. *Manley's* capital work [i.e. the *New Atalantis*], all of which I hope are forgotten.'[1] Clearly Haywood's tendency to identify her narratorial persona with that of her deceived heroines in her early fiction had its dividends in this later assessment of her work, in which she could be presented as the victim of the seductive strategies of those earlier and older temptresses, Behn and Manley.

It has long been a commonplace in criticism of the eighteenth-century novel to view the publication of Samuel Richardson's *Pamela* in 1740 as inaugurating a new era in the history of the English novel, whether in the establishment of sentiment as the dominating principle of novelistic fiction or domestic bourgeois values as opposed to aristocratic gallantry as the mainstay of novelistic ideology.[2] The pains which Haywood and her later supporters such as Reeve took to represent her shift to domestic realism in the 1740s as a personal moral conversion, might be interpreted as an attempt to conceal a less worthy motive on the author's part, that of personal material need in the face of changing taste. Quite simply, 'by the mid-century, Haywood could no longer make money by selling her short romances of passion. In 1768 a version of an early romance originally entitled *The Agreeable Caledonian* (1728) and ostensibly corrected by Haywood shortly before her death in 1756 was printed only to be roundly dismissed in the *Monthly Review* as 'like the rest of Mrs. Haywood's novels, written in a tawdry style, now utterly exploded; the romances of these days being reduced much nearer the standard of nature, and to the manners of the living world'.[3] Clearly the market for hyperbolic passion, romance names, and exotic settings had diminished by the 1760s and was, indeed, not to revive until the last decades of the eighteenth century with the Gothic novels of Ann Radcliffe, who significantly restored the use of the term 'romance' to describe her fiction.[4]

---

[1] Clara Reeve, *The Progress of Romance and the History of Charoba, Queen of Aegypt* (Facsimile Text Society Ser. 1: Literature and Language, 4; New York, 1930) 121 (texts separately numbered).

[2] On sentiment, see R. S. Crane, 'Suggestions toward a Genealogy of the Man of Feeling', *ELH* 1 (1934), 205–30 and R. F. Brissenden, *Virtue in Distress: Studies in the Novel of Sentiment from Richardson to Sade* (London, 1974). On domestic bourgeois values, see ch. 3 of Armstrong, *Desire and Domestic Fiction*, 59–95 and ch. 3 of Spencer, *Rise of the Woman Novelist*, 75–103.

[3] Review of *Clementina*, *Monthly Review*, 38 (1768), 412.

[4] Only Radcliffe's first novel, *The Castles of Athlin and Dunbayne: A Highland Story* (1784), did not employ the term 'romance' in its title or subtitle.

The brusque comments of the *Monthly Review* reveal, however, the extent to which formal realism had come to be equated with moral realism. The accusation of improbability had come to stand for that of immorality. The likelihood of a serving-maid finally marrying her wealthy and status-obsessed master was, after all, no more or less probable in the English society of the 1740s, than that of an Italian nun eloping from a convent with a Scottish nobleman in that of the 1720s.[5] Richardson's narratives were, then, taken as the new model for fiction more by virtue of their overt claims to moral purity than the probability of their plots.

In concluding my consideration of Behn's, Manley's and Haywood's amatory fiction, I will turn to a discussion of the importance of their role as negative precedents in the formation of the 'new' domestic novel of sentiment of the mid- to late eighteenth century, of which Richardson was, of course, the pre-eminent example. The late eighteenth century, in particular, saw an extensive process of what might be termed canon-formation. Magazines found the backbone of their material in publishing new and classic works of fiction in serial form and in reviewing fiction of the period. The growing popularity of circulating libraries and the availability of texts in cheaper formats from the 1750s onwards meant that a new body of readers were perceived to be in search of some guidance in their choice of texts. The lapse of copyright on a number of eighteenth-century novelists such as Defoe, Richardson, and Fielding saw the emergence of the cheap edited collection of novels in the late eighteenth and early nineteenth centuries.[6]

The late seventeenth-century and early eighteenth-century fiction of Behn, Manley, and Haywood is distinguished in this process of canon-formation by the frequency with which it is noted and dismissed in the same breath in critical commentaries and by an almost total lack of republication. Neither Scott and Ballantyne nor

---

[5] Haywood's novel may have been republished under the title *Clementina* to capitalize on the success of Richardson's *Sir Charles Grandison* (1753–4), in which the stalwartly patriotic and Protestant hero found himself entangled with an Italian Catholic aristocrat named Clementina.

[6] On magazines, see Robert Mayo, *The English Novel in the Magazines 1740–1815* (London, 1962). The best-known edited collections of novels are Anna Laetitia Barbauld's fifty-volume *The British Novelists* (London, 1810) and Ballantyne's ten-volume *Novelist's Library* (London, 1821–4), with biographical 'memoirs' of the authors prefixed to the volumes provided by Sir Walter Scott. On canon-formation in the late eighteenth and early nineteenth century see Armstrong, *Desire and Domestic Fiction*, 37–8.

Barbauld included any novels by Behn, Manley, or Haywood in their influential collections of novels. Indeed, Scott, in his 'biographical memoir' of Horace Walpole, claiming to provide a history of the romance in England, politely ignored early English amatory fiction altogether, arguing that the 'unnatural taste' for: 'those dullest of dull folios, the romances of Calprenede and Scuderi, works which hover between the ancient tale of chivalry and the modern novel . . . began to give way early in the eighteenth century; and, about the middle of it, was entirely superseded by the works of LeSage, Richardson, Fielding and Smollett.'[7] Anna Laetitia Barbauld did include a brief commentary on Behn, Manley and Haywood in her preface to the first volume of her *The British Novelists* (1810) with an essay 'On the Origin and Progress of Novel-Writing'.[8] Barbauld claimed that:

Of the lighter species of this kind of writing, *the Novel*, till within half a century we had scarcely any. *The Atalantis* of Mrs. Manley lives only in that line of Pope which seems to promise it immortality:

'As long as *Atalantis* shall be read'.

It was, like *Astrea*, filled with fashionable scandal. Mrs. Behn's Novels were licentious; they are also fallen; but it ought not to be forgotten that Southern borrowed from her his affecting story of *Oroonoko*. Mrs. Haywood was a very prolific genius; her earlier novels are in the style of Mrs. Behn's, and Pope has chastised her in his *Dunciad* without mercy or delicacy, but her latter works are by no means void of merit. She wrote *The Invisible Spy*, and *Betsy Thoughtless*, and was the author of *The Female Spectator*. ('Origin', 34–5)

In this one paragraph, Barbauld in fact embodies the dominant perspective on the 'fair Triumvirate of Wit' of the mid- to late eighteenth century. Manley, whose sophisticated party political interventions had become virtually meaningless to non-contemporary readers, was dismissed out of hand. The only fiction by Behn that had continuing appeal was her *Oroonoko* by virtue principally of its sentimental reworkings in the drama.[9] Haywood was given some credit for her shift in moral perspective in the later novels, but

---

[7] Sir Walter Scott, 'Horace Walpole', in *Biographical Memoirs*, vol. iii of *Miscellaneous Prose Works of Sir Walter Scott* (Edinburgh, 1827), 106.

[8] Anna Laetitia Barbauld, 'On the Origin and Progress of Novel-Writing', in *The British Novelists, with an Essay, and Prefaces, Biographical and Critical*, new edn., vol. i (London, 1820), 1–59. All references are to this edition unless otherwise noted, cited as 'Origin' and included in the main body of the text.

[9] Wylie Sypher comments that a dramatic version of *Oroonoko* was given at least once every season in London from 1696 to 1801 (*Guinea's Captive Kings*, 116).

this did not result in a concerted attempt to rejuvenate her earlier works.

Any consideration of Behn, Manley, and Haywood habitually released a meditation on the moral advancement of the novel in the mid- to late eighteenth century as a result of changing sexual ideology. Thus the entry on Aphra Behn in David Erskine Baker's *Companion to the Play-House* of 1764 argued that she had no alternative but to comply with prevailing taste, reluctantly conceding that to some extent it corresponded to her own:

The best, and perhaps the only true Excuse that can be made for it is, that altho' she might herself have as great an Aversion as any One to loose Scenes or too warm Descriptions, yet, as she wrote for a Livelihood, she was obliged to comply with the corrupt Taste of the Times.—And, as she was a Woman, and naturally, moreover, of an amorous Complexion, and wrote in an Age, and to a Court of Gallantry and Licentiousness, the Latter Circumstances, added to her Necessities, compell'd her to indulge her Audience in their favorite Depravity. (B3^r)

Elizabeth Griffith's introduction to her three-volume *Collection of Novels, Selected and Revised* (1777), which consisted in fact of seven English and French novels of the late seventeenth and early eighteenth century only one of which is by a male author, was in many ways an early prototype of Barbauld's more ambitious project to provide a history of the rise of the novel. In her 'Editor's Preface', describing the effect of the restoration of the Stuart monarchy on the sphere of the arts, Griffith comments:

Mirth and wit, both which had been anatematized during the gloomy interregnum of Cromwell's usurpation, broke forth, like light, with the returning sun of royalty. Exiled with the Monarch, they accompanied him home again; but, like him also, unreformed by chastisement, and untutored by adversity. Sermons and homilies gave place to Shaftesbury's Characteristics; mystic hymns were exchanged for wanton sonnets; and the stately romance resigned its station in the female library, to the gross effusions of amorous nonsense; which was, at that era, first introduced into these kingdoms, under the more modern title of *Novels*.[10]

Griffith, then, took a more pragmatic approach to the best means of preventing her readers from corruption at the hands of these decadent narratives than her successors in editing the novel. Where Barbauld and Scott had simply warned their readers against such

[10] Elizabeth Griffith (ed.), *A Collection of Novels, Selected and Revised by Mrs. Griffith* (3 vols.; London, 1777), i. A2^{r-v}.

early fiction by women or simply ignored them in constructing their new canons for the novel, Griffith edited Behn's and Haywood's texts so as to make them conform to the sentimental and domestic moralism that dominated the novelistic discourse of her time. In her editorial preface she notes that:

all young minds require a certain supply of entertainment, as well as the body of nutriment; both which, if not properly provided, will anxiously be sought after; and writings of the most dangerous tendency, conveyed through the vehicle of an amusing or interesting story, like the most unwholesome viands, if rendered palatable, will be swallowed with avidity, by the unformed taste and unexperienced judgement of our youth of both sexes. (i. A3ʳ)

Young people will succeed in obtaining these dangerous foods in their unadulterated form, Griffith suggests, unless older and wiser heads make it their business to doctor them to insure no harmful effects are attendant on their consumption.

Behn's *Oroonoko* is of particular interest here. In 1759, Hawkesworth prefaced his dramatic reworking of Southerne's already anaesthetized version of Behn's *Oroonoko* with the claim to have done away with all vestiges of indecency in order to leave the purely sentimental effect of the original narrative, removing the sub-plot of female cross-dressing and same-sex marriage that Southerne had added. In his 'Preface' to the printed edition of the play, Hawkesworth defended his decision by arguing that:

Attention is, throughout, invariably fixed upon the two principal Characters, *Oroonoko* and *Imoinda*: who are so connected as to make but one Object, in which all the Passions of the Audience, moved by the most tender and exquisite Distress, are concentered.

It was therefore justly regretted, that these Scenes were degraded by a Connexion with some of the most loose and contemptible that have ever disgraced our Language and our Theatre....[11]

Hawkesworth, like Barbauld, stresses the sentimental power of Southerne's version of Behn's *Oroonoko*, the ability to move the audience to 'the most tender and exquisite Distress'.

It is this sentimental power, in fact more a product of Southerne and Hawkesworth than Behn, that Griffith sought to emphasize in her republication of the novel and which she underscored by careful

---

[11] John Hawkesworth, 'Preface', *Oroonoko: A Tragedy by Thomas Southern, with Alterations* (London, 1775), n.p.

excision of a number of passages. Griffith in fact made three excisions. First, she omitted the love-making scene between Oroonoko and Imoinda in the seraglio, in which Oroonoko is cast by Behn in the traditional mould of the seducer, seizing the advantage of the moment to 'ruin' the only half-reluctant virgin; second, Behn's description of Oroonoko's contempt for the Christian religion and mockery of it when she attempts to convert his wife by telling her stories of nuns; and third, Behn's comment that although she herself was absent at Oroonoko's brutal execution, her mother and sister watched the entire proceeding. These excisions clearly indicate the attempt on Griffith's part to present *Oroonoko* within the sentimental and moral frame of fiction that her readers had come to expect from women's writing in the second half of the eighteenth century.

Oroonoko, although it includes scenes of brutal violence, is, of all Behn's novels, the least given to lengthy passages of erotic description. Griffith, in fact, removed the only scene that might have given offense in this respect. Her own 'Character of Oroonoko', which precedes the edited narrative, argues that the Christian reader is left with the 'humiliating reflection' that 'Europeans, though enlightened by Christianity, have, in this, and many other instances, shewn less regard to the laws of truth and humanity, than the most ignorant savages' (200), an assertion only made possible by her silencing of the almost atheistical implications of Behn's endorsement of her hero's critique of the Christian religion. Oroonoko thus appears most vividly as 'more Christian' than his European counterparts. Finally, by excising the mention of the women's presence at the execution, Griffith complies with the new idealization of femininity in her own period, and the belief that middle-class women were too delicate and refined to view scenes of violence or the naked exercise of political power enacted in the public execution. With the republication of *Oroonoko* in Griffith's 1777 *Collection*, then, Behn's novel was suitably sanitized for consumption both on the public stage and in the private boudoir, policed into a newly sentimental form and stripped of its more incendiary sexual and political meanings.

Oroonoko was clearly a favourite with eighteenth-century audiences, but always associated more closely with its dramatic redactions than its original authoress. It was republished in serial form in two eighteenth-century magazines, *The Oxford Magazine, or Family Companion* (1736) and the *Ladies Magazine, or the Universal*

Entertainer (1749–53). No copy remains of the former,[12] but Jasper Goodwill, editor of the latter, provided a prefatory note to the first instalment of the 'History of the Royal Slave' that, again, cited the Southerne adaptation:

Mr. *Goodwill* having received Letters from many of his female Correspondents, desiring he will insert in his *Magazine*, such Novels as may, at the same time, divert and instruct.—He resolved immediately to comply with this Request; and as he knows of nothing more engaging than the *Royal Slave*, of the celebrated Mrs. *Behn*, from which Mr. *Southern* took his Play of that Name, he hopes it will be agreeable to his Readers.[13]

Such magazine fiction, of course, always enjoyed somewhat more licence than the genteel and more expensive small-print volumes of mid- to late eighteenth-century novel publication. However, among the numberless volumes of amatory fiction produced by Behn, Manley, and Haywood, only Behn's *Oroonoko* and the later fiction of Haywood (largely poached from the short moral tales she included in her *Female Spectator*) received the privilege of serialization in eighteenth-century magazines.[14]

Griffith's editing of Haywood's *The Fruitless Enquiry* in 1777 reveals a similar sentimental and moral emphasis to that which she employed toward *Oroonoko*. Haywood's text consists of a series of stories of marital unhappiness, held together by the thin frame narrative of a mother who is told by a fortune-teller that her lost son will only be restored to her if she can persuade a perfectly content woman to make him a shirt. The mother, Miramillia, visits a number of her friends in search of a suitable seamstress, only to discover that all conceal some terrible secret that makes their happiness incomplete. The pathos of the mother in search of her lost child made *The Fruitless Enquiry* an attractive novel to include in Griffith's *Collection* for an age much preoccupied with the sentimental appeal of maternal love.[15] Griffith chose to cancel whole stories in her

[12] Mayo, *English Novel in the Magazines*, 66.

[13] *Ladies Magazine, or the Universal Entertainer* (14/28 April) 4 (London, 1753), 115.

[14] Mayo draws attention to the fact that the most popular magazine devoted solely to reprinting classic fiction in serial form, the *Novelist's Magazine* (1780–9), included no Behn or Manley in its many numbers and printed only three selections from Haywood's 'reformed' period. From the earlier period of the late seventeenth and early eighteenth century, it reprinted only the *Arabian Nights*, *Tales of the Genii*, *Gulliver's Travels*, and *Robinson Crusoe*. See Mayo, *English Novel in the Magazines*, 366–7.

[15] Mothers play a remarkably small part in earlier amatory fiction in contrast with later domestic fiction. To mention only a few instances from the later period,

republication of Haywood's novel, but did not tamper with the
material of those that remained. Her choices for omission are again
significant. She excises the history of Celesina, in which a mother
discovers that her daughter was raped by the man she has recently
married prior to his courtship of her; the history of Bellazara, in
which a woman is first raped and then blackmailed into providing
further sexual favours by her husband's valet; the history of
Coquiana, in which the heroine obtains a wealthy husband by posing
as an heiress only to discover that he too is a fraud; the history of
Violathia who is driven to marital infidelity by her husband's
jealousy; and the history of Clara and Ferdinand, in which the
heroine, whose cousin rapes her and then boasts of his conquest,
takes her revenge by castrating him. Griffith, then, purged the novel
of its most violent and grotesque content. The remaining stories
contain some far from delicate elements, such as Anziana's daily
rituals in front of the skeleton of an early lover who her husband
has murdered in a fit of (unfounded) jealousy, and the story of
Montrano's castration at the hands of an Inca queen whose advances
he rejects out of continuing love for his wife, Iseria. However,
Griffith significantly removes from the text those stories most
concerned with marital infidelity, male sexual violence, active female
desire and female duplicity or personal ambition. The remaining
stories emphasize a pathetic melancholy on the part of women who
have suffered at the hands of fate, rather than (as in Haywood's
original) masculine power.

By the 1820s, we find that even Behn's *Oroonoko* could no longer
be excepted from the wholesale exclusion of women's early amatory
fiction from the annals of novelistic fiction. In an epistolary
anecdote to Lady Louisa Stuart, Sir Walter Scott, prime mover in
the early nineteenth-century initiative toward constructing a
prestigious novelistic canon, demonstrates that the name of Aphra
Behn had become synonymous with indecency, if not pornography.[16]
Scott describes a visit to his great-aunt, one Mrs Keith, an elderly

maternal love which finally 'tames' Richardson's lively Charlotte Grandison in her
marriage to Lord G— in *Sir Charles Grandison* (1753–4), is also the activating
principle behind Fielding's most sentimental portrayal of womanhood, Amelia, in
Amelia (1751) and the final cause of the reunion of Fanny Burney's heroine with her
family in *Camilla* (1796).

   [16] The anecdote is reprinted in full in Scott's words from a letter of 1826 in vol. iii
of John Gibson Lockhart's *Memoirs of the Life of Sir Walter Scott* (Boston and New York,
1902), 596–7.

lady 'of some condition' who 'lived with unabated vigour of intellect to a very advanced age' (596). Mrs Keith asks Scott to obtain a copy of Aphra Behn's novels for her, since she remembers them 'being very much admired' in her youth (596). Scott reluctantly concurs, and informs his reader:

I sent Mrs. Aphra Behn, curiously sealed up, with 'private and confidential' on the packet, to my gay old grand-aunt. The next time I saw her afterwards, she gave back Aphra, properly wrapped up, with nearly these words: 'Take back your bonny Mrs. Behn; and if you will take my advice, put her in the fire, for I found it impossible to get through the very first novel. But is it not', she said, 'a very odd thing that I, an old woman of eighty and upwards, sitting alone, feel myself ashamed to read a book which, sixty years ago, I have heard read aloud for the amusement of large circles, consisting of the first and most creditable society in London?' This, of course, was owing to the gradual improvement of the national taste and delicacy. (596–7)

Scott, then, uses the anecdote to demonstrate the advancement of taste in relation to the novel, from degraded populism to middle-class gentility. My interest in this anecdote, however, is in the importance of a shift in the perceived nature and location of novel consumption registered by Mrs Keith. Novel-reading, as Scott's great-aunt comments, was by the 1820s conceived of as a private and solitary act. The 'large circle' has dwindled to one and a novel that used to be displayed with pride and read in public has now to be wrapped up and concealed, sealed with the title 'private and confidential'. Scott represents and packages Behn's novels as pieces of pornography to be consumed covertly and, most importantly, privately.

Earlier in the century, Fielding had represented the reading of Behn's novels in a similar vein. A minor character in his *Tom Jones* (1749), the amorous Irishman, Mr Macklachlan, is introduced to the reader lying in bed 'reading one of Mrs. *Behn's* Novels; for he had been instructed by a Friend, that he would find no more effectual Method of recommending himself to the Ladies than the improving his Understanding, and filling his Mind with good Literature'.[17] When he hears a commotion in the neighbouring room, Macklachlan leaps from his bed and rushes in, thoroughly excited. Fielding's irony in terming Behn's novels 'good Literature', but to be consumed in

[17] Henry Fielding, *The History of Tom Jones, a Foundling*, ed. Martin C. Battestin and Fredson Bowers (Oxford, 1974) ii. 530 (bk. X, ch. 2).

bed by candlelight, reveals the extent to which they were interpreted as a form of pornography.

A similar incident in Charlotte Lennox's *Henrietta* (1753) with regard to the appropriateness of Eliza Haywood's early romances as bedtime reading, sets up Fielding as the unlikely moral antonym to the pornographic pleasures of early eighteenth-century fiction. Lennox's virtuous heroine, alone in London, is trying to select a novel to take to bed with her from the shelves of her landlady. Faced only with a selection of light fiction, which includes Manley's *New Atalantis*, she is forced to fall back on Fielding's anti-romance of *Joseph Andrews*. Her landlady is appalled at such highbrow taste, and attempts to persuade her to take up Haywood, with the words, 'there is Mrs. Haywood's Novels, did you ever read them? Oh! they are the finest, love-sick, passionate stories; I assure you, you'll like them vastly: Pray take a volume of Haywood upon my recommendation'.[18] Henrietta's landlady, then, assumes that a young lady in search of a book to take to bed must be in search of the sexually lubricious and, oddly perhaps given the overtly sexual content of much of Fielding's novel, that Haywood's early romances are best suited to such a desire.[19]

It is clear, then, from Scott's anecdote and Charlotte Lennox's satire that by the mid- to late eighteenth century a major shift had taken place in conceptualizing both the expectations and conditions of novelistic consumption in Britain. Although novel fiction remained largely feminocentric in terms of its content and thematic interests (concerned with sexual pursuit and amatory conflict), the 'female form' of the novel was now rigidly conceived as an essentially private one, to be consumed in the boudoir or bedroom for personal pleasure. The hegemony of the figure of the virtuous woman in this new novelistic discourse simultaneously provided the figure of the woman with a new cultural authority beyond the purely party political resistance she had represented in the works of Behn and Manley, and severely restricted the possibilities for the woman writer herself to undermine and manipulate fictions of gender identity as she had done earlier in the century. In other words, in the shift from the specificities of party political struggle to the more generalized conflict of class, the figure of the woman was

---

[18] Charlotte Lennox, *Henrietta* (London, 1753), i. 36.
[19] Since all Haywood's fiction after 1740 was published anonymously, the landlady can only be referring to her early works if she cites them by naming the author.

instrumental in evolving a 'naturalized' domestic bourgeois ideology established in contradistinction to, rather than in alliance with, the realm of the 'political'. As Marlene LeGates contends, 'the idea of the morally superior woman contributed an ideological prop to the family seen as a means of social consolidation in an increasingly class-conscious society'.[20]

The virtuous bourgeois woman (Clarissa, Sophia Western, Elizabeth Bennet) is now perceived as a force for social cohesion, precisely by virtue of her very distance from the corruptions of political identity and class conflict. Even in the work of perhaps the most party politically motivated of all the mid-century novelists, Henry Fielding, we can see this separation and idealization of the morally superior bourgeois woman as a regulatory social force in the contrast between his heroine, Sophia Western, her aunt Mrs Western, and her false protectress, Lady Bellaston. Lady Bellaston and Mrs Western are satirically reworked portraits of the Restoration and early eighteenth-century heroines and anti-heroines that have been the main focus of this thesis. Whereas Lady Bellaston recollects the type of the libidinous older woman who seeks sexual pleasure without foregoing her independent fortune or her reputation (a mid-century Duchesse de l'Inconstant or Ciamara), Mrs Western reincarnates the politically astute and manipulative villainesses of Bussy-Rabutin and Manley (Madame de Châtillon, Queen Zarah). However, through Fielding's satirical manipulations, these early models of female power become comic and ludicrous, clinging to outworn tricks and discourses (Lady Bellaston's masquerade disguise, Mrs Western's empty displays of learning) beside the incandescent beauty and moral conviction of the author's 'favourite child', Sophia, whom he can never 'quit . . . for any long Time without the utmost Reluctance' (book XVI, ch. 6, p. 660).

Fielding and Richardson's conservative paradigms of domesticated female individualism resisting social coercion and self-interest were, then, no more or less, political in the broadest sense of the term, than Behn's, Manley's and, to a lesser extent, Haywood's Tory scandal chronicles of beset virginity. In many ways, while they disclaimed any connection to these early 'romances', they owed profound debts to them. The virtuous female victim had, after all, been a staple ingredient of these early feminocentric narratives, if

[20] Marlene LeGates, 'The Cult of Womanhood in Eighteenth Century Thought', *Eighteenth Century Studies*, 10 (1976–7), 26.

not the only, or always dominant, means of representing female possibilities for power. However, in idealizing the figure of the morally superior woman, these influential mid-century novels succeeded in radically diminishing the possibilities of female self-representation for the woman writers that succeeded and imitated them. From this point onwards, women writers of the novel were forced to go to sometimes extraordinary lengths to avoid any identification between themselves and the disreputable Behn, Manley, or Haywood and to encourage in its place an identification between themselves and their morally upright heroines. The distance between Frances Burney's concern to remain anonymous upon the publication of her first novel, *Evelina* (1778), and the self-displaying narcissism of Aphra Behn seems almost immeasurable. In 1688 we find Aphra Behn expressing the hope that 'the Reputation of [her] Pen is considerable enough to make [Oroonoko's] Name to survive to all Ages, with that of the brave, the beautiful and the constant Imoinda' (*Works*, v. 208). The conjuring power of her own name, she boldly asserts, should be enough to commit that of her hero to posterity. In contrast, just under a century later, Frances Burney, in a private letter, admits that she had hoped to conceal her name behind that of her heroine. 'An *Authoress*', Burney writes, 'must always be assumed to be flippant, assuming and loquacious, and indeed, the dread of these kind of censures have been my principal motives for wishing *snugship*'.[21] In both cases, the woman writer seeks to be identified with the central protagonist of her fiction, Behn with the heroic Oroonoko, refusing to be silenced by his oppressors, proudly and publicly displaying his wounds, and Burney with the seemingly gentle Evelina, silent and retiring in public yet indulging her satiric pen in the privacy of the familial letter.

In the case of both Behn and Burney, I would argue, the attempt at self-representation is also self-consciously ironic. Both recognize that the figure of the female authoress is as much a 'fiction' as that of the female characters they represented. However, by the time that Burney came to write *Evelina*, the possibilities for the female writer to adopt a self-consciously 'public' voice and ensure critical acclaim or 'reputation' for her fictional work, had radically diminished. The dilemma that faces one of Jane Austen's earliest heroines, Susan Vernon, in her *Lady Susan*, illustrates the restrictive effects of the

---

[21] Fanny Burney, *Diary MSS*, suppressed fragments, New York Public Library, box 2; as quoted in Joyce Hemlow, *Fanny Burney* (Oxford, 1958), 63.

'new' ideal of the domestic bourgeois woman upon the range of
fictional identities available to the female writer.[22] Lady Susan is, in
many ways, another relic of late seventeenth- and early eighteenth
century amatory fiction, or 'a successful adventuress in the mode of
Restoration drama'.[23] She is a mistress of disguise, a self-observing
and narcissistic manipulator of discourse who takes an 'exquisite
pleasure in subduing an insolent spirit, in making a person pre-
determined to dislike, acknowledge one's superiority' (*Lady Susan*,
254). Like the Baroness de Tortillée in Haywood's *The Injur'd
Husband*, Lady Susan wins her young lover by presenting herself as
a virtuous woman who succumbs despite herself to passion.
However, whereas this role is only one of many in the Baroness's
arsenal of seductive strategies deployed according to the different
temperaments of a variety of lovers, it is revealed to be the only
option for Lady Susan. When the virtuous, maternal, and domesticated Mrs Vernon first meets her sister-in-law, she comments:

One is apt I beleive [*sic*] to connect assurance of manner with coquetry, & to
expect that an impudent address will necessarily attend an impudent mind;
at least I was myself prepared for an improper degree of confidence in Lady
Susan; but her Countenance is absolutely sweet, & her voice & manner
winningly mild. I am sorry it is so, for what is this but Deceit? . . . She has
already almost persuaded me of being warmly attached to her daughter, tho'
I have so long been convinced of the contrary. (251)

The adventuress, then, like the authoress, is expected to be 'flippant,
assuming and loquacious'. Lady Susan disarms her critics by
appearing 'sweet' and 'mild'. The ultimate test of her 'virtue',
however, is not so much the proof of her chastity (although the
discovery of her relationship with a married man is the final cause
of Reginald breaking off his engagement with her), as the proof of
her maternal devotion. Lady Susan's sweet and mild airs do not
extend to her behaviour toward her daughter Frederica, and it is the
latter's arrival at the Vernon's country house that begins to undermine Lady Susan's deceits. Frederica embodies the new, artless
heroine of sentimental fiction, the young lady entering the world

---

[22] *Lady Susan* was not published until 1871, when J. E. Austen-Leigh included it
with his *Memoir* of the author. However, it was probably composed early in Jane
Austen's career, around 1793–4. See B. C. Southam's note prefacing R. W. Chapman's
edition of the novel, in vol. vi, *Minor Works*, of *The Works of Jane Austen*, ed. R. W.
Chapman (1954; London, 1972), 243. All subsequent references are to this edition,
cited as *Lady Susan* and included in the main body of the text.

[23] Armstrong, *Desire and Domestic Fiction*, 97.

who needs a mother's guidance and protection. Her mother comments with contempt: 'I never saw a girl of her age, bid fairer to be
the sport of Mankind. Her feelings are tolerably lively, & she is so
charmingly artless in their display, as to afford the most reasonable
hope of her being ridiculed and despised by every man who sees her'
(274). Lady Susan seriously miscalculates here in that, although
Frederica is powerless to expose her mother's stratagems, her
'charmingly artless' display of distress when her mother tries to
force her into an unwanted marriage, cannot be misinterpreted by
either Reginald de Courcy or his sister. Ultimately, it is Frederica
who triumphs in this novel, waiting patiently in the wings until de
Courcy recovers from his disappointment in her mother and is ready
to respond to her devotion.

If we interpret Lady Susan's history as a paradigm of the fate of
the woman writer of early amatory fiction in a newly moralistic
order, we can see the extent to which the dominance of a feminocentric idealization of woman as the signifier of moral purity and
incorruptible truth from the 1740s onwards had come to limit her
possibilities for negotiation within the world of fiction. Fiction and
femininity are now thoroughly at odds. Refining the female form of
the novel, making it newly respectable, was also an act of redefinition that severely limited Behn's, Manley's, and Haywood's female
successors in the genre. Women may have entered the field of
novelistic fiction in far greater numbers than they had done in the
late seventeenth and early eighteenth century, but they did so on
more confined terms.

In particular, the new generation of women writers could only
acquire their own literary 'reputation' by asserting their difference
from the 'fair Triumvirate'. Like Frederica, who casts off Lady
Susan in favour of Mrs Vernon at the end of Austen's novel, their
only possibility of success in the newly created world of fiction, was
to cast off the old mother lest her amatory sins should be visited
upon the daughter, and to retire to a domestic tranquillity overseen
by an adoptive female presence of indisputable virtue. Behn, Manley,
and Haywood appear to have been written out of the history of the
rise of the novel not in order to ensure the pre-eminence of the male
novelist, but rather to secure the reputations of his female counterpart. Thus, Anna Laetitia Barbauld could proudly assert in 1810 that

notwithstanding the many paltry books of this kind published in the course
of every year, it may safely be affirmed that we have more good writers in

this walk living at the present time, than at any period since the days of Richardson and Fielding. A very great proportion of these are ladies: and surely it will not be said that either taste or morals have been losers by their taking the pen in hand. The names of D'Arblay, Edgeworth, Inchbald, Radcliffe, and a number more will vindicate this assertion. ('Origin', 56)

It has only been in recent years that this history of the novel has begun to be reassessed and revised, ensuring that Aphra Behn, Delarivier Manley, and Eliza Haywood be accorded the serious attention their prose writings deserve.

Bibliography

ADDISON, JOSEPH and STEELE, RICHARD, *The Spectator*, ed. Donald F. Bond (5 vols.; Oxford, 1965).
—— *The Tatler*, ed. Donald F. Bond (3 vols.; Oxford, 1987).
ANDERSON, PAUL BUNYAN, 'The History and Authorship of Mrs. Crackenthorpe's *Female Tatler*', *Modern Philology*, 28 (1931), 354–60.
—— 'Delariviere Manley's Prose Fiction', *Philological Quarterly*, 13 (1934), 168–88.
—— 'Mistress Delariviere Manley's Biography', *Modern Philology*, 33 (1936), 261–78.
ARMSTRONG, NANCY, *Desire and Domestic Fiction: A Political History of the Novel* (Oxford, 1985).
ARONSON, NICOLE, *Mademoiselle de Scudéry*, trans. Stuart Aronson (Boston, 1978).
ASTELL, MARY, *The First English Feminist: Reflections on Marriage and other Writings*, ed. Bridget Hill (Aldershot, 1986).
—— *A Serious Proposal to the Ladies, Part II: Wherein a Method Is Offer'd for the Improvement of their Minds* (London, 1697).
AUBIN, PENELOPE, 'Preface', *The Life of Charlotta du Pont* (1723), rpr. in *Eighteenth Century Novelists on the Novel*, ed. George L. Barnett (New York, 1968), 35.
AUSTEN, JANE, *Lady Susan*, in *The Works of Jane Austen*, vi: *Minor Works*, ed. R. W. Chapman, rev. B. C. Southam (London, 1972), 243–428.
BAKER, DAVID ERSKINE, *The Companion to the Play-House, or, An Historical Account of All the Dramatic Writers (and their Works) That Have Appeared in Great Britain and Ireland, from the Commencement of our Theatrical Exhibitions, Down to the Present Year 1764. Composed in the Form of a Dictionary* (2 vols.; London, 1764).
BAKER, ERNEST, *The History of the English Novel*, iii: *The Later Romances and the Establishment of Realism* (London, 1929).
BAKER, SHERIDAN, 'The Idea of the Romance in the Eighteenth Century', *Publications of the Michigan Academy of Arts, Sciences and Letters* 48 (1964), 507–22.
BARBAULD, ANNA LAETITIA, 'On the Origin and Progress of Novel-Writing', in *The British Novelists, with an Essay, and Prefaces, Biographical and Critical* new edn., vol. i (London, 1820), 1–59.
BARKER, JANE, *Exilius: Or, the Banish'd Roman* (1715) (Garland Foundations of the Novel, 25; New York and London, 1973).
BARNETT, GEORGE L. (ed.), *Eighteenth Century British Novelists on the Novel* (New York, 1968).

BARRELL, JOHN, *English Literature in History 1730–80: An Equal, Wide Survey* (London, 1983).

BARTHES, ROLAND, *Mythologies* (1957), trans. Annette Lavers (London and New York, 1973).

BATSLEER, JANET et al, *Rewriting English: Cultural Politics of Gender and Class* (London, 1985).

BEASLEY, JERRY C., 'Politics and Moral Idealism. The Achievement of Some Early Women Novelists', in Macheski and Schofield (eds.), *British Women Novelists 1670–1815*, 216–36.

BEELER, JAMES RUSH, 'Madame d'Aulnoy: Historical Novelist of the Late Seventeenth Century' (Univ. of North Carolina Ph.D. diss., 1964).

BEHN, APHRA, *All the Histories and Novels of the Late Ingenious Mrs. Behn, Entire in One Volume. Together with the History of the Life and Memoirs of Mrs Behn. By One of the Fair Sex*, 3rd edn. (London, 1698).

—— *All the Histories and Novels Written by the Late Ingenious Mrs. Behn*, 5th edn. (London, 1705).

—— *The Histories and Novels of the Late Ingenious Mrs. Behn* (London, 1696).

—— *The History of Oroonoko, or, The Royal Slave* (abridged), ed. Elizabeth Griffith, *Collection of Novels* vol. i. (London, 1777), 199–278.

—— *Love-Letters between a Nobleman and his Sister* (London, 1684).

—— *Love-Letters between a Nobleman and his Sister*, ed. Maureen Duffy (London, 1987).

—— *Prologue to Romulus* (London, 1682).

—— *The Works of Aphra Behn*, ed. Montague Summers (6 vols.; London, 1915).

—— *The Younger Brother, or, The Amorous Jilt*, ed. Charles Gildon (London, 1696).

BELANGER, TERRY, 'Publishers and Writers in Eighteenth-Century England', in Isabel Rivers (ed.), *Books and their Readers in Eighteenth-Century England* (Leicester, 1982), 5–26.

BLACKMORE, RICHARD, *A Treatise of Spleen and Vapours, or, Hypochondria and Hysterical Affections* (London, 1725).

BOUCÉ, PAUL GABRIEL, (ed.), *Sexuality in Eighteenth-Century Britain* (Manchester, 1982).

BRISSENDEN, R. F., *Virtue in Distress: Studies in the Novel of Sentiment from Richardson to Sade* (London, 1974).

BRONSON, BERTRAND, *Printing as an Index of Taste in Eighteenth-Century England* (New York Public Library Reprint; New York, 1958).

BROWN, LAURA, 'The Romance of Empire: *Oroonoko* and the Trade in Slaves', in Laura Brown and Felicity Nussbaum (eds.), *The New Eighteenth Century: Theory, Politics, English Literature* (London, 1987) 41–62.

BROWN, THOMAS, *Familiar Letters of Love, Gallantry and Several Occasions, by the Wits of the Last and Present Age* (London, 1718).

BRUNT, ROSALIND, 'A Career in Love: The Romantic World of Barbara Cartland', in Christopher Pawling (ed.), *Popular Fiction and Social Change* (London, 1984), 127–57.

BURGIN, VICTOR, DONALD, JAMES, and KAPLAN, CORA (eds.), *Formations of Fantasy* (London, 1986).

Calendar of State Papers, Domestic Series, Public Record Office (London, 1668–9).

CAMERON, WILLIAM J., *New Light on Aphra Behn* (Auckland, 1961).

CARSWELL, JOHN, *The South Sea Bubble* (London, 1960).

CASTLE, TERRY, *Masquerade and Civilization: The Carnivalesque in Eighteenth-Century English Culture and Fiction* (Stanford, Calif., 1986).

—— 'The Carnivalization of Eighteenth-Century English Narrative', *PMLA* 9 (1984), 903–16.

CHAMBERS, ROSS, *Story and Situation: Narrative Seduction and the Power of Fiction* (Manchester University Press, Theory and History of Literature Ser., 12; Manchester, 1984).

CHAPMAN, R. W., 'The Course of the Post in the Eighteenth Century', *Notes and Queries*, 183 (1942), 67–9.

CHEYNE, GEORGE, *The English Malady, or, A Treatise of Nervous Disorders of all Kinds* (London, 1733).

CHURCHILL, SARAH, *Private Correspondence of Sarah, Duchess of Marlborough*, i. (London, 1838).

CIXOUS, HÉLÈNE, 'The Laugh of the Medusa', in *New French Feminisms: An Anthology*, trans. and ed. Elaine Marks and Isabelle de Courtivron (Brighton, 1981), 245–64.

—— and CLÉMENT, CATHERINE, *The Newly Born Woman*, trans. Betsy Wing (Theory and History of Literature Ser., 24; Manchester, 1986).

CLARK, ALICE, *Working Life of Women in the Seventeenth Century* (London, 1919).

CLMENT, CATHERINE, 'The Guilty One', in Cixous and Clément, *The Newly Born Woman*, 1–59.

COLLINS, A. S., 'The Growth of the Reading Public during the Eighteenth Century', *Review of English Studies*, 2 (1926), 284–94, 428–38.

CRANE, R. S., 'Suggestions toward a Genealogy of the Man of Feeling', *ELH* 1 (1934), 205–30.

CRESSY, DAVID, *Literacy and the Social Order* (Cambridge, 1980).

CURLL, EDMUND, *A Compleat Key to the Dunciad* (London, 1728).

DANGERFIELD, THOMAS, *Don Tomazo, or The Juvenile Rambles of Thomas Dangerfield* (London, 1680).

DAVIS, LENNARD J., *Factual Fictions: The Origins of the English Novel* (New York, 1983).

DAVIS, ROBERT CON (ed.), *Lacan and Narration: The Psychoanalytic Difference in Narrative Theory* (Baltimore and London, 1983).

DAY, ROBERT ADAMS, *Told in Letters: Epistolary Fiction before Richardson* (Ann Arbor, Mich., 1966).

D'AULNOY, MARIE CATHERINE LA MOTTE, Baronne d', *The Ingenious and Diverting Letters of the Lady——Travels into Spain*, 2nd edn. (London, 1692).

—— *Memoirs of the Court of England* (London, 1707).

DEFOE, DANIEL, *The History of the Life and Adventures of Mr. Duncan Campbell, a Gentleman, Who, tho' Deaf and Dumb Writes Down Any Stranger's Name at First Sight, with their Future Contingencies of Fortune* (London, 1720).

—— *The Fortunes and Misfortunes Of the Famous Moll Flanders, &c.* (1722), ed. G. A. Starr (London and New York, 1971).

DELMAR, ROSALIND, 'Eighteenth Century Amazons', *Feminist Review*, 26 (Summer 1987), 105–16.

DERRIDA, JACQUES, 'The Law of Genre', *Critical Inquiry*, 7 (1980), 55–92.

DOWNIE, J. A., *Robert Harley and the Press: Propaganda and Public Opinion in the Age of Swift and Defoe* (Cambridge, 1979).

DRYDEN, JOHN, 'A Discourse concerning the Original and Progress of Satire' (1693), in *Essays of John Dryden*, ed. W. P. Ker, vol. ii. (New York, 1961), 15–114.

DUFF, DOLORES DIANE CLARKE, 'Materials toward a Biography of Mary Delariviere Manley (Univ. of Indiana Ph.D. diss., 1965).

DUFFY, MAUREEN, *The Passionate Shepherdess: Aphra Behn 1640–89* (London, 1977).

DUNCOMBE, JOHN, *The Feminiad: A Poem* (1754) (The Augustan Reprint Society Ser., 207; Los Angeles, 1981).

EAGLETON, TERRY, *Criticism and Ideology: A Study in Marxist Literary Theory* (London, 1976).

—— *The Function of Criticism* (Oxford, 1984).

ELKIN, P. K., *The Augustan Defence of Satire* (Oxford, 1973).

FAIRCHILD, HOXIE NEALE, *The Noble Savage: A Study in Romantic Naturalism* (New York, 1928).

FELMAN, SHOSHANA, 'Rereading Femininity', *Yale French Studies*, 62 (1981), 19–44.

FERGUSON, MOIRA (ed.), *First Feminists: British Women Writers 1578–1799* (Bloomington, 1985).

FIELDING, HENRY, *The History of Tom Jones, a Foundling*, (eds). Martin C. Battestin and Fredson Bowers (2 vols.; Oxford, 1974).

Five Love-Letters from a Nun to a Cavalier (1678), trans. Roger L'Estrange, in Natascha Würzbach (ed.), *The Novel in Letters. Epistolary Fiction in the Early English Novel 1678–1740* (London, 1969), 1–23.

FOUCAULT, MICHEL, *The History of Sexuality, i: An Introduction*, trans. Robert Hurley (Harmondsworth, 1981).

216 BIBLIOGRAPHY

FOUCAULT, MICHEL, *Madness and Civilization: A History of Insanity in the Age of Reason*, trans. Richard Howard (New York, 1988).

FOULCHÉ-DELBOSC, RAYMOND, 'Madame D'Aulnoy et l'Espagne', *Révue hispanique*, 67 (1926), 1–151.

FOXON, DAVID, *Libertine Literature in England 1660–1745* (New York, 1965).

FREUD, SIGMUND, 'On Narcissism: An Introduction', in *Essential Papers on Narcissism*, ed. Andrew P. Morrison (New York, 1986), 17–43.

—— *The Standard Edition of the Complete Psychological Works of Sigmund Freud*, trans. and ed. James Strachey *et al.* (24 vols.; London, 1953–74).

FRYE, NORTHROP, *Anatomy of Criticism* (Princeton, NJ, 1957).

GARDINER, JUDITH KEGAN, 'Aphra Behn: Sexuality and Self-Respect', *Women's Studies*, 7 (1980), 67–78.

GILBERT, SANDRA, and GUBAR, SUSAN, *The Madwoman in the Attic: The Woman Writer and the Nineteenth-Century Literary Imagination* (London and New Haven, Conn., 1979).

GILLESPIE, GERALD, 'Novel, Nouvelle, Novelle, Short Novel?—A Review of Terms', *Neophilologus*, 51 (1967), 117–27.

GODENNE, RENÉ, *Les Romans de Mademoiselle de Scudéry* (Geneva, 1983).

GOLDGAR, BERTRAND A., *Walpole and the Wits: The Relation of Politics to Literature 1722–42* (London and Lincoln, Nebr., 1976).

GOREAU, ANGELINE, *Reconstructing Aphra: A Social Biography of Aphra Behn* (Oxford, 1980).

GRAHAM, WALTER, 'Thomas Baker, Mrs. Manley and the Female Tatler', *Modern Philology*, 34 (1936–7), 267–72.

GREEN, F. C., *French Novelists, Manners and Ideas from the Renaissance to the Revolution* (Toronto and London, 1928).

—— 'Who was the Author of the "Lettres Portugaises"?' *Modern Language Review*, 21 (1926), 159–67.

GREEN, V. H. H., *The Hanoverians 1714–1815* (London, 1948).

GREGG, EDWARD, *Queen Anne* (London, 1980).

GRIFFITH, ELIZABETH (ed.), *A Collection of Novels, Selected and Revised by Mrs. Griffith* (3 vols.; London, 1777).

HAGSTRUM, JEAN, *Sex and Sensibility: Ideal and Erotic Love from Milton to Mozart* (Chicago, 1980).

HAMMOND, RON, 'Why "Who Wrote the Portuguese Letters?" Matters', unpublished paper.

HAWKESWORTH, JOHN, 'Preface', *Oroonoko: A Tragedy by Thomas Southern, with Alterations* (London, 1775).

HAYWOOD, ELIZA, *The Adventures of Eovaai, Princess of Ijaveo. Written Originally in the Language of Nature, (of Later Years but Little Understood). First Translated into Chinese, at the Command of the Emperor, by a Cabal of Seventy Philosophers; and Now Retranslated Into English, by the Son of a Mandarin, Residing in London* (London, 1736).

HAYWOOD, ELIZA, *The Agreeable Caledonian, or, Memoirs of Signora di Morella, a Roman Lady, Who Made Her Escape from a Monastery at Viterbo, for the Love of a Scots Nobleman* (2 pts.; London, 1728, 1729).

—— *The Arragonian Queen: A Secret History,* (London, 1724).

—— *Bath Intrigues, in Four Letters to a Friend in London* (London, 1725).

—— *La Belle Assemblée, or The Adventures of Six Days* (London, 1724).

—— *Clementina, or The History of an Italian Lady, Who Made Her Escape from a Monastery, for the Love of a Scots Nobleman* (London, 1768).

—— Review of *Clementina, Monthly Review,* 38 (1768), 412.

—— *Cleomelia, or, The Generous Mistress. To Which Is Added, I. The Lucky Rape: Or, Fate the Best Disposer. II. The Capricious Lover: Or, No Trifling With a Woman,* 2nd edn. (London, 1727).

—— *The Disguis'd Prince, or, The Beautiful Parisian* (London, 1728).

—— *The Female Spectator* (4 vols.; London, 1745).

—— *The Fortunate Foundlings, being the Genuine History of Colonel M—rs, and his Sister, Madam du P—y, the Issue of the Hon. Ch—es M—rs, Son of the late Duke of R—L—D—* (London, 1741).

—— *The Fruitless Enquiry, being a Collection of Several Entertaining Histories and Occurrences, Which Fell under the Observation of a Lady in Her Search after Happiness* (London, 1727). Abr. in Griffith (ed.) *Collection of Novels,* ii. 161–269.

—— *The History of Jemmy and Jenny Jessamy* (3 vols.; London, 1753).

—— *The History of Leonora Meadowson* (London, 1788).

—— *The History of Miss Betsy Thoughtless* (4 vols.; London, 1751).

—— *Irish Artifice, or, The History of Clarina, in The Female Dunciad,* ed. Edmund Curll (London, 1728), 17–41.

—— *Letters from a Lady of Quality to a Chevalier. Translated from the French,* 2nd edn. (London, 1724).

—— *Letters from the Palace of Fame, Written by a First Minister in The Regions of Air, to an Inhabitant of This World. Translated from an Arabian Manuscript* (London, 1727).

—— *Life's Progress through the Passions, or, The Adventures of Natura* (London, 1748).

—— *Love in Excess, or, The Fatal Enquiry* (London, 1720).

—— *The Masquerade Novels of Eliza Haywood,* ed. Mary Anne Schofield, (Delmar, NY, 1986).

—— *The Masqueraders, or Fatal Curiosity, Being the Secret History of a Late Amour* (London, 1724).

—— *The Masqueraders, or, Fatal Curiosity, Being the Secret History of a Late Amour. Part II* (London, 1725).

—— *Memoirs of the Baron de Brosse, Who Was Broke on the Wheel in the Reign of Louis XIV* (London, 1725).

—— *Memoirs of a Certain Island Adjacent to the Kingdom of Utopia. Now Translated into English* (London, 1725).

HAYWOOD, ELIZA, *The Plays of Eliza Haywood*, ed. Valerie C. Rudolph (Garland Eighteenth Century English Drama Series; New York and London, 1983).

—— *Reflections on the Various Effects of Love, according to the Contrary Dispositions of the Persons on Whom It Operates* (London, 1726).

—— *Secret Histories, Novels and Poems. In Four Volumes*, 2nd edn. (vols. i and ii; London, 1725).

—— *Secret Histories, Novels and Poems. In Four Volumes*, 3rd edn. (vols. iii and iv; London, 1732).

—— *The Secret History of the Present Intrigues of the Court of Caramania* (London, 1727).

—— *A Spy on the Conjurer, or, A Collection of Surprising and Diverting Stories, with Merry and Ingenious Letters. By Way of the Memoirs of the Famous Mr. Duncan Campbell. Revised by Mrs. Eliza Haywood* (London, 1724).

—— *The Works of Mrs. Eliza Haywood, Consisting of Novels, Letters, Poems and Plays* (4 vols.; London, 1724).

HEATH, STEPHEN, 'Joan Rivière and the Masquerade', in Burgin, Donald, and Kaplan (eds.), *Formations of Fantasy*, 45–61.

HEMLOW, JOYCE, *Fanny Burney* (Oxford, 1958).

HOBBY, ELAINE, *Virtue of Necessity: English Women's Writing 1649–88* (London, 1988).

HOLMES, GEOFFREY and SPECK, W. A. (eds.), *The Divided Society: Party Conflict in England 1696–1716* (London, 1967).

IRIGARAY, LUCE, 'Any Theory of the "Subject" Has Always Been Appropriated by the "Masculine"', in *Speculum of the Other Woman*, trans. Catherine Porter (New York, 1985), 133–46.

—— 'The Power of Discourse and the Subordination of the Feminine', in *This Sex Which Is Not One*, trans. Catherine Porter (London, 1985), 68–86.

—— 'Women on the Market', in *This Sex Which is Not One*, 170–92.

JACKSON, ROSEMARY, *Fantasy: The Literature of Subversion* (London, 1981).

JAKOBSON, ROMAN and HALLE, MORRIS, *Fundamentals of Language* (The Hague, 1956).

JENSEN, KATHERINE A., 'Male Models of Feminine Epistolarity: or, How to Write Like a Woman in Seventeenth-Century France', in Elizabeth C. Goldsmith (ed.), *Writing the Female Voice: Essays on Epistolary Literature* (Boston, 1989), 25–45.

KAMM, JOSEPHINE, *Hope Deferred: Girls' Education in English History* (London, 1965).

KAMUF, PEGGY, *Fictions of Feminine Desire: Disclosures of Heloise* (Lincoln, Nebr. and London, 1982).

—— 'Writing like a Woman', in Sally McConnell-Ginet, Ruth Borker, and Nelly Furman (eds.), *Women and Language in Literature and Society* (New York, 1980), 284–329.

KAPLAN, CORA, 'The Thorn Birds: Fiction, Fantasy, Femininity', in *Sea Changes: Culture and Feminism* (London, 1986), 117–46.

—— (ed.), *Salt and Bitter and Good: Three Centuries of English and American Women Poets* (London, 1975).

KAUFMANN, LINDA S., *Discourses of Desire: Gender, Genre and Epistolary Fictions* (Ithaca, NY, and London, 1986).

KENYON, JOHN, *The Popish Plot* (London, 1972).

KERN, EDITH, 'The Romance of the Novel/Novella', in Peter Dernetz, Thomas Greene, and Lowry Nelson, jun. (eds.), *The Disciplines of Criticism: Essays in Literary Theory, Interpretation and History* (New Haven, Conn., 1968), 511–30.

KING, GREGORY, 'Natural and Political Observations and Conclusions about the State and Condition of England' (1696), in *Two Tracts*, ed. George E. Barnett (Baltimore, 1936).

KOFMAN, SARAH, *The Enigma of Woman: Woman in Freud's Writings*, trans. Catherine Porter (Ithaca, NY, and London, 1985).

KOON, HELENE, 'Eliza Haywood and the *Female Spectator*', *Huntington Library Quarterly*, 42 (1978–9), 43–57.

KÖSTER, PATRICIA, 'Delariviere Manley and the *DNB*: A Cautionary Tale about Following Black Sheep with a Challenge to Cataloguers', *Eighteenth-Century Life*, 3 (1977), 106–11.

KROPF, C. R., 'Libel and Satire in the Eighteenth Century', *Eighteenth Century Studies*, 8 (1974–5), 153–68.

LACAN, JACQUES, *Écrits: A Selection*, trans. Alan Sheridan (London and New York, 1977).

Ladies' Magazine, or the Universal Entertainer (14 April 1753), 115.

LAFAYETTE, MARIE MADELEINE DE LA VERGNE, comtesse de, *The Princess of Cleves* (London, 1679).

LAPLANCHE, J. and PONTALIS, J.-B., 'Phantasy' and 'Transference', in *The Language of Psycho-Analysis*, trans. Donald Nicholson-Smith (The International Psycho-Analytical Library, 94; London, 1983), 314–19, 455–62.

LEGATES, MARLENE, 'The Cult of Womanhood in Eighteenth Century Thought', *Eighteenth Century Studies*, 10 (1976–7), 21–39.

LENNOX, CHARLOTTE, *Henrietta* (4 vols.; London, 1753).

LINK, FREDERICK, *Aphra Behn* (New York, 1968).

LOCKHART, JOHN GIBSON, *Memoirs of the Life of Sir Walter Scott*, iii. (Boston and New York, 1902).

LONDON, APRIL, 'Placing the Female: The Metonymic Garden in Amatory and Pious Narrative 1700–1740', in Macheski and Schofield (eds.), *British Women Novelists 1670–1815*, 101–23.

LOWENTHAL, LEO and FISKE, MARGARET, 'The Debate over Art and

Popular Culture: English Eighteenth Century as a Case Study', in Leo Lowenthal (ed.), *Literature, Popular Culture and Society* (Englewood Cliffs, NJ, 1961), 52–108.

LUTTRELL, NARCISSUS, *A Brief Relation of State Affairs from September 1678 to April 1714* (6 vols.; Oxford, 1857).

MCBURNEY, W. H., 'Mrs. Penelope Aubin and the Early Eighteenth-Century Novel', *Huntington Library Quarterly*, 20 (1957), 245–67.

MACCARTHY, BRIDGET, *Women Writers: Their Contribution to the English Novel 1621–1744* (Cork, 1944).

MCDOUGALL, DOROTHY, *Madeleine de Scudéry: Her Romantic Life and Death* (London, 1938).

MACHESKI, CECILIA and SCHOFIELD, MARY ANNE (eds.), *Fetter'd or Free? British Women Novelists 1670–1815* (Athens, Ohio, 1985).

MCKEON, MICHAEL, *The Origins of the English Novel 1600–1740* (Baltimore and London, 1987).

MCKILLOP, ALAN D., 'The Personal Relations between Richardson and Fielding', *Modern Philology*, 28 (1931), 423–5.

MACUBBIN, ROBERT M. (ed.), *'Tis Nature's Fault: Unauthorized Sexuality during the Enlightenment* (Cambridge, 1987).

MANLEY, DELARIVIER, *Court Intrigues, in a Collection of Original Letters from the Island of New Atalantis, & Co.* (London, 1711).

—— *The Duke of M———h's Vindication in Answer to a Pamphlet Lately Publish'd Call'd Bouchain, or A Dialogue between the Medley and the Examiner* (London, 1711).

—— *The Honour and Prerogative of the Queen's Majesty Vindicated and Defended against the Unexampled Insolence of the Author of the* Guardian, *in a Letter from a Country Whig to Mr. Steele* (London, 1713).

—— *A Learned Comment upon Dr. Hare's Excellent Sermon Preach'd before the Duke of Marlborough, on the Surrender of Bouchain* (London, 1711).

—— *Letters Written by Mrs. Manley, to Which is Added a Letter from a Supposed Nun in Portugal to a Gentleman in France, in Imitation of the Nun's Five Letters in Print, by Colonel Pack* (London, 1696).

—— 'Mrs. Manley's Will', *Notes and Queries*, 7th ser. 8 (1889), 156–7.

—— *Mrs. Manley's History of her Own Life and Times* (London, 1725).

—— *A Modest Enquiry into the Reasons of the Joy Expressed by a Certain Sett of People upon the Spreading of a Report of Her Majesty's Death* (London, 1714).

—— *The Novels of Mary Delariviere Manley 1705–1714*, ed. Patricia Köster (2 vols.; Scholars' Facsimiles and Reprints; Gainesville, Fla., 1971).

—— *The Power of Love, in Seven Novels* (London, 1720).

—— *The Royal Mischief: A Tragedy* (London, 1696).

—— *A Stagecoach Journey to Exeter* (London, 1725).

—— *A True Narrative of What Pass'd at the Examination of the Marquis de Guiscard at the Cock-Pit, the 8th of March 1710/11* (London, 1711).

MANLEY, DELARIVIER, *A True Relation of the Several Facts and Circumstances of the Intended Riot and Tumult on Queen Elizabeth's Birth-day* (London, 1711).

MASSON, J. M., *Freud: The Assault on Truth* (London, 1984).

MAYO, ROBERT, *The English Novel in the Magazines 1740–1815* (London, 1962).

MODLESKI, TANIA, *Loving with a Vengeance: Mass-Produced Fantasies for Women* (London and New York, 1984).

MOERS, ELLEN, *Literary Women: The Great Writers* (London, 1977).

MOLIÈRE, JEAN BAPTISTE, *Les Précieuses Ridicules/The Affected Ladies* (1659), in *The Plays of Molière in French and English*, ed. A. R. Waller (Edinburgh, 1907), ii. 1–55.

MONTAGU, MARY WORTLEY, *The Complete Letters of Lady Mary Wortley Montagu*, ed. Robert Halsband (4 vols.; Oxford, 1966).

MORGAN, CHARLOTTE E., *The Rise of the Novel of Manners: A Study of Prose Fiction between 1600 and 1740* (New York, 1911).

MORGAN, FIDELIS, *A Woman of No Character: An Autobiography of Mrs. Manley* (London, 1986).

MULLAN, JOHN, 'Hypochondria and Hysteria: Sensibility and the Physicians', *The Eighteenth Century: Theory and Interpretation*, 25 (1984), 141–74.

MURAT, MADAME DE, *The Memoirs of the Countess of Dunois* (London, 1699).

NEEDHAM, GWENDOLYN, 'Mary de la Rivière Manley, Tory Defender', *Huntington Library Quarterly*, 12 (1948–9), 255–89.

—— 'Mrs. Manley: An Eighteenth-Century Wife of Bath', *Huntington Library Quarterly*, 14 (1950–1), 259–85.

NELSON, CAROLYN, and SECCOMBE, MATTHEW (comps.), *British Newspapers and Periodicals 1641–1700: A Short-Title Catalogue of Serials Printed in England, Scotland, Ireland and British America* (New York, 1987).

NEUBURG, VICTOR E., *Popular Literature: A History and Guide from the Beginning of Printing to the Year 1897* (Harmondsworth, 1977).

NUSSBAUM, FELICITY, *The Brink of All We Hate: English Satires on Women 1660–1740* (Lexington, Ky., 1984).

OSBORNE, DOROTHY, *The Letters of Dorothy Osborne to William Temple*, ed. G. C. Moore Smith (Oxford, 1928).

OVID, *'Heroides' and 'Amores'*, trans. Grant Shaverman (Loeb Classical Library; Cambridge, Mass, 1914).

PAINTER, WILLIAM, *The Palace of Pleasure: Elizabethan Versions of Italian and French Novels from Boccaccio, Bandello, Cinthio, Straparoal, Queen Margaret of Navarre and Others* (1566), ed. Joseph Jacobs, 2nd edn. (London, 1890).

PALMER, MELVIN D., 'Madame d'Aulnoy in England', *Comparative Literature*, 27 (1975), 237–53.

PARKER, PATRICIA, 'Literary Fat Ladies and the Generation of the Text', in *Literary Fat Ladies: Rhetoric, Gender, Property* (London, 1987), 8–35.

PAULSON, RONALD, *Satire and the Novel in Eighteenth-Century England* (London and New Haven, Conn., 1967).

PEPYS, SAMUEL, *The Diary of Samuel Pepys* (1660–1669), ed. Robert Latham and Robert Matthews (10 vols.; London, 1970–83).

PERRY, RUTH, *Women, Letters and the Novel* (New York, 1980).

—— *The Celebrated Mary Astell: An Early English Feminist* (Chicago and London, 1986).

POLLAK, ELLEN, *The Poetics of Sexual Myth: Gender and Ideology in the Verse of Swift and Pope* (Women in Culture and Society Series; Chicago, 1985).

POPE, ALEXANDER, *The Dunciad*, ed. James Sutherland, vol. v of *The Poems of Alexander Pope*, ed. John Butt, 3rd edn. rev. (6 vols.; London, 1963).

PORTER, ROY, *English Society in the Eighteenth Century* (Pelican Social History of Britain; London, 1982).

—— 'The Secrets of Generation Display'd: *Aristotle's Masterpiece*', in Macubbin (ed.), *Unauthorised Sexuality*, 1–21.

RABUTIN, ROGER DE, Count de Bussy, *The Amorous History of the Gauls* (London, 1725).

RADWAY, JANICE, *Reading the Romance: Women, Patriarchy and Popular Literature* (London, 1984).

REEVE, CLARA, *The Progress of Romance and the History of Charoba, Queen of Aegypt* (Facsimile Text Society Ser. 1: Literature and Language, 4; New York, 1930).

RICHARDSON, SAMUEL, *The History of Sir Charles Grandison* (1753–4), ed. Jocelyn Harris (Oxford, 1986).

—— *Pamela, or, Virtue Rewarded* (London, 1740).

RICHETTI, J. J., *Popular Fiction before Richardson: Narrative Patterns 1700–39* (Oxford, 1969).

RIVIÈRE, JOAN, 'Womanliness as a Masquerade' (1929), repr. in Burgin, Donald, and Kaplan (eds.), *Formations of Fantasy*, 35–44.

SACKVILLE-WEST, VITA, *Aphra Behn: The Incomparable Astrea* (New York, 1927).

SAVAGE, RICHARD, *An Author to Be Lett. Being a Proposal Humbly Address'd to the Consideration of the Knights, Esquires, Gentlemen, and Other Worshipful and Weighty Members of the Solid and Ancient Society of the Bathos. By their Associate and Well-Wisher, Iscariot Hackney* (London, 1732).

—— *The Authors of the Town: A Satire, Inscribed to the Author of The Universal Passion* (London, 1725).

SCHOFIELD, MARY ANNE, '"Descending Angels": Salubrious Sluts and Petty Prostitutes in Haywood's Fiction', in Macheski and Schofield (eds.), *British Women Novelists 1670–1815*, 186–200.

—— *Eliza Haywood* (Boston, 1985).

SCHULZ, DIETER, '"Novel", "Romance", and Popular Fiction in the First Half of the Eighteenth Century', *Studies in Philology*, 70 (1973), 77–91.

SCOTT, SARAH, *A Description of Millenium Hall and the Country Adjacent* (1762; London, 1986).

SCOTT, WALTER, 'Horace Walpole', in *Biographical Memoirs*, vol. iii of *Miscellaneous Prose Works of Sir Walter Scott* (Edinburgh, 1827), 355–86.

SCUDÉRY, MADELEINE DE, *Clelia: An Excellent New Romance*, trans. J. Davies and G. Havers (London, 1678).

—— 'Preface', *Ibrahim, or The Illustrious Bassa, written in French by Monsieur de Scudery, and Now Englished by Henry Cogan, Gent* (London, 1674).

SEDGWICK, EVE KOSOFSKY, *Between Men: English Literature and Male Homosocial Desire* (New York, 1985).

SERGEANT, PHILIP W., *Liars and Fakers* (London, 1926).

Seven Portuguese Letters, being a Second Part to the Five Love-Letters from a Nun to a Cavalier. One of the Most Passionate Pieces, That Possibly Ever Has Been Extant (London, 1681).

SHKLOVSKY, VIKTOR, 'Art as Technique' (1917), repr. in *Russian Formalist Criticism: Four Essays*, trans. and ed. Lee T. Lemon and Marion J. Reis (Lincoln, Nebr., 1965), 3–21.

—— 'Sterne's *Tristram Shandy*: Stylistic Commentary' (1921), repr. in *Russian Formalist Criticism: Four Essays*, 21–57.

SHOWALTER, ELAINE, *A Literature of their Own: British Women Novelists from Bronte to Lessing*, rev. edn. (London, 1982).

SKURA, MEREDITH ANNE, *The Literary Use of the Psychoanalytic Process* (London and New Haven, Conn., 1981).

SMITH, JOHN HARRINGTON, 'Thomas Baker and *The Female Tatler*', *Modern Philology*, 49 (1951–2), 182–8.

SNITOW, ANN BARR, 'Mass Market Romance: Pornography for Women Is Different', in Ann Barr Snitow, Christine Stansell, and Sharon Thompson (eds.), *Desire: The Politics of Sexuality* (London, 1984), 258–75.

SOUTHERNE, THOMAS, *Oroonoko: A Tragedy* (London, 1696).

SPACKS, PATRICIA MEYER, 'Ev'ry Woman Is at Heart a Rake', *Eighteenth Century Studies*, 8 (1974), 27–74.

SPECK, W. A., *Stability and Strife: England 1714–1760* (Cambridge, Mass., 1977).

SPENCER, JANE, *The Rise of the Woman Novelist: From Aphra Behn to Jane Austen* (Oxford, 1986).

SPENDER, DALE, *Mothers of the Novel: One Hundred Good Women Writers before Jane Austen* (London, 1986).

SPERLING, JOHN G., *The South Sea Company* (Kress Library Series of Publications; Boston, 1962).

SPIVAK, GAYATRI CHAKRAVORTY, 'Explanation and Culture: Marginalia', in *In Other Worlds: Essays in Cultural Politics* (London, 1987), 103–17.

SPUFFORD, MARGARET, *Small Books and Pleasant Histories: Popular Fiction and its Readership in Seventeenth-Century England* (London, 1981).

STANTON, DOMNA C., 'The Fiction of Préciosité and the Fear of Women', *Yale French Studies*, 62 (1981), 107–34.

State Trials: Political and Social, ed. H. L. Stephen, vol. ii (London, 1899).

STAVES, SUSAN, *Players' Scepters: Fictions of Authority in the Restoration* (Lincoln, Nebr. and London, 1979).

STEARNS, BERTHA MONICA, 'Early English Periodicals for Women', *PMLA* 48 (1933), 38–60.

—— 'The First English Periodical for Women', *Modern Philology*, 28 (1930), 45–59.

STRAUS, RALPH, *The Unspeakable Curll, Being Some Account of Edmund Curll Bookseller, to Which Is Added a Full List of His Books* (London, 1927).

STUKELY, WILLIAM, *Of the Spleen: Its Description and History, Uses and Diseases, Particularly the Vapors, with their Remedy* (London, 1723).

SWIFT, JONATHAN, *The Correspondence of Jonathan Swift*, ed. Harold Williams, vol. iii (Oxford, 1963).

—— *The Examiner and Other Pieces Written in 1710–11*, vol. iii of *The Prose Works of Jonathan Swift*, ed. Herbert Davis (Oxford, 1940).

—— *Journal to Stella*, ed. Harold Williams, vol. i (Oxford, 1948).

—— *A Tale of a Tub, to Which is added The Battle of the Books and the Mechanical Operation of the Spirit* (1704), eds. A. C. Guthkelch and D. Nichol Smith, 2nd edn. (Oxford, 1958).

SYPHER, WYLIE, *Guinea's Captive Kings: British Anti-Slavery Literature of the XVIIIth Century* (Chapel Hill, NC, 1942).

THOMPSON, ROGER, *Unfit for Modest Ears: A Study of Pornographic, Obscene and Bawdy Works Written or Published in England in the Second Half of the Seventeenth Century* (London, 1979).

THURSTON, CAROL, *The Romance Revolution: Erotic Novels for Women and the Quest for a New Sexual Identity* (Urbana and Chicago, 1987).

TODD, JANET, *The Sign of Angellica: Women, Writing and Fiction 1660–1800* (London, 1989).

—— *Women's Friendship in Literature* (New York, 1980).

—— (ed.), *A Dictionary of British and American Women Writers 1600–1800* (London, 1984).

TREVELYAN, G. M., *England under Queen Anne, iii: The Peace and the Protestant Succession* (London, 1934).

TURNER, JAMES G., 'The Properties of Libertinism', in Macubbin (ed.), *Unauthorized Sexuality during the Enlightenment*, 75–87.

VILLEDIEU, MARIE CATHERINE HORTENSE DE DESJARDINS, Madame de, *The Annals of Love, Containing Select Histories of the Amours Of Divers Princes' Courts, Pleasantly Related* (London, 1672).

—— *Les Désordres de l'Amour* (1677), ed. Micheline Cuénin (Geneva, 1970).

VILLEDIEU, MARIE CATHERINE HORTENSE DE DESJARDINS, Madame de, *The Disorders of Love Truly Expressed in the Unfortunate Amours of Givry with Mademoiselle de Guise* (London, 1677).

WAGNER, PETER, *Eros Revived: Erotica of the Enlightenment in England and America* (London, 1988).

WATT, IAN, *The Rise of the Novel: Studies in Defoe, Richardson and Fielding* (London, 1957).

WEINSTEIN, ARNOLD, *Fictions of the Self: 1550–1800* (Princeton, NJ, 1981).

WHICHER, GEORGE FRISBIE, *The Life and Romances of Mrs. Eliza Haywood* (New York, 1915).

The Whisperer, no. 1 (11 October 1709) (Augustan Reprint Society Series 47: Los Angeles, 1954).

WHITE, ALLON, and STALLYBRASS, PETER, 'The Grotesque Body and the Smithfield Muse: Authorship in the Eighteenth Century', *The Politics and Poetics of Transgression* (London, 1986), 80–124.

WILLIAMS, IOAON (ed.), *Novel and Romance: A Documentary Record* (London, 1970).

WILLIAMS, RAYMOND, *Marxism and Literature* (Oxford, 1977).

WOODCOCK, GEORGE, *The Incomparable Aphra* (London and New York, 1948).

WOOLF, VIRGINIA, 'Aphra Behn', in *Virginia Woolf: Women and Writing*, ed. Michèle Barrett (London, 1979), 89–91.

WRIGHT, ELIZABETH, *Psychoanalytic Criticism: Theory in Practice* (London, 1984).

Zelinda, an Excellent New Romance, trans. 'T. D.' (London, 1677).

Index